HELICOPTER BOYS

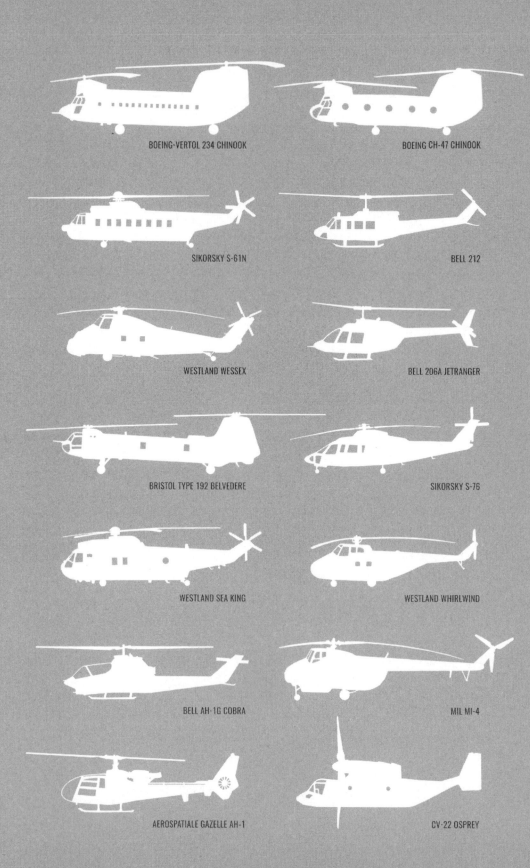

BOEING-VERTOL 234 CHINOOK

BOEING CH-47 CHINOOK

SIKORSKY S-61N

BELL 212

WESTLAND WESSEX

BELL 206A JETRANGER

BRISTOL TYPE 192 BELVEDERE

SIKORSKY S-76

WESTLAND SEA KING

WESTLAND WHIRLWIND

BELL AH-1G COBRA

MIL MI-4

AEROSPATIALE GAZELLE AH-1

CV-22 OSPREY

HELICOPTER BOYS

TRUE TALES FROM OPERATORS OF MILITARY
AND CIVILIAN ROTORCRAFT

RICHARD PIKE

GRUB STREET / LONDON

Published by
Grub Street
4 Rainham Close
London
SW11 6SS

Copyright © Grub Street 2018
Copyright text © Richard Pike 2018

A CIP record for this title is available from the British Library

ISBN-13: 978-1-910690-55-0

Design by Daniele Roa

Printed and bound by Finidr, Czech Republic

CONTENTS

AUTHOR'S DEDICATION

THIS BOOK IS dedicated, firstly, to the late Mr Bill Deacon GM, the aircrewman for a series of unusual and somewhat challenging flights we undertook together in the spring of 1995 to St Kilda, the westernmost islands of the Outer Hebrides of Scotland. A couple of years later, in November 1997, Bill faced rather more extreme challenges during a search and rescue mission off the coast of Bressay, Shetland Islands. In mountainous seas whipped up by Hurricane Force 12 winds, Bill was winched down to the deck of the vessel *Green Lily* which was foundering close to the rocky shoreline. Once on board, he placed ship's crew members two at a time into rescue strops to be winched aboard the coastguard helicopter. Eventually alone on the deck and with the ship by then on the rocks, Bill's own rescue could not be completed before he was washed overboard and engulfed by the waves. He was awarded the George Medal posthumously.

I'd also like to mention Mark Ashton who, through his parents, my wife and I met not long before his first offshore job as trainee technician on the Piper Alpha platform. Mark was the youngest victim of the disaster which overwhelmed that platform on 6 July 1988. He was just nineteen years old.

On a rather less sombre note, sincere thanks to the many people from countries across the world who have shown such enthusiasm and illuminating support for this project.

CHAPTER 1
STORMY START

Richard Pike's introduction to North Sea
helicopter flying

"THE WEATHER'S NOT looking great," said Bill as we stared up at the sky. He grunted and glanced at me, "but I've known worse." While we walked towards our allocated helicopter, Sikorsky S-61N registration G-BAKA parked on the heliport at Aberdeen Airport, I noted how the wind howled and the sky was filling with enormous clouds, or not quite clouds, just shapeless drifts. It was July 1981 and while I'd been warned to anticipate eccentric weather with elastic seasons, these mid-summer conditions seemed rather more eccentric and elastic than I'd hoped. There were at least three levels of cloud, all moving in different ways. The old round clouds, now joined in masses, moved slowly across the airfield with a vast piled dignity; a second layer, made up of fantastic torn shapes, twisted bodies with giant limbs that all pointed in odd directions, swam fast like the debris of a flood. Below, moving faster still, as fast as a racehorse could canter, white fragments, wisps trailing their flimsy fringes not much higher than adjacent buildings, appeared like ghosts of clouds rushing seawards, lost creatures below the tumult on high.

"Right-o," I said to Bill in the absence of a more useful remark that sprang readily to mind. Bill, a somewhat gruff individual, was outwardly friendly and personable although on better acquaintance he could seem reticent as if with a serious secret to guard. He'd given me endless briefings over the last few days for it was his job, as a training captain with Bristow Helicopters, to indoctrinate new pilots like me into company procedures. As an ex-military pilot I had the benefit of several thousand hours of flying experience, nevertheless I was struggling to adapt to civilian routines and attitudes. Indeed, my thoughts felt as turbulent as the weather conditions as I tried to grapple with a number of lessons that needed to be learnt fast.

There was, for a start, quite a lot to learn about the S-61 helicopter itself. In his introductory briefings, Bill described how this machine was dubbed 'the workhorse of the North Sea'. He then explained how it was developed in the 1950s from the XHSS-2 Sea King prototype which first flew in March 1959. The Sea King was the military version but it didn't take long for Sikorsky to introduce a commercial model, the S-61L, which first flew in November 1961.

The following year the S-61N, optimised for over-water and oil-rig support, made its first flight. This was the type we flew for Bristow.

He went on to describe an accident seven years earlier, in 1974, when a S-61N (PH-NZC) owned by KLM Noordzee Helikopters crashed into the sea following a probable blade failure to one of the five main rotor blades. "They reckoned the root cause of the accident was metal fatigue," said Bill, "so nowadays the blade inspections are more regular. As a matter of interest, the machine was recovered from the seabed and rebuilt. As far as I know it's currently flying in the USA."

Bill had covered numerous other issues for he knew that, in addition to technical aspects, I needed to digest a variety of topics connected to civil aviation, civilian attitudes and the general contrasts to life in the military. "This company," said Bill, "is influenced by what you might call an autocratic approach." To make his point, with an amused twinkle in his eye Bill went on to relate a story about an errant co-pilot whose actions had so annoyed the company boss that the co-pilot had been summoned to explain himself.

He'd entered the great man's office and waited. The great man apparently said nothing at first although the co-pilot noticed that the great fists were clenched. He almost expected the great man to start shaking. The co-pilot's eyes were riveted when the great mouth started to speak and his gaze held a morbid fascination while he stared at the fellow, half-horrified, half-mesmerised. Bill reckoned that the boss's tactic was to make the opening salvo sound calm enough but this was merely a ruse to clear a path for what lay ahead. The contrast was stark when, quite quickly, any possibility of cheeriness, any form of humour, faded to infinity. The co-pilot suspected that he gave an involuntary shiver; his pale face might have twitched suspensively as, in awesome persistence, the castigation crescendoed. Forest fires could have been set ablaze; the moon itself might have started to glow green. As if to dwell on the agonies of the condemned, the great man recited the great crime in detail, explained how the very fabric of society had been emasculated.

"I must apologise for my error," said the co-pilot eventually, "but I think that by now I have got the message." "That is immaterial," exploded the great man. His gruesome expression, his hideous reaction at this remark suggested that the co-pilot had not said the right thing. Indeed, the monstrous impertinence of the interjection seemed to spark a further few minutes of rebuke. But it was then, just as the levels of outrage reached their peak, that he was abruptly dismissed when the telephone rang.

Naturally, I was mindful of this and other anecdotes when I walked with Bill towards G-BAKA on that July day in 1981. I was burdened too, with this need to acquire great volumes of knowledge, some subtle, some less so, all of it whirling through my head. The planned flight that day was a fairly short one, around two hours, and would introduce me to North Sea helicopter flying. Our task was to fly passengers out to the Beatrice 'A' in the Moray Firth, assist with disembarkation after landing, then refuel before we picked up homeward-bound passengers. Sometimes this route involved a landing on both the Beatrice 'A' and the Beatrice 'B' platforms, but today only one stop was required.

"Morning," said Bill as we walked up to the ground crewman who stood by G-BAKA to assist with start procedures.

"Aye, aye," said the ground crewman, a reaction that sounded a bit peculiar to me for I was used to a smart military response.

"You do the external checks," Bill said to me, "while I check over the cabin."

Starting my external checks with a general overview, our helicopter's red, white and blue paint scheme looked, I felt, rather good compared to the ubiquitous khaki of military machines. On the underside, Day-glo chevrons had been painted to aid searchers in the event of the helicopter turning turtle after ditching in water. I moved back towards the undercarriage assembly to check the starboard sponson. The S-61N's two dual-purpose sponsons acted as a buoyancy aid in water, and housed the retractable undercarriage. "Sikorsky has designed this machine as an amphibian," Bill had said, "but frankly not a very good one, hence the inflatable bags for extra support." I bent low to inspect the underside of the sponson for damage and, while there, checked over the wheels, tyres and brakes. Moving further back, I gazed up at the large stabiliser which, placed opposite the tail rotor, was set at four degrees negative angle of attack to produce, Bill had told me, a down force at cruise airspeed. Then I checked the tail rotor itself, mounted on the helicopter's port side, before stepping back to scrutinise the rear blades of the five-bladed main rotor with its semi-articulated head. Bill had explained that in order to ensure an equal amount of lift along the full length of each blade, they were designed with about six degrees less pitch at the tips than at the roots.

Soon, with these and other external checks completed, I walked up steps built into the helicopter's air-stair door to enter the cabin before moving forward to join Bill as he strapped himself into the cockpit's left-hand seat. As a trainee captain, I would occupy the right-hand seat: this was the accepted convention in helicopters, the exact opposite to airliners where the captain normally occupied the left seat. The reason for this remained something of a mystery although Bill had attempted an explanation one time: "Most people are right-handed," he'd said, "and the helicopter captain, with his left hand grasping the collective lever, uses his right hand to control the cyclic stick which is far more sensitive than an airliner's joystick."

He continued, "When the helicopter captain needs to operate the undercarriage, radio and other systems, he can use his left hand while still gripping the cyclic stick with his right hand while the airliner captain uses his left." "Right,"

I'd said. "No, left," Bill said, "because in an airliner the throttles, undercarriage and flap controls are designed for the convenience of a right-handed individual." "I see the point," I'd said tactfully even though I hadn't really seen the point at all.

But now, as I stooped low to enter G-BAKA's cockpit, I manoeuvred myself towards the right-hand seat as briefed. "Settle yourself in," said Bill, "and when you're ready we'll run through the pre-start checks, then start up the engines." As a keen student, I'd already spent time in a hangar-bound aircraft to learn these checks. It was not long, therefore, before the ground crewman responded to my 'engine start' signal and, raising my left hand, I grasped one of the speed select levers used to control the engines (though not in the same way as fixed-wing aircraft throttles). My thumb felt for a small button at the base of the lever. When I pressed the button, a high-pitched squeal confirmed that the start cycle of the associated engine had commenced. Soon, when the cockpit engine instruments verified that all was well, I glanced up again at the ground crewman whose ruddy complexion reflected an outdoor lifestyle. Moreover, his long-faced expression suggested that he was bored. I raised my hand and gave a signal to request clearance to turn the rotors. The ground crewman re-checked behind the helicopter and to the sides, then returned my signal. With my left hand gripping the rotor brake lever, I released it carefully. The rotors reacted at once, turning slowly at first but soon picking up speed to cause the cockpit noise level to increase markedly.

With the associated racket of the rotors turning, I began to feel a sense of additional excitement – a tingling in the pit of the stomach. After another check of the cockpit dials it was time to start the helicopter's second engine. At length, with everything 'burning and turning' we were ready – finally – to proceed but it had seemed, I thought, something of a marathon effort to get to this stage. Later, especially when I was involved with search and rescue duties, these start-up checks, so laborious for the new kid on the block, would be rattled off rapidly yet safely by an experienced pilot during a scramble start procedure.

Now, though, we were ready to move at last and Bill called on the aircraft radio for clearance to taxi to the passenger pick-up point. The routine, although new to me, was well rehearsed by the others and I was impressed by the way that the passengers, dressed in bright orange survival suits, trooped out in an orderly queue to board the helicopter. Their facial expressions hardly portrayed enthusiasm and I learnt later that many of them, unlike me, did not like flying. While we waited for them to board, Bill pointed out some high grass banks that surrounded the heliport: "Those grass banks are intended to protect the airport's main terminal from dangerous debris flying about if there's a mishap with one of the helicopters." Ironically, some fifteen years in the future, a 'Tiger' helicopter would turn too sharply and end up on its side. Regretfully, the planned safety measure proved ineffective for the helicopter's dismembered rotor blades shot over the top of the grass banks to bury themselves in various parts of the air-port's main terminal. By sheer good fortune no-one was injured or worse.

With the passengers on board and strapped in, the air-stair door closed and a thumbs-up sign from the ground crewman, Bill used the aircraft radio to call for taxi clearance. With this given, I manoeuvred the helicopter away from the heliport area towards the active runway. As we moved, I noticed the way that the clouds still raced in various directions. A few drops of rain had begun to patter against G-BAKA's windscreen. Across the airfield, beyond the runway, a line of buildings displayed the signs of a rival helicopter company. Beyond that, past the airfield perimeter, lay the suburbs of Dyce with the city of Aber-deen to the south, though little was visible in the murky conditions. As we neared the active runway, Bill spoke again to the local controller who responded: "You're clear to line up and take off."

For the take-off, Bill moved the twin speed select levers fully forward and held them there; this ensured that the engines were at the top end of their governed range. Now, as I lifted G-BAKA into a hover, I held the helicopter steady for a moment or two while we checked the instrument readings. As a former fighter pilot I'd feel a curious exhilaration at this stage: the act of lifting into the air without first having to thunder down the runway at enormous speed could feel alien even after a number of years of helicopter flying. There was little time to ponder that now, though, for as soon as I was satisfied with the cockpit indications I lowered the aircraft's nose to commence the required take-off profile. The take-off may have been sedate compared to the likes of an English Electric Lightning or a McDonnell Douglas Phantom with their pilots' reputation for a 'kick the tyres, light the fires, the last one airborne is a sissy' mentality – exaggerated nonsense, of course, for the tyres should not be kicked – nonetheless the profile had to be flown accurately to ensure the best chance of a safe outcome in the event of an engine failure.

"Well done," said Bill as we climbed away after take-off to head north towards the Beatrice platforms, "that was nicely flown." He read out more checks and we changed radio frequencies to speak to another air traffic controller after which the hectic activity seemed to calm down a bit. In between further checks and radio calls, Bill talked to me on a broad range of subjects. "When it comes to operations," he said at one point, "this company's pretty good. Quite different to the union-orientated opposition," he muttered referring, I assumed, to British Airways Helicopters. "They're an odd bunch. Some claim to be peerage, gentry, this and that. Pompous lot if you ask me, full of self-importance," he sniffed. "No, no, here at Bristow we're down-to-earth, get-on-with-the-job types though the man-management leaves much to be desired. In fact, between you and me," he added in a confidential tone, "they haven't got a clue." I was a little taken aback by the frankness.

"Which perhaps explains," went on Bill, "the strike of four or so years ago." That strike, evidently an ongoing sore point within the company, had aroused much ill-feeling which, I was told, still lingered especially between certain individuals with strong views. "For many of the ex-military men like me," said Bill, "the thought of going on strike was anathema. The all-through civilian types, however, had a different approach." Bill grimaced: "It was bad, though. Friends became enemies overnight. It'll take time, but we'll get over it eventually."

When I glanced back to check that the passengers were okay, I noticed that some of them were asleep, some read newspapers and one man stared straight ahead, an obvious tension about him. One moment he was sitting very still before he started to shift about in his seat and rub the back of his neck, then he placed both hands on his knees and began to tap his fingers against his kneecaps.

"Out of interest," I asked Bill, "what's the normal routine for these offshore workers?"

"Contracts vary," said Bill, "but most have a two week on, two week off routine – domestically disruptive, but the guys are well paid and seem to cope." Bill described a particular atmosphere within offshore installations. "A degree of give-and-take is needed. Occasionally tempers will flare and there'll be trouble, but that's unusual. An offshore worker's dread is to return to shore with a 'NRB' [not required back] note to deliver to the boss."

After twenty or so minutes, as we approached the coast near the town of Banff, the two Beatrice platforms began to paint as blips on G-BAKA's radar. Before long, Bill spoke to the Beatrice 'A' radio operator who cleared us to land. By now descending to a height of one thousand feet as we flew above the Moray Firth, we carried out the pre-landing checks. When the yellow 'H' on the platform's helideck loomed, I planned my approach to ensure a landing into wind. For the landing itself I brought the S-61N to a hover at a height of about ten feet above the 'H', then lowered the helicopter judiciously onto the deck. As we landed, I noticed fire crews behind fire pumps placed around the deck edge. "Good stuff," said Bill. "Normally," he continued, "we carry out 'rotors running' refuels, especially for short trips like this one, so you nip out now and supervise the refuelling while I remain at the flight controls."

Walking down the steps of G-BAKA's air-stair door I noticed the particular odour of an offshore oil installation – a heady, petroleum-filled tang mixed with sea air and a whiff of fish. The helideck itself was overlayed with heavy rope secured to the sides; Bill had told me that sometimes, when we operated at the maximum permissible wind limits, the passengers had to hang on to this deck rope as they crawled on hands and knees to and from the helicopter. The surrounding scene, dominated by a mass of pipes, generators, specialist containers and other heavy equipment, appeared functional and bleak. Glancing down, the sea's surface looked hazardous as I made out the movement of the waves. With rain clouds approaching, the darkening sea was disturbed by the swell of waves and I could see small plumes of sea foam begin to ride with the wind. Attached to the base of Beatrice 'A' were hoses which sprayed jets of water into the sea.

Standing nearby and watching me was the helicopter landing officer (HLO). He used hand-signals to ask if we needed to refuel G-BAKA; normal speech was inhibited by the din of the helicopter, in any case I wore my noise-reducing headset and the others all wore ear defenders. I signalled a thumbs-up sign to the HLO. His eyes, I noticed, moved quickly about the helideck, never settling or resting on one thing for more than a moment. There seemed to be a hint of resignation about his demeanour as if he knew that his duties had to be taken seriously even though he was tired of it all.

During the refuelling process I glanced up to see a dark rain cloud speed across the sky towards us. The ambient light began to fade, the surroundings dissolved into grey as a few fat beads of rain started to stutter earthwards, a prelude to the deluge that was about to follow. Soon, when heavy rushes of water tumbled from the sky then bounced back up, it was as if the helideck's surface was enervated by the rain and wished it gone. But it would not go; the rain was almost overwhelming as it fell heavier, harder, louder – so loud that it began to mingle with the racket of the helicopter. Even yelling became an effort. Before long, though, with the refuelling completed and the returning passengers seated and strapped in, I scrambled back on board G-BAKA to walk forward and resume my seat in the cockpit.

As I sat down, re-connected my headset and strapped in, Bill gazed at me gloomily. When I glanced at him, in the dim light he seemed to have pale, almost colourless eyes. Suddenly, however, a broad grin began to spread across his face: I must have looked like a drowned rat. He didn't comment at first but eventually, still grinning, he said: "Welcome to the weird and wonderful world of North Sea helicopter flying." I nodded and attempted a smile by way of reply. My focus, however, was on the rig departure procedure. The Beatrice 'A' infra-structure looked uncomfortably close: there was no room for error when we took off. But this was not the moment for prevarication. Rain or shine it was time to get going, time to get immersed in the intriguing, unpredictable, amazing world about to be entered...

CHAPTER 2
BREEZY STRUGGLE

Robbie Duff sent to the rescue

A FIXED OFFSHORE platform or a moveable semi-submersible oil rig can seem to the visitor like an island – isolated, sea-washed, other-worldly. But at the approach of dusk with drab, wintry skies and dampness and rain and the wind blowing in great gusts and volleys across the sea, the island can appear to turn into a complete, arcane world, a universe in its own right. And life within that confined universe can feel more than a little intimidating when heavy seas roll and tear at the structure's legs so that even the hardiest of souls might experience a sense of trepidation. To those whose work will take them outside, a forecast of stormy weather could induce a shudder of apprehension.

So it was for Robbie Duff one October day in 1987. "We've got a helicopter stranded on one of the Ninian platforms," his boss at British Airways Helicopters (BAH) had said to him. "There's a problem with one of the main rotor blades. I'd like you to go there to sort it out." Robbie was a member of BAH's engineering team.

"And you'll have to get a shift on, Robbie," said the boss, "the flight taking you there is about to leave, the weather's stormy and they're forecasting worse to come!" The boss went on to brief Robbie that he'd be flown in a Sikorsky S-61N helicopter from the BAH base at Aberdeen Airport to an oil rig close to the Ninian. As the Ninian helideck was occupied by the problem S-61N, he'd be transferred there in a winch-equipped Bell 212 operated by Bristow Helicopters whose crew would winch him down next to the unserviceable machine. Robbie sighed: with the three Ninian platforms – north, central, south – situated some two hundred and forty miles north-east of Aberdeen, he was destined for a long flight.

This, indeed, proved the case and when, eventually, the BAH S-61N landed on the designated oil rig, it was a tired and troubled Robbie that clambered out clutching his engineering equipment: toolbox, nitrogen bottle and charging kit. Though bulky, all of this was necessary for him to deal with the problem rotor blade. Now all he needed was for the Bell 212 to turn up for the transfer to the Ninian platform. While he waited, Robbie was surprised to note that the weather was, in fact, quite good – clear visibility, a light breeze, a generally nice day. He spent time chatting with members of the oil rig's crew including the HLO whose office at one side of the helideck provided a convenient refuge. Inside this office, schedules had been pinned to a noticeboard alongside obligatory safety notices, a few postcards from abroad, a company calendar, a cut-out newspaper article. "Shouldn't be too long now," the HLO said with an optimistic air as Robbie gazed anxiously skywards for signs of the Bell 212.

By this stage, after a wait of an hour or more, the sun had begun to sink towards the horizon, the wind had started to pick up and Robbie realised that he faced escalating challenges. When, at last, the distinctive beat of a Bell 212's rotor blades could be heard clattering in the sky, Robbie gathered up his toolbox, nitrogen bottle and charging kit ready for the transfer flight. Before long, when the Bell 212 had landed, a crewman emerged from the cabin and hastened towards Robbie. "We'll have to hurry," the crewman yelled above the din of the helicopter, "we're getting close to our maximum permissible wind limits." Glancing gloomily at Robbie's toolbox and other equipment, the crewman added: "Do you really need all of this stuff?" "If I didn't need it," said Robbie huffily, "why would I have brought it here?"

The question, however, began to make sense when the crewman pointed at a special net to indicate that the equipment would have to be loaded in the net, then winched into the Bell 212's cabin. By now the wind was blowing ever stronger across the deck and Robbie's uneasiness was hardly assuaged by the first drops of rain that started to fall from darkening skies as dusk turned to night. Quite quickly airborne and feeling freezing and miserable, Robbie could see little as he stared out of the Bell 212's windows although he could imagine the clouds that swirled and spiralled all around him. As the helicopter headed directly for the Ninian field, the machine bumped and jerked as if in a Wild West fairground ride. Robbie felt grateful that the sea's perilous surface, with great waves welling up high and white horses riding against the wind with plumes of spray behind them, was hidden within the veil of dark.

The transfer flight took around forty minutes at the end of which, as the bright lights from the Ninian platform loomed, Robbie might have experienced a sense of cold feet growing steadily colder. As the helicopter pilot brought the Bell 212 to a hover above the Ninian's deck, the crewman shouted to Robbie: "Which do you want us to winch down first? The equipment or you?"

"The equipment!" yelled Robbie with thoughts that if the equipment didn't make it down safely there'd be no point in him following. The crewman therefore attached the net to the winch and as the equipment was lowered, Robbie glimpsed the legs of the Ninian platform intermittently illuminated by searchlights. A shiver of angst went through him. Surging against the Ninian's black legs, the waves raged, frothed and boiled like a riotous crowd.

As Robbie's equipment was lowered, he noticed how it sloped back when caught in the wind. A group of oil workers stood ready to grab the net, secure it with ropes and release the winch hook before dragging the equipment to one side of the deck. On completion of all this, the hook was winched back up ready for the next load: Robbie himself. Robbie swallowed hard and glanced at the crewman who appeared to grin grimly as he placed a strop over Robbie's head and under his arms. "Just try to relax," advised the crewman, "and enjoy the ride! If you start to spin, start walking in the air and swimming with your arms. You may look a bit peculiar but never mind. It should help to stabilise you."

"Are you coming down with me?" asked Robbie.

The winchman shook his head. "Nah," he said, "our combined weight would be too much for the winch." That's odd, thought Robbie, unsure if he'd been 'had'. "Let's be having you, then," went on the winchman who indicated that Robbie should step onto the Bell 212's landing skid. When he complied, Robbie was struck suddenly by the strength of the wind in his face which forced him to half-close his eyes as if he was standing up in an open-top car driving at speed along a motorway. When signalled by the crewman, Robbie stepped off the landing skid, a step into space that felt like entering the abyss. As he was lowered, the wind immediately whisked him backwards beneath the helicopter's fuselage. He passed close to a flashing red anti-collision light and thoughts such as 'what the hell am I doing here?' hurtled through his head. His journey was a short one but events ensued in slow motion; a few seconds appeared to stretch into rather a lot of minutes. He experienced a curious, disembodied feeling. In a nerve-racking manoeuvre the helicopter rotated through about sixty degrees so that the crew, deduced Robbie, could keep him in sight. His descent then seemed to stabilise and he began to feel a little better although at that stage he could see nothing apart from the white belly of the Bell 212, its spinning main rotor blade and the flicker of the anti-collision lights.

However, as he was lowered further, Robbie started to see lights on the Ninian's upper framework before the main superstructure began to appear. Won't be long now, he encouraged himself: helideck here I come! He'd made up his mind that, on landing, he'd grab hold of the rope netting that was stretched across the deck and hang on tightly in the hope that crewmen would rush out to help him. Ideally, he reckoned, the men would unclip the winch hook, release him carefully from the strop then carry him respectfully down into the depths of the Ninian where a cup of tea and a nice sticky bun would await.

The reality, regretfully, failed to match the aspiration. As he neared the helideck he passed close to the stranded S-61N and noticed that one of the Sikorsky's tie-down (blade-restraining) ropes had snapped. This blade, consequently, bounced and whipped about as if a deranged Ninian ninja was wielding a sword. Moreover, flailing around like a cowboy's whip was the tie-down rope itself. Fearful of a hundred lashes followed by possible decapitation, Robbie twisted round to face the group of crewmen who, as anticipated, had gathered in one corner of the helideck. Robbie tried to indicate that now was a good moment to run across and assist him. His efforts, alas, were in vain. Far from rushing to his aid, the slow-witted group stood like cretins with cameras to take photographs of our poor, hard-pressed protagonist. As he touched the helideck, Robbie fell flat on his back. He fumbled with the winch hook and strop to release himself. As he did so, evil thoughts might have raged through his furious mind for the Ninian's crewmen still failed to offer any form of assistance. Eventually Robbie managed to extricate himself at which point the strop was winched straight back up to the Bell 212 which immediately turned away to head off into the wide blue yonder.

Still lying on his back, and having been dumped like a sack of potatoes, Robbie felt abandoned, vulnerable, lost. His night vision had been impaired by camera flashes from the Ninian crewmen who still remained detached, and with the strength of the wind it seemed dangerous to stand up. Furthermore, his back hurt after the fall and he felt disinclined to move. 'Well I can't lie here all night,' he thought to himself. At length, with notions in his mind of mountains and Mohammed, he decided that his best course of action would be to crawl on hands and knees towards the Ninian crewmen. As he did so, he looked nervously around him. He was aware of strange structural groans that reverberated on all sides. Set away from the main superstructure, flame from the Ninian's flare stack flickered through the deepening darkness. An orange-coloured windsock waved in the wind. In the air he picked up the occasional whiff of cooking as the evening meal was prepared.

Robbie struggled on, not too concerned, perhaps, about the Ninian's record-breaking heritage. At that moment he may not have given much thought about how the Ninian Field, discovered in 1974 and brought on-stream four years later, was one of the oldest fields in the North Sea. The fact that oil was transported under the seabed via the amazing Ninian pipeline system to the Sullom Voe terminal in the Shetland Islands may have passed him by. Lost, too, may have been the point about the Ninian Central's record in 1978 as the world's largest man-made movable object when the six hundred thousand-tonne platform was towed into position and fixed to the seabed. Also possibly of little interest to Robbie may have been the statistical revelation that the Ninian Central's circular concrete gravity structure was one hundred and forty metres in diameter at its base, with seven concentric walls of stepped heights intersected by radial walls at forty-five-degree angles, and that a fourteen-metre-wide central shaft was surrounded by a breakwater wall forty-five metres in diameter, and that up to forty-two wells could be drilled.

Instead, when he reached the edge of the helideck, Robbie might have heaved a sigh of relief and harboured thoughts that his actions surely marked a triumph of human perseverance. When he stood up to join the group of Ninian crewmen,

Robbie noticed that the S-61N captain and co-pilot were amongst them. "Why the hell didn't you help me?" he wanted to cry out, "thanks for nothing!" But no, he didn't say that and instead followed them into a nearby office to discuss details of the S-61N's defect. The symptoms, Robbie concluded, suggested low pressure in the affected rotor blade spar or a crack in the blade. "In either case," said the captain, "if we don't leave soon we won't be leaving at all. The wind is already at our maximum limit of sixty knots and forecast to increase to one hundred knots." Robbie gazed into the small, black eyes of the captain seeing the sparks of excitement dancing in their centre-points. The co-pilot seemed similarly anxious. "I know, I know," sighed Robbie, "I get the message. But that blade has got to be checked."

Leaving the office to battle the elements once again, Robbie collected his tools and other paraphernalia before clambering up the side of the helicopter. He chose the windward side judging that, with the wind at his back, it would be safer to be blown towards the helicopter in the event of a mishap. He opened a hatch to gain access to the transmission inspection deck then, crouching low, he gave a signal to the pilot in the cockpit to release the helicopter's rotor brake. Gripping one of the rotor blades, Robbie now turned the rotor head manually until the problem blade was positioned directly in front of him. He worked with one hand while using the other to steady himself in the wind. He was forced to hold on to the main rotor spindle or the pitch link or the scissors – or anything else he could find which seemed reasonably secure.

Robbie discovered that the blade inspection method (BIM) indicator revealed slightly low blade pressure. Using his much-travelled tools and equipment he therefore topped up the pressure before climbing down to speak to the captain. "To confirm that I've rectified the problem," said Robbie, "I need you to start up and run the helicopter for about ten to fifteen minutes." The captain's jaw dropped, his eyes opened wide and he began to gesticulate. "Look," said Robbie, "either we do it now or we risk losing the aircraft when the wind picks up even more!" At this, the captain's pale, hollow-eyed look, his near-messianic gestures became a sight to behold as he recited chapter and verse from the S-61N flight manual. The captain then moved a few steps sideways to consult in private with his co-pilot. The two of them, Robbie observed, remained in deep discussion for some while as they waved their arms, shook their heads flamboyantly, adopted worried expressions. They seemed to tut and grimace but at length the two men pivoted on their heels and sidled up to Robbie. "Okay," announced the captain, "we've made a decision. We've decided to give it a go. But this decision, mind, is against our better judgement. So it's just this once."

"Right," said Robbie, "let's get on with it."

"To limit blade 'sailing'," asked the captain, "can we accelerate the rotor faster than normal?"

"I don't see why not. It shouldn't cause too much damage – but just this once, mind."

"Understood."

"If the BIM warning comes on during the ground run," said Robbie, "shut down at once. The helicopter will then just have to take its chances in the storm."

Robbie now hauled his gear into the helicopter's baggage hold while the two pilots strapped into their cockpit seats. With his gear stowed and the pre-start routines underway, Robbie stood in the companionway between the pilots. He had to hold on tightly while the S-61N bounced from side to side as stormy gusts struck the side of the machine. The wind whistled eerily through the fuselage; rain pounded against the windows; the entire helicopter seemed to rattle alarmingly. The three men felt increasingly nervous for they'd noted that the wind speed had picked up to seventy knots. Before long, though, with both engines started, the two pilots prepared for the crucial, hazardous moment of rotor brake release. Their faces pale and sharp, the men gazed fiercely at the cockpit instruments. With his hands gripping the flight controls, the captain's white knuckles showed up ominously. The co-pilot, meantime, used his right hand to ease the twin speed select levers gradually forward. Just at the point when the rotor brake could no longer restrain the rotors from turning, the captain nodded and said to his co-pilot: "Release it now!" At once, as the unleashed rotor blades shot round, there was a loud bang: the root section of one of the rotor blades had 'sailed' in the violent winds and struck the cockpit roof. Robbie ducked instinctively, then glanced up. Fortunately, no serious damage had been done.

Soon, once the rotor blades picked up speed, the S-61N began to settle and it was not long before the captain turned to Robbie to shout: "I'm going to take off now!" Robbie, who was without a headset for communication, merely shrugged his shoulders: the ten to fifteen minutes ground run he'd wanted was, he had to concede, probably unrealistic under the current circumstances. He therefore turned around and went back to sit in a passenger seat. He strapped himself in and gave a thumbs-up sign to the captain who acknowledged with a nod. Within moments, in firm, swift movements, the captain raised the helicopter's collective lever, thrust the cyclic stick forward and lifted away from the Ninian's helideck.

While the S-61N battled the elements, Robbie sat patiently in the hope that the flight time to Aberdeen, normally around two-and-a-half hours from the Ninian Field, would pass reasonably quickly. There was not much to do except gaze out of the window into dark space. He had to discipline himself against over-frequent checks of his watch although at one point, when he calculated that nearly an hour had elapsed since take-off, he decided to go forward to speak with the captain. "We're not making very good progress against these strong headwinds," the captain yelled above the din of the helicopter. "The wind speed's gusting up to ninety knots. We may not even have sufficient fuel to make it back to Aberdeen."

Despite the gloomy prediction, however, the S-61N struggled on and after a further two-and-a-half hours the captain eventually managed to land at Aberdeen.

"The problem blade seemed to cope," said the captain when, after landing, he walked with Robbie to sign the technical log.

"To be on the safe side," said Robbie, "I'll ask for the blade to be removed and put on an extended stress test."

The result, when it came through, revealed that after a two-day period the blade failed the stress test. This, Robbie reckoned, was an indication of a cracked main spar. "Hardly ideal," said the captain when he heard the news, "when flying in such stormy weather conditions. Did you hear what happened to the wind overnight? After landing at Aberdeen, wind speeds of one hundred and ten knots were recorded."

"Is that right?" Robbie asked.

"Yup. It meant that if we'd been flying directly into the wind our speed over the ground would have been a big, fat zero."

Robbie kept his fingers firmly crossed in the hope that his services would not be required for another such flight.

CHAPTER 3
MIRACLE MUM

Richard Pike in the Outer Hebrides

THERE WAS A moment of confusion and hesitation. The doctor walked assertively towards the helicopter while the nurse and her patient, a young woman with pregnancy complications, seemed to slow their pace. I glanced at my fellow pilot, Steve: "Perhaps we should shut down the engines?" I suggested. "The noise of the helicopter seems to be making her nervous." Steve, the aircraft captain for the flight, shrugged. "I suppose we could," he said, "but the case is urgent. We need to get her to hospital ASAP."

We watched as the doctor turned back when he realised that his patient had faltered. He went to her, seemed to offer some words of comfort, then helped the nurse to escort her gently towards the helicopter's air-stair door. While they walked up the steps, our winchman guided them on board and, as directed by the doctor, helped the patient to lie down on a stretcher. With a worried frown, she scrutinised the unfamiliar surroundings inside the helicopter. The helicopter itself, a Sikorsky S-61N registration G-BIMU, had been adapted for the search and rescue role: cabin seats had been removed to make room for a stretcher, other specialist paraphernalia had been fitted including comprehensive medical gear, additional communications equipment, and a powerful winch by the cargo door.

Above the racket of the helicopter we were unable to hear the conversation clearly but the doctor seemed to be reassuring her: "...don't worry...you're in good hands...it won't be a long flight..."

Within moments, when the winchman had closed the air-stair door, checked that the passengers were safely strapped in, assured himself that everything was in order, he gave a thumbs-up sign. The winch operator, secured by a special 'long' strap, then checked out of the open cargo door and said on the aircraft intercommunications system: "All clear above and behind, captain...okay to take off." Steve now firmly, smoothly raised G-BIMU's collective lever to lift the helicopter into a hover. When satisfied, he continued the take-off from a large field on the island of South Uist and turned onto a north-easterly heading for the hospital in Stornoway. He flew at fairly low level on a direct route to the hospital; clearly he was anxious to avoid any delay to our flight of thirty or so minutes.

Earlier, as we'd remained on standby in the search and rescue set-up at Stornoway Airfield, we had talked about this relatively new unit's activities and experiences, including the loss of a helicopter (G-BDII) the year before, in October 1988: the S-61N had crashed into the sea after the captain lost control during a night-time hover manoeuvre. Fortunately the crew members suffered only minor injuries and were rescued by the crew of another search and rescue unit flying a Royal Air Force Sea King helicopter. We talked, too, about the case which had prompted the contract awarded in 1987 to Bristow Helicopters to run the Stornoway unit.

It was just a few days before Christmas 1985 when the fishing vessel *Bon Ami* (BF323) ran aground while trying to make for the harbour at Kinlochbervie on the north-west coast of mainland Scotland. As the tide turned and the wind picked up to gale force, it became shockingly clear that the crew members were in grievous danger. Other fishing vessels and coastguard units rushed to the area where they found the *Bon Ami* listing heavily with waves crashing over the side. The skipper was on the radio in the wheelhouse while other crew members, waist-deep in foaming sea water, clung on to handrails. Only one man wore a life jacket; other life jackets were evidently inaccessible below deck. There was shouted communication; crew members said that they were freezing cold and could not hold on for much longer. With frigid fingers and numb legs, movement was hard and the crews' minds, clouded by the cold, must have struggled to act logically. There seemed to be plenty to say but little appetite to say it and as thought processes slowed, the will to live must have started to weaken. For those observing, the growing gravity of the situation surely haunted their minds: they may not get out of this one...this could be it...

Rescue efforts persisted, although tragically without success. Attempts to float life rafts onto the *Bon Ami* were thwarted by backwash from the shore. Rocket lines fired towards the stricken vessel became tangled in aerials. A search and rescue helicopter from RAF Lossiemouth was scrambled but was forced by icing conditions to take a long route. A helicopter based at Stornoway could have reached the area in time, but despite lobbying no dedicated unit had been established there. It was about 1 p.m. when the shouting stopped, hopes of rescue died away, the struggle ceased. No amount of preparation could stem the observers' sense of impotence as they witnessed the final moments when the *Bon Ami* succumbed to nature's clutches and rolled over to sink stern first taking all six members of the crew.

At that juncture, there was a period of silence as the four of us – the winchman, the winch operator, the captain (Steve) and myself – thought about the *Bon Ami* disaster. In the unit's new scrapbook, we studied press cuttings and crew reports about this and other cases then, as he turned the pages of the book, Steve pointed to details covering another, quite recent, case. "It was traumatic too," he said, "but at least there was a happy outcome." The case was in early April 1989, when a young mother, Catherine, was due to give birth in Daliburgh Hospital in South Uist. Complications had arisen and the on-call doctor decided that she should be taken to the better-equipped hospital at Stornoway. It was a Sunday afternoon, the Stornoway coastguard helicopter was scrambled and when the machine landed poor Catherine was watched by most of the village folk as she walked in her dressing gown across a car park into the helicopter. "I could have told them we wouldn't make it in time," she said later, "but nobody asked!"

The helicopter took off and Catherine, accompanied by a midwife, was helped along by the helicopter's onboard supply of Entonox, a pain-relieving mix of nitrous oxide and oxygen. She even began to enjoy the ride. "I remember looking out of the helicopter window," she said later, "and thinking: 'what a beautiful day...a beautiful spring morning...the sea was so blue.'"

"As you see," said Steve pointing to the press articles, "her reverie didn't last." We read that it was just ten minutes before landing when the midwife asked the winchman to give the pilot a message: "Tell him to slow down and take it steady! This baby is not going to wait!" The baby, indeed, did not wait and the article revealed how Catherine recalled that when the birth took place everyone in the helicopter became unexpectedly emotional. "The crew members were all in tears," she said later, "I suppose they were used to picking up people with terrible injuries and here they were with a birth. The captain radioed ahead to the hospital and told them to expect us to land with an extra passenger on board."

Suddenly, our reminiscences were interrupted when the coastguard telephone rang. The man nearest to the phone, the winch operator, lifted the receiver while the rest of us listened. "Mmmm...okay," he said, "understood...we'll be ready." He replaced the receiver and glanced up. "A potentially tricky one," he said, "the coastguard reckons that we may be required down in South Uist. The medics are worried about a pregnant woman there. She may need a helicopter transfer to Stornoway Hospital."

Instinctively we glanced at the scrapbook: was history about to be repeated? "It was only a warning call," said the winch operator, "which may come to nothing."

Topical conversation now wandered through various issues while we put the world to rights, including the dramatic changes in Mikhail Gorbachev's Soviet Union as well as events in East Germany's *Deutsche Demokratische Republik* and the astonishingly courageous efforts of 'tank man' in Tiananmen Square. At length, however, with the world more or less righted bar the odd detail, the telephone rang again and this time the winchman answered. All eyes watched him as silence fell across the room. "Right," he said, scribbling down details, "no problem...we're on our way." At this, he sounded the scramble siren and we began to dash towards the red and white liveried G-BIMU. Steve, as captain, made directly for the cockpit's right-hand seat while I occupied the co-pilot's seat on the left. Soon, as we strapped in and swiftly went through the start-up procedures, the two rear crew members hastily re-checked the cabin, slammed the air-stair door closed and strapped in before take-off.

"To speed things up," Steve said to me, "ask for a direct take-off from here." The wind direction was suitable and with the S-61N parked on hard-standing away from obstructions, the controller soon cleared us to proceed. Steve lifted G-BIMU into a hover then set heading on a south-westerly course as we took off in considerably less time than the stipulated maximum of fifteen minutes (forty-five at night).

After the frenetic activity, the atmosphere calmed down a little during our transit down to South Uist. We even had opportunities to take in some of the local scenes. To our right, overlooking the town of Stornoway itself and in the grounds of Lews Castle, was a slipway used in World War Two to launch Supermarine Walrus aircraft, an amphibious biplane operated by 700 Naval Air Squadron, the unit tasked in the 1950s to introduce into service the Westland Whirlwind which later earned distinction as a search and rescue helicopter. South of Lews Castle, the harbour was marked by the movements of large numbers of fishing vessels, and ahead, as we flew away from Stornoway, we could see the two lochs which marked the boundary between Lewis and Harris. For some reason not reasonably explained to me, the Isle of Lewis and the Isle of Harris consisted of one island with two names. The northern of the two, Lewis, was generally flat although helicopter pilots had to be wary of the southern isle, hilly Harris, which had more than thirty peaks above one thousand feet and one peak, Clisham, at over two thousand five hundred feet.

Before too long, when we crossed the waters of the Sound of Harris, I made a courtesy radio call to the controller at Benbecula Airport, a secluded outpost used, among other things, for flights to a nearby missile-testing range. Part of the range included a remote radar tracking station on the main island of St Kilda, a solitary spot with fickle winds known to make helicopter landings hazardous and to which I'd flown a few times recently to deliver specialist equipment and personnel.

The flight time worked out as calculated and when we drew close to the South Uist landing site the two rear crew members started to pace around the cabin as they double-checked this and that. Everything, though, had been carefully prepared as usual. Below, the patchwork of peat bog over North Uist contrasted with South Uist beyond, the latter with long, sandy beaches on the west coast and high ground, including a peak of over two thousand feet, on the east. Aviation chart in hand, I guided Steve towards the grid reference given by the coastguard until, quite soon, the field allocated for our landing came into view. We could see a crowd of onlookers and a fire engine and a police van parked nearby.

"Clear to open the cargo door, captain?" asked the winch operator.

"Go ahead," said Steve.

The winch operator, still attached to the 'long' strap which allowed him freedom of movement, slid back the cargo door at the front of G-BIMU's cabin. Leaning out, he began to give directions to the captain: "Forward ten as you approach the landing spot...down four and right two," glancing up I noticed an ambulance driving up to one corner of the field, "a further five to run, captain... landing spot on the nose...steady...steady...clear below to land."

As soon as the S-61N touched down, the winchman opened G-BIMU's air-stair door and headed for the ambulance. Meantime, the rest of the crew remained on board with the helicopter's engines and rotors still 'burning and turning'. When the patient appeared, she looked rather bedraggled in her dressing gown and woolly slippers. The accompanying nurse helped her along while the doctor followed our winchman who, efficient as ever, carried medical equipment to the helicopter. When the patient faltered, the doctor turned back to reassure her and to help the nurse guide their patient into the helicopter. As she walked up the steps and into the cabin, she seemed bewildered. Steve, however, conscious of the need for speed, spoke with the winch operator who soon confirmed that the air-stair door was shut and that the passengers were strapped in. From his position by the still-open cargo door, the winch operator then called: "clear above and behind for take-off".

Swiftly airborne and heading for Stornoway Hospital, at first the flight proceeded as planned. It was at about the halfway point when Steve and I became aware that something was wrong. We both glanced back into the cabin. The patient's blanket had been cast aside; the medical team stumbled around as if in a state of sudden panic. Our thoughts seemed to coincide...another airborne birth? The winch operator started to say something: "Spot of trouble back here... standby..." at which his headphone connecting plug was promptly disconnected. Isolated in our cockpit, as pilots we had to concentrate on the flight's safe progress. At one point, despite the helicopter's racket, we picked up an unusual sound – a sharp *crumph,* followed by another, then another.

By the time the winch operator had reconnected his headset we'd begun our approach to the helicopter emergency landing pad at Stornoway Hospital. Mindful that we needed to concentrate on the landing procedures, the winch operator merely said: "Bit of bother back here...tell you after landing." The procedures went according to plan and as soon as G-BMIU had touched down, the doctor and nurse assisted their patient to get up from her stretcher and head for the air-stair door. She walked down the steps to a wheeled stretcher which was used to whisk her away into the hospital. The doctor and nurse then came back on board and when the area was clear, we lifted the S-61N from the landing pad to head due east for our base at Stornoway Airport.

It was not until we'd completed the short flight back to the airport and closed down G-BIMU that Steve and I had a chance to speak with the doctor. "You okay?" Steve asked him.

"Yes and no," the doctor shook his head. "A close call but she's in good hands now."

"What happened exactly?"

"Her heart..." said the doctor haltingly "...her heart stopped during the flight. At one point I thought we'd lost her – she was technically dead."

I stared at the good doctor. Some moments of silence ensued and I was conscious that the heavy weight of responsibility seemed to bear down on him like a storm cloud. His facial expression reflected inner turmoil and in the ongoing hush I heard the haunting cries of gulls in the background. "So..." I went on eventually "...so she walked onto the helicopter...she died during the flight...then she walked off after landing? That's some kind of miracle is it not?"

"The process of birth is a miracle."

"Yes, but..."

The doctor gazed at us with dark, emotional eyes. "Perhaps," he said, "there are some things in life which are not meant to be understood."

I nodded and said quietly: "Indeed, doctor. This was a miracle mum. Let's just be grateful for that."

CHAPTER 4
NIGERIAN CHALLENGES

Peter Donaldson's unplanned plunges

THE OUTLOOK WAS good. That is to say, the outlook was reasonably good bearing in mind his situation. For Peter Donaldson, after a five-year spell as a helicopter pilot in the Royal Navy, had been posted by his company, Bristow Helicopters, to Nigeria where life was certainly not without challenges. In Nigeria Peter flew the Bell 206A Jetranger helicopter, a single-engine machine powered by an Allison 250-C18 turboshaft engine. The Jetranger could carry one pilot and four passengers – one seated next to the pilot and three behind. It was this type of aircraft that he'd been scheduled to fly in mid-August 1970 on a day when all did not go exactly to plan.

Peter was based in southern Nigeria at Warri, the commercial capital of Delta State and a city known nationwide for its unique form of pidgin English, and his task on this momentous day was to fly three passengers from Warri to the British Petroleum/Shell base at Forcados in the mouth of the Niger River. At Forcados he was scheduled to pick up another passenger before continuing offshore to the oil tanker *Niso* to drop off all four passengers.

As he drove to work that day, Peter noted an overcast, milky-coloured sky and he was relieved that conditions were dry even though this was the middle of the rainy season. He had not been long in Nigeria but he'd already experienced problems caused by the road to his accommodation in Warri, a house which he shared with other company personnel. This road was liable to flooding, although fortunately the company's trusty Volkswagen Beetle car seemed to cope amazingly well. Indeed, on one occasion the Beetle had needed to negotiate a flooded pothole which was so deep that the vehicle ended up floating like an amphibian. Carried along by its own momentum, the small car eventually reached the other side safely after which, as if with a shrug, it carried on non-chalantly, its passengers still dry although the brakes proved a little suspect (a not-too-uncommon feature of cars on Nigeria's roads).

While he continued his drive to work, Peter reflected that Nigeria's recent civil war (better known as the Biafran War) had ended just a few months earlier in mid-January 1970, and the country remained in a state of turmoil. This conflict, which had at root deep local tensions preceding Britain's decolonisation of Nigeria in the early 1960s, had led to severe hardship and suffering on a barely comprehensible scale. It was estimated that some two million civilians had died from starvation and disease during the two-and-a-half-year blockade of Biafra. Now, as the population recovered, a key aspect was the rebuilding of the Nigerian oil industry. For this, Peter and his colleagues were regularly asked to convey industry engineers and their equipment to out-of-the-way villages and other places where helicopters provided the most practical form of transport. After landing in what felt like the remotest of remote spots, Peter never failed to be intrigued by the way the helicopter's arrival brought dozens of children to the scene within minutes, swiftly followed by the adults as surely as if a bugle call had summoned them. The local people always seemed more than glad to see Peter and his colleagues. As a kindly act, Peter learnt to take glossy magazines with him so that, after landing, he could rip out the pictures and distribute them to the youngsters whose glee was marvellous to see.

However, mused Peter as he drove along, less marvellous were the area's climatic hazards and the potential perils of flying in a tropical equatorial region. When he'd first arrived in Nigeria he'd been briefed on the two distinct seasons, wet and dry, and the implications for flying operations. Although the wet season, which generally ran between March/April through to October/November, created particular challenges including massive thunderstorms, in some ways, he reckoned, this was the better season for their operations: the dry season winds would swing round to the north-east to carry Sahara Desert dust across West Africa, an effect known in Nigeria as the Harmattan, and the Jetranger's Allison engine could give problems. As a single-engine machine, the reliability of the engine was, one could say, fairly fundamental, which was about to be highlighted in Peter's forthcoming flight.

When he drove up to the company's base set-up, Peter soon commenced the pre-flight planning which included, among other matters, a check of the meteorological forecast – such as it was; Port Harcourt Airport was just a few miles away but the information was still rudimentary. When satisfied, he signed the necessary paperwork before walking out to his allocated Jetranger which had been carefully parked on a specific spot. With his three passengers cleared to board, he went through the pre-start routines. When completed, he signalled 'ready to start' to the ground crewman who checked behind and to the sides of the helicopter before giving a 'clear to start' sign. It was not long before the distinctive sound of the Allison engine crescendoed to a high-pitched whine and Peter spoke to a local controller who cleared him to take off and assume a south-westerly heading for the short flight from Warri to Forcados.

As he flew across the Niger Delta, Peter felt a sense of privilege at the opportunities to fly above such an interesting region and at a time when its peoples were more than a little relieved that the recent war had ended. The densely populated delta acted as the lifeblood of the region which was sometimes called the Oil Rivers, a reference not so much to modern petroleum production as to Victorian times when the area was a major producer of palm oil. The ecosystem, Peter knew, contained one of the highest concentrations of biodiversity in the world with the ability to support a wide variety of crops, trees and freshwater fish. Local fishermen built traps which provided a large source of local food that included the delicious red snapper suppers presented by the elderly Nigerian who acted as cook/steward in Peter's accommodation. Pollution could be a problem although high humidity and temperature acted to break down any spills fairly rapidly. Corruption at government level was endemic, and even though Nigeria's profit from oil was considerable, the River States saw little benefit at that time.

Peter's flight to Forcados and onwards to the oil tanker *Niso* proceeded as planned and it was on the return flight from the *Niso* that trouble loomed. He'd taken his passengers to the tanker, closed down for lunch, then picked up four other passengers for the return journey. He flew one passenger to Forcados, and took off again to take the remaining three to Warri. Flying above the Niger Delta, he was able to appreciate the fine views of coastal barrier islands, mangrove swamp forests, freshwater swamps and, in the distance, lowland rain forests. Conditions, as usual, were hot and humid and he was looking forward to a cold drink at Warri when, suddenly, a strange 'schlooop' sound was followed without further warning by engine failure.

At once, Peter lowered the Jetranger's collective lever to enter autorotation. He turned into wind and transmitted a Mayday distress call on the aircraft radio. During the autorotational descent, and with the Jetranger rapidly losing height, he inflated the floats stowed in skids on either side of the fuselage. With thoughts of analysis and remedial action racing through his mind, he searched for reference points on the water's surface. The surface, however, was smooth and misleading although he managed to focus on a patch of floating weed. This opportune reference point was basic but enough to guide him as he pulled back the cyclic stick to convert forward airspeed into lift. With skill and judgement acquired over years, he manoeuvred the Jetranger to achieve a successful landing on the water. Within moments of settling, he checked around the cockpit to turn off electrical systems then removed his headset and told the passenger in the left seat: "Push the life raft onto the water!" Needing no further encouragement, the man quickly complied. Meantime, Peter spotted bubbles burst up from the right-hand skid. "We've a problem with the right-hand float," he said to the passengers, "we'll have to evacuate into the life raft!"

The four men now scrambled out of the helicopter and into the life raft, a drill facilitated by previous briefings and practice. On successful completion, Peter assured his passengers that a Mayday message had been transmitted and that they just needed to wait for rescue. Encouraged in this way, the four men settled down to sit patiently in the hope that help would come soon.

With very little wind and attached by rope to the Jetranger they felt reasonably safe although Peter worried about the helicopter's list to starboard as the float slowly deflated. While the four men sat disconsolately, conversation was sporadic for the heat and humidity soon made them drowsy. From time to time Peter bailed out water then sank lower in the life raft in attempts to escape the sun's rays. He glanced frequently at his watch and wondered if rescue would be by launch or a winch-equipped helicopter. Suddenly he lifted his head as if to focus his ears for he thought he could hear the distant hum of a boat engine. He sat up and turned to see a launch heading their way. Before long the engine noise was intermingled with the shouts of the crew as the launch, despatched from a nearby oil rig, pulled up alongside. Peter helped his three passengers to evacuate the life raft, then followed himself. When on board the launch, he discussed with the captain what to do about the Jetranger. "We'll tow it along behind us," said the captain.

"It might sink," said Peter, "can we secure the faulty skid to the side of the launch?"

After some disagreement, the captain eventually relented and manoeuvred his craft alongside the helicopter which, duly secured, acted like an outrigger canoe as it was hauled towards the oil rig from where the passengers were flown back to dry land in another helicopter.

When the Jetranger was examined, engineers discovered that the company contracted to overhaul the engine had used incorrect procedures as a result of which the fuel pump failed. The outside of the helicopter was hosed down with fresh water, no other faults were found and the machine was flying again within a week. A further, somewhat unexpected, upshot was that the four passengers revealed to the authorities that they'd lost solid gold Rolex watches during the proceedings. In this way, future passengers were reassured when word spread that an engine failure was survivable, moreover it was possible to claim a brand new, solid gold Rolex watch.

Some three months later, in November 1970, Peter was posted to the Bristow base in Port Harcourt, the capital city of Nigeria's Rivers State and a key centre for the country's petroleum industry. As, by then, it was considered safe for wives and families to live in Nigeria, Peter was joined by his wife. They were allocated a bungalow within a compound run by the Shell oil company, a property, as was customary, given the same name as the occupiers. Situated to the north-east of Port Harcourt, the Shell compound, called Umukoroshe, occupied an area of a couple of square miles with hundreds of houses, a club with a theatre, a swimming pool and a nine-hole golf course. Surrounded by a very high fence, the compound offered a life protected from the danger of robbers and other criminals. Children could cycle in safety to the compound's primary school and they could play outdoors. Many better-off Nigerians also lived in such compounds.

In mid-December 1970, on a day which dawned dull but dry, Peter was scheduled to carry out checks on a newly fitted engine in Jetranger registration 5N-AIO. On completion of the checks he would land then pick up four passengers to fly them from Port Harcourt to the coastal oil base on Bonny Island.

The engine checks duly proved satisfactory so that, with the paperwork completed and the passengers ready to board, Peter was cleared to start up and take off to head for the Bonny base. As was routine, rather than risk an engine failure over mangrove trees he flew over the waters of Bonny River which widened significantly towards the coast. While he flew along, Peter spotted the numerous water taxis which plied the river to connect Port Harcourt and Bonny Island. To the west and south of the island, he could see in the far distance long stretches of beach, popular with locals and tourists and renowned for colourful beach carnivals on 26 and 31 December annually.

In his mind, perhaps, were thoughts of satisfaction at the way life was turning out in Nigeria for he and his wife were happy there and she had applied successfully for a post in a local secondary school for girls. Of course, he mused, their situation in Nigeria was a privileged one which, at times, could lead to a sense of guilt. For one thing, every residence in the compound had a servant and theirs, a cook/steward called Joseph, was a skilled chef who'd been employed on an oil rig before the civil war. Peter and his wife felt, in a liberal kind of way, that it was not right for Joseph to work just for them. They were told, however, that as hundreds of thousands of Nigerians had been displaced because of the war, jobs were scarce especially those where the pay amounted to £12 to £15 a month as in Joseph's case. When they discovered that this sum supported not only Joseph's wife and children but numbers of his family in a remote village, they were amazed and agreed to Joseph's appeal to employ his cousin, called Akpan, as a gardener on a salary of £6 a month. Peter was aware that some of the Umukoroshe residents were unkind to their Nigerian staff who, he was warned, were inclined to steal. Joseph, though, proved honest and dependable and sometimes Peter would give him an extra allowance to do all the domestic shopping.

It was about ten minutes after take-off, and while he continued to fly above the Bonny River, that such thoughts were promptly put out of Peter's mind. By then he'd reached a wide section of the river estuary known as the Cawthorne Channel where he'd observed the way that the colour of the water looked grey and muddy along the coastline, unlike the clearer water in the channel's centre. Flying at a height of two thousand feet all seemed well until the helicopter was suddenly rocked by an explosion above Peter's head. A second or two elapsed while he absorbed the implications. Possibilities raced through his mind – bird strike?...technical failure?...servicing error?...until he realised that he was still in a serviceable helicopter, albeit one with an engine that had stopped. Now he went through the same drills as a few months ago including the Mayday call which, this time, he made on the Port Harcourt Airport Tower frequency..."Five India Oscar – engine failure – ditching Cawthorne Channel."

"Oh...India Oscar," replied the controller, "PLEASE say again."

After a pause, the captain of a passing British airliner said in a very public school accent: "He's had an engine failure and he's ditching in the Cawthorne Channel. For God's sake listen man!"

With the Jetranger autorotating down, Peter saw that the water below, as before, was smooth and deceptive. With thoughts, perhaps, that this was becoming a habit, he managed to focus on a roughened surface patch to help his judgement for the flare and landing. Within moments the passengers felt a vigorous manoeuvre as Peter pulled back the cyclic stick. Just as the helicopter was about to land, he raised the collective lever to the maximum limit thus enabling the rotor's kinetic energy to check the helicopter's descent before touchdown. The Jetranger, though, had heavy baggage in the rear hold and was fuel-heavy after only ten minutes of flight. The tail rotor consequently touched the water thereby twisting the drive shaft which later needed to be replaced along with the engine.

Peter now evacuated his four passengers into the Jetranger's life raft after which he decided to climb back aboard the helicopter. Unlike his last experience, both the helicopter's floats appeared to be serviceable so he elected to stay with the machine until a rescue boat arrived to tow him to safety. Using the Jetranger's radio he called up base to confirm that the Mayday call had been received. Affirmative, he was told, the call had been logged and a winch-equipped Wessex helicopter had been despatched to retrieve his passengers. It was not long before the Wessex arrived and the four passengers, duly winched-up, were flown back to base where, yes, they claimed new gold watches.

Meanwhile, back in the Jetranger, Peter was drifting downstream at a pace rather quicker than was comfortable. In fact, he began to feel increasingly vulnerable and he worried that he'd be swept out to sea never to be found again. Later, he would learn that the boat sent to rescue him had turned back due to a misunderstanding, although by chance another boat, a passing canoe paddled along by a river state fisherman, approached him at one stage: "Why for you in de river, master?" asked the river state man.

"My engine," replied Peter, adopting the local form of pidgin English, "done go big bang and I have to be in de river."

The fisherman paddled around looking distressed. "Sorry, master," he said, "so sorry." He held up his catch and said: "I dash you some fish!" Reckoning that the kindly fellow assumed that Peter would be stuck in the helicopter for weeks, he put the fisherman's mind at rest after which he waved farewell and paddled his canoe away from the scene to leave Peter alone again.

As the time ticked by, Peter speculated on the cause of the engine failure. He'd learn in due course that the engine's main turbine spool had been incorrectly torque-loaded. The turbine's end nut consequently flew off and hit the inlet guide vanes at which juncture, with turbine rotors operating at about fifty-two thousand revolutions per minute, the engine blew up.

At length, after an hour of drifting and with the sight of land becoming progressively distant, Peter decided to call base again. He managed, fortunately, to make radio contact and when he'd explained his situation he thought that he could hear curses in the background. Half-an-hour later a rescue boat arrived, took Peter on board, rigged-up a towline to the Jetranger and during the subsequent journey to safety a crestfallen skipper explained that he'd spotted the helicopter earlier. However, some weeks ago he'd taken part in a staged exercise and, assuming this to be another such exercise, had turned around to go back to his oil rig. The skipper was gently reminded that staged exercises did not usually include a ditched helicopter.

Peter spent another eighteen months in Nigeria during which period he experienced intensive flying, though luckily without further engine failures. By the time of their move, he and his wife realised how much they had grown to appreciate the country, the ups and downs of life there, the eccentricities and challenges, the open friendliness of the good people they'd met. They sympathised with the ordinary folk who continued to struggle with the aftermath of the civil war and its brutality. They looked back with memories sparked, perhaps, by thoughts of a warm, dark African night, the distant flickers of lightning against the face of the moon, the dawn chorus that heralded a magnesium sun rising to hover and blaze across the country to create deep shadows of dark and light, a fitting facsimile of the complex contrasts they'd experienced during their time in Nigeria.

CHAPTER 5
CHINOOK DOWN

Captain Pushp Vaid VrC

Author's note: with the distressing nature of events described in this chapter I felt it inappropriate to add further analysis or dramatisation. The chapter therefore follows Captain Vaid's own words as he sent them to me.

ON 6 NOVEMBER 1986 at 1132 hours a Boeing-Vertol 234 Chinook helicopter crashed just two miles short of its destination of Sumburgh Airport in the Shetland Islands. It was the worst ever civilian helicopter crash. Of the forty-seven people on board, the lives of forty-five were taken.

I was the captain of the helicopter and, together with one passenger, I survived the crash. How or why we survived remains a mystery. There's no explanation, it was just pure luck. For a long time after the accident I would ask myself: "Why were the other passengers not so lucky?" I guess that nobody can answer such a question. When the helicopter wreckage was retrieved from the sea, the accident investigating inspector met me. He was wondering how I could possibly have survived the crash. But not only did I survive, I came out with very minor injuries.

I joined British Airways Helicopters in 1975 after leaving the Indian Air Force. In 1982 I converted to Chinooks, the largest civilian helicopter in the world, and by 1986 I'd flown over two thousand five hundred hours on this type. In my flying career, which spanned over forty-four years, I amassed nearly eighteen thousand hours on helicopters, but in spite of the accident I would still say that the Chinook was the best helicopter I ever flew because of the aircraft's tremendous power. With a full fuel load the Chinook had over six hours of endurance and could always carry a full load of passengers.

There were six Chinooks in our company, one of which would fly to Sumburgh on a Monday morning to operate from there for a five-day period before returning to Aberdeen on the Friday evening. For this, we had two sets of crews. One crew did the morning two flights to the East Shetland basin, situated just over one hundred miles north-east of Sumburgh, then the second crew came in at 1300 hours for one flight in the afternoon.

On Monday 3 November 1986 I flew Chinook G-BWFC from Aberdeen up to Sumburgh for one of these Monday to Friday sessions. My co-pilot was 43-year-old First Officer Neville Nixon who, a few years earlier, had left Bristow Helicopters to help his wife Pauline set up a chemist shop in York. After three years, the chemist shop was doing so well that Pauline could manage by herself which meant that Neville could return to his first love, that of flying. He joined British Airways Helicopters in the summer of 1986 and because he hadn't flown for nearly three years he was very keen to make the most of opportunities to fly. On that fateful day in November 1986 he was rostered to fly the afternoon shift. However, because the morning shift involved two flights and he wanted to boost his flying hours, he arranged to change shifts with First Officer Mike Stanley. This change cost Neville his life.

Thursday 6 November 1986 was a beautiful day at Sumburgh Airport with light winds, it didn't feel cold and I anticipated good flying conditions. By the time I arrived for work that morning Neville was already in the operations set-up to carry out the planning for our flight. When he'd finished, I remember that he rang home. It was the last time that he spoke to his wife.

At about 0730 that morning, our cabin attendant, Mike Walton, arrived and went to the Chinook to do his checks on the helicopter which included confirmation that the cabin was clean and that all the safety equipment was on board. With all pre-flight procedures completed, by 0900 we had started up G-BWFC and begun to taxi the helicopter from our company hangar at 'Virkie' to the other side of the runway where, at 'Wilsness', we picked up our passengers from the Sumburgh passenger terminal. By this stage we had learnt of a last-minute change to our original plan: in addition to landing on the Brent Bravo and Brent Delta we were required, too, to land on the Brent Alpha to drop a load. This added some ten minutes to our flight, ten minutes that would turn out to be crucial for the accident happened just two minutes before our planned landing back at Sumburgh...destiny, yes?

On the outbound flight I was the handling pilot while my co-pilot operated the radios, attended to load sheets, maintained a flight log and carried out other administrative tasks. The flight proceeded as planned and after our landings on the Brent Alpha, Charlie and Delta everything seemed fine and at 1043 we set course to return to Sumburgh. We had a full complement on board: forty-four passengers and three crew. For this stage of the flight Neville was the handling pilot while I dealt with the radios and administrative duties. We flew at a height of two thousand five hundred feet on 'Track Mike' and I recall that we flew in and out of clouds although the weather was generally very nice and we had an enjoyable flight. Neville and I talked about all sorts of things and he told me about his brother who had been to India and liked it there.

At a range of forty miles from Sumburgh Airfield we changed radio frequency and initiated a slow descent down to one thousand feet. We carried out approach checks and at a range of ten miles from Sumburgh I changed radio frequency to the control tower. We descended to five hundred feet and I contacted my company to give a routine 'two minutes to landing' call. Meanwhile, in the Bristow hangar the coastguard crew were preparing for a training flight. Their Sikorsky S-61 search and rescue helicopter call-sign 'Oscar Charlie' was fuelled and ready but the crew had to wait for one of their members to return from an errand. The delay meant that the S-61 was airborne shortly after 1129, just as our Chinook was on finals for landing.

It was at this juncture, when the Chinook was about three and a half miles from the runway, that we began to hear a whining noise that seemed to get louder. The noise did not sound dangerous. Mike Walton, our cabin attendant, opened the door to the cockpit to tell us that he'd checked the cabin and that the passengers were all strapped in and ready for landing. He heard us discuss the whining noise and said that it came from the front gearbox which was just above his head. He didn't seem alarmed by the noise.

By now two minutes from landing, we were descending through a height of approximately two hundred and fifty to three hundred feet above the sea. Our airspeed was reducing below one hundred knots. I remember that we decided to inform the engineers about the noise so that they could sort it out before the next flight. I radioed to the tower that we were on finals. The controller cleared us to land. I saw the coastguard helicopter ahead. Our cabin attendant opened the cabin door then closed it behind him, though I don't believe that he had a chance to sit down and strap in. A fraction of a second later, at exactly 1132, we heard a very loud bang.

Suddenly, the Chinook pitched nose-up violently. The helicopter pointed vertically upwards; I could see the sky ahead of me. I had no time to make a Mayday call. Then the Chinook began to fall backwards towards the sea. Instinctively, I grabbed the cyclic control stick and pushed it fully forward to try to level the helicopter. As if we were performing an outside loop, I felt negative 'g' (gravity force) and the Chinook appeared to move from pointing vertically upwards to vertically downwards. Now I could see the sea in front of me. The helicopter was rushing nose-down vertically towards the sea. As we went down I was aware that everything around me was breaking up. My mind was thinking in double-quick time, trying to work out if there was anything I could do to save the helicopter and all of us in it. To me, it felt as if we were in a fairground roller-coaster ride. I was hoping that the helicopter would level out at the bottom of the ride, we would land on the water and everybody would come out safely. Not for one moment did it occur to me that anybody would die.

When the Chinook hit the water, the rear end took the impact. The cockpit, with me still inside it, broke off from the helicopter and fell gently into the sea as if from twenty feet. The cockpit kept going down to at least thirty feet below the surface before it stopped moving. I could make out the sunlight so I knew which way to swim. Despite this, when I left the seat and started to swim I suddenly discovered that I was going the wrong way; it was getting darker. At once, I turned around to head towards the sunlight. I passed through the emergency window which had been blown away and I started to swim up towards the surface.

Beautiful sunshine met me at the surface. I was feeling very cold and my breathing was excessively fast and hard. I spotted what looked like a big bowl which I think was part of the fuel tank cover. I managed to climb into it but two seconds later a wave tipped me over and I was back in the water. I wasn't worried, though: in the back of my mind I knew that the search and rescue helicopter would be overhead soon. It was just a case of waiting for it to come and pick us all up.

At this point a body popped up next to me, then another and another. Before long there must have been at least seven bodies floating close to me and not moving. That was the first time it occurred to me that perhaps some people had died. There was a lot of hydraulic fluid and broken pieces of the Chinook floating in the sea near me. When I looked up, I saw the coastguard helicopter heading towards the area. I waved my arms and the helicopter moved to a position above me. Then the winchman was lowered and he placed a strop around me to winch me up. My shoes were coming off and for some reason I was hanging onto them, although in the end I never saw them again.

When I was settling inside the coastguard helicopter I became aware that someone else was being winched up. My survival suit was full of cold water so even though I was out of the sea I was still in cold water. Every time a member of the crew came to check me I made a hand signal to cut my survival suit so the water could drain away. However, with all of the helicopter noise he could not understand me although eventually he realised and cut the suit. By now both of my eyes were closing up, as were the eyes of the other survivor. The crewman therefore told the captain to take us to the hospital at Lerwick.

When we arrived at the hospital my body temperature was down to around thirty-three degrees centigrade. The hospital staff cut away all of my clothes and wrapped me in a tin foil space blanket. At last I began to warm up. My eyes were still closed but suddenly I heard a doctor speaking to me in Hindi, my native language. They don't speak Hindi in heaven do they? I knew then that I was still alive.

Later, when the remains of G-BWFC had been recovered from the sea, I listened to the tape from the cockpit voice recorder which had been taken to the workshop of the Aircraft Accident Investigation Board. I could hear the noise from the front gearbox as the modified bevel ring gear was breaking up – a noise that lasted for the entire thirty minutes of the tape. Once the bevel ring gear fractured, the Chinook's front rotor slowed down a fraction after which it was a matter of just twenty or thirty seconds before the helicopter's two counter-rotating rotor blades collided with each other. That was the loud bang which we heard. The rear rotor blades began to shake so much that they, along with the rear gearbox which weighed more than a ton, parted company from the Chinook to splash down in the water about a mile away from us. A gentleman standing on top of a hill some five miles from the accident site saw the Chinook fall towards the sea. He was able to point out to the salvage team where to look for the rear rotor.

Now without a rear rotor, there was nothing to hold up the back end of the Chinook. As the machine's back end fell, so the nose of the aircraft went up, pointing vertically upwards at the sky. Because the helicopter, which had been travelling at around one hundred knots, came to such an abrupt stop, the whiplash effect probably killed many of the passengers. My co-pilot, too, probably died at that instant. As the handling pilot, he was sitting slightly forward, his back not against the seat's backrest. Because I was the non-handling pilot my back was resting on the backrest so that the whiplash effect was not as great – although thinking about it (like right now) I begin to feel pain in my back.

By this stage the whole structure of the helicopter was weakened and starting to break up. When I'd pushed the cyclic stick forward, the front rotor blades, which were still responding to control inputs, had flipped over the cockpit section of the Chinook. Only the floor of the cockpit had remained attached to the main body of the helicopter. My action of pushing the cyclic stick forward was probably responsible for saving the two of us who survived. With the whole helicopter falling backwards towards the sea, and with the cockpit askew, a large hole appeared at the top of the cabin where the cockpit had been. The other survivor, Eric Morrans, was thrown through this hole when he was unconscious under water.

I found out later that the front rotor blades had chopped off the part of the windscreen in front of the co-pilot. Broken bits from the windscreen had been flying around, some hitting me in the face as the Chinook fell towards the sea. The left side of my face was cut and I suffered a broken nose but amazingly nothing struck my eyes. Another amazing detail discovered later was that I'd never unbuckled my seat belt. When the cockpit was salvaged the accident investigators found that one strap had broken but the other three were still locked in position. How did I come out of those straps? I have no idea!

A further remarkable aspect was the way events worked out with the coast-guard helicopter. The crew were preparing for a training sortie but were delayed by a colleague late back from an errand. Eventually able to get going at last, the captain wanted to head directly for his planned training area. Once airborne, he asked the air traffic controller to confirm the position of the Chinook. The controller looked up but was astonished that he couldn't see the Chinook which he'd just cleared to land. The crew of the coastguard machine then spotted debris floating in the sea so immediately made for that area. The crew saw me waving, winched me up and began an urgent search for other survivors. There was only one, twenty-year-old Eric Morrans who'd been sitting in the front row of seats which faced backwards. By a quirk of fate he survived the crash because he was sitting in the wrong seat. Later, Eric described how he saw the fear of death on the facial expressions of the other forty-three passengers when the Chinook was plunging vertically backwards into the sea. "Looking towards me was an audience of faces totally shocked. I did almost nothing to save myself. It was just luck, the grace of God if you want to call it that." He could see that all of them knew they were going to die, although in fact some of them had already died because of the whiplash effect.

Eric, like me, was just plain lucky. When he'd heard the loud bang, out of instinct he'd zipped up his survival suit. There were, he said, a lot of broken bits and pieces flying around the cabin and he was knocked unconscious. As the Chinook plunged into the sea he went with it. When he was about thirty feet underwater his survival suit, which was full of air, acted like a football under water: natural buoyancy thrust him upwards, through the hole behind him and on up to the surface. At the surface, waves from the sea lapped over his face and woke him up. As he opened his eyes he found, quite by chance, an inflated dinghy next to him. He grabbed the dinghy and tied his hand to it with a rope – just in time for he then passed out again. Woken by the noise of the coastguard helicopter, he looked across to see me being winched up. Worried that he may be left behind, he started to wave his hands frantically. The coastguard crew spotted him, winched him up and took the two of us to the Gilbert Bain Hospital, Lerwick.

The mechanical failure that caused the gearbox to break up was a one-in-a-million chance. The Chinook was withdrawn from United Kingdom civil operations, though it remained in use with the military. I was advised by friends not to return to flying, and the company (by then British International Helicopters) offered to pension me off. I knew, however, that money alone wouldn't fill the hours; flying was all that I ever wanted to do. By February 1987 I felt ready to fly again. The company, though, insisted on psychiatric tests and I did not return to flying until April 1987. I flew for a further twenty years and enjoyed every minute of it.

CHAPTER 6

HELI-MISCELLANY (1)

Dietary solution (from Alan Boulden)

A SENIOR ROYAL Air Force officer, evidently not well liked and not world famous for his tact, was sent from London in the mid-1980s to visit the RAF contingent on the Falkland Islands, including the helicopter elements. When the officer toured a Swedish-built floating accommodation barge known as a coastel which housed airmen supporting the nearby Stanley airfield, he was shown into the coastel's dining area where a number of airmen were assembled. The coastel's design was nothing if not basic; indeed, when eventually sent to the USA to be used as a prison ship, significant upgrading was required. The senior officer, though, did not seem too bothered about this. He strode into the dining area, glanced menacingly about him and barked the age-old question favoured by senior officers who inspected dining rooms: "Any complaints?"

One man, a helicopter specialist technician, raised his hand timidly: "I have one, sir."

"Well?"

"It's to do with the choice at meal times."

"What about it?"

"There's never any salad."

At this the senior officer turned around, whispered instructions to his aide-de-camp who went up to the airman and took a note of his name.

Several weeks went by until an official-looking letter was received by the airman. He tore open the envelope to read the senior officer's terse post-script attached to a packet of lettuce seeds with the words: bon appétit!

Wessex ditching (from Mike Lehan)

THE TRAINING FLIGHT in a Wessex Mk 3 helicopter had been underway in the English Channel for some forty-five minutes; it was a dark February night in 1970 and the instructor, Lieutenant Mike Lehan, was pleased with progress up to that point. His students, young naval pilots, were under Mike's guidance as they searched for a submarine by use of sonar, however the wind was increasing to gale-force strength and the sea had been whipped up to a very rough state. By now the training exercise had achieved three hovers and a fourth was in progress with the sonar unit at full depth and pinging away as sonar units do. Mike, though, was worried about the sea state. He knew that the conditions were becoming too rough to effect a safe recovery in the event of a ditching. So he'd decided that this should be the last hover before he and his students flew the Wessex back to base.

Imagine his shock and disbelief, therefore, when the Wessex cockpit suddenly filled with smoke and the fire warning light illuminated. At once he leant across the cockpit, swiftly brought back the fuel control lever to stop the engine as, simultaneously, he transmitted a terse Mayday call. The Wessex now sank down for a crash landing which fortunately proved relatively gentle. As soon as the helicopter touched the sea's surface, inflatable bags operated to keep the machine afloat. After a few minutes, though, these bags were almost thrashed to shreds by the rough sea – but not before the four crew members had had time to abandon the helicopter and to launch four single-man rubber dinghies.

Proceeding with well-rehearsed drills, each crew member grasped his dinghy pack's attachment cord, and threw the pack into the sea while jumping clear of the Wessex and tugging at the dinghy's inflation device. With the reassuring sound of rushing gas and the creak of unfolding rubber, the dinghies rapidly inflated. Clambering into their individual dinghies the men found that waves pounded against them to cause the small dinghies, which sat high in the water, to roll alarmingly until canvas sea anchors were deployed to help steady the movement. With the wind's howl rising to a shriek, the air was filled with wind-blown spray. Marauding waves persisted to toss the rubber dinghies this way and that. From the crest of a wave one moment, a mountain would collapse to leave a great emptiness into which the dinghies would plunge.

Mike had not been long settled in his dinghy when he looked up at the Wessex to see that the rotors were still turning: he'd forgotten to apply the rotor brake! What, he wondered with a curse, would his commanding officer say when he learnt that Mike had failed to close down the aircraft correctly? In a remarkable act prompted by deeply instilled training (some might call it brainwashing), he climbed out of his dinghy, scrambled up the undercarriage oleo leg, re-entered the helicopter's cockpit, engaged the rotor brake, turned off the battery master switch then clambered down the oleo leg and returned to his dinghy. A few seconds later both floatation bags exploded and the Wessex sank to the deep.

The four survivors now tethered their dinghies one to the other with Mike in the lead dinghy. The maelstrom surrounding them could overwhelm the senses but these were four highly trained, highly disciplined aircrew who understood the significance of the 'will to live'. If fear was felt (which it surely was), such fear had to be fought before it turned to despair. For if fear, real fear, was allowed to take control, it would be all too easy for a survivor to be led towards a mortal end. So it was that the four men ensured that their dinghies were kept as ship-shape as possible – sea water regularly bailed out, dinghy floors and protective canopies kept fully inflated, location aids to hand for quick use. These and other routines had been practised over and over again in regular naval survival drills.

Although held within the gloom of a February night, the survivors were not in complete darkness for small lights, activated by contact with sea water, shone dimly like beacons of hope. The lights, which reflected the Day-glo colouring of the dinghies' canopies, helped to boost morale and the four men, unlike the lone fighter pilot, could shout encouragement to one another. With limbs and torsos inclined to become numb with cold, minds had to stay focused and alert.

The sound, when heard, must have stirred many emotions for now, wavering in the wind, the four men listened to the distant clatter of a helicopter. Hearts thumping, they watched the machine's lights probe the darkness. Making hasty preparations for rescue, the survivors set off night flares and listened appre-hensively as the noise crept ever closer. Before long they watched when the machine came to a hover above the rear dinghy of the linked-up group that must have looked like castaways. The helicopter, which turned out to be an Australian Sea King of the foreign training unit based at the Royal Naval Air Station at Culdrose, manoeuvred to a winching position to take the first survivor on board. The Sea King crew, who'd reacted to Mike's Mayday call, had by chance been in the vicinity on their own training exercise.

Mike was the last to be winched up. During the winching process he was astonished by the strength of the Sea King's downwash – a bombardment of water which struck his face painfully, as if in a violent hailstorm, and which almost blinded him. Almost blinding, too, were the Sea King's powerful down lights which made it very hard to see the rescue strop. Feeling frigid with cold, when he was winched into the Sea King's cabin, Mike was amazed to see that the duty crewman had remote control of the hover – as a former aircrewman himself, he thought how wonderful! Stepping out of the rescue strop, he then went forward to thank the pilots. Standing in the space behind the pilots, how-ever, Mike was horrified to observe the Sea King's hydraulic gauges which thrashed left and right to full-scale deflection. Convinced that a hydraulic failure was imminent and in anticipation of another ditching, he ran back to sit down in the doorway ready to abandon yet another helicopter.

The helicopter's puzzled crewman, having established the cause of Mike's concern, explained to him that this early version of the Sea King did not have damped hydraulic gauge instruments. Mike's worries were assuaged, the flight continued and the return to base was without further problems.

As a postscript to the accident, the Wessex was recovered from the seabed and eventually rebuilt to fly again. Examination of the machine revealed that the engine's jet exhaust pipes had detached causing hot gases to be directed into the engine bay and the cockpit. Whether the rotor brake was found to be applied as proof of Mike's correct shut-down drills, and whether this point was brought to the attention of his commanding officer, remains, though, a matter of conjecture.

French encounter (from Richard Pike)

THERE WERE FOUR of us, two pilots and two aircrewmen, all dressed in service-issue military combat gear as we walked through the French village of La Courtine in the Nouvelle-Aquitaine region of central France. We were heading for a local cafe which, we'd been told, was the best in town. A couple of days earlier, we'd flown two 18 Squadron Westland Wessex helicopters from our base at Royal Air Force Gütersloh, Germany, to a military camp in the La Courtine complex – a camp with the capacity to house up to four thousand troops and which, when opened in 1904, had inevitably caused a local stir. We'd been told that the villagers, *paysants* during the day, became bar keepers at night so that, according to rumour, there were soon more bars than inhabitants. We certainly saw plenty of bars that evening as we continued to stroll through the village streets after a fairly hectic day of flying. This flying, part of a NATO training exercise, had involved several sorties over lakes, forestry, farmland and mountains, some of which rose to over six thousand feet and which were part of the renowned diversity found in the *massif central* area that covered almost one-sixth of France.

Before we'd left Gütersloh, the four of us had been briefed on a number of aspects, including the still-sensitive issue of the World War Two Vichy regime. For this was in the late-1970s, the war had ended a mere thirty-five years earlier and memories, particularly amongst the older generation, remained raw. The town of Vichy, a spa resort situated a couple of hundred miles south of Paris and not far from La Courtine, had been the seat of government of Vichy France from 1940 to 1944 and so, in view of its position back then as a *de facto* client state of Nazi Germany, retained an ignominious legacy. We'd been advised to be wary of using the pejorative term *Vichyste* which indicated collaboration with the Vichy regime. Our 18 Squadron briefing officer had emphasised that a key component of Vichy ideology was Anglophobia stirred up by its leader, the octogenarian Marshal Pétain. This man had held a personal dislike of the British, once declaring: "England has always been France's most implacable enemy." The briefing officer told us, therefore, that we needed to be more than a little circumspect when in contact with local people.

"Germany kept some two million – yes, two million – French soldiers as prisoners carrying out forced labour," the briefing officer had said. "These soldiers were, in effect, hostages to ensure that the Vichy regime would reduce its military forces and would make payments to Germany in the form of gold, food and supplies. The French police were ordered to round up Jews and other 'undesirables'. It was a bad business and after the liberation of France, collaborationists, or perceived collaborationists, were sent to prison or to an internment camp. Women thought to have had romantic liaisons with Germans or who were deemed to have been prostitutes, had their heads shaved as a mark of public humiliation. Men and women regarded as war profiteers or black marketers, popularly called 'BOF' *(buerre, oeufs, fromage)*, were stigmatised."

With this and other background information fresh in the memory, perhaps we four Brits walked through the streets of La Courtine with a degree of vigilance that evening. It was hardly a case of 'left – right – left – right – qui-ick march' for it had been a long time since any of us had been under the command of a drill sergeant. Nonetheless, we were military personnel representing our country and despite the past, or maybe because of it, instinctively we all made efforts to look smart and military-like in our service-issue disruptive-pattern combat gear. At one point my crewman, Mike, stopped to gaze in a shop window. I felt it best to stay with him while the other two went on ahead. It was an unplanned separation but one which appeared to offer an opportunity for a local Frenchman to come up to us. "Messieurs," he cried, "Excusez-mois! Vous êtes Anglais, je crois?" We turned, surprised, to see a man aged, I reckoned, in his late fifties or early sixties. In view of the severe background briefings, Mike and I were instantly on our guard. "Mais oui, nous sommes Anglais," I replied stiffly but politely.

A moment of silence ensued and I noticed that something was happening to the eyes of the man who'd hailed us. His face was sunburnt and calm with an expression that did not change. It seemed to me, as we stared at one another, that he knew all about us. The barriers were down, as if at a confessional; it was an odd feeling. There was a particular inflection in his voice as the man said: "Please to come with me – just for a moment, please." He had deduced, correctly, that our standard of French was likely to be worse than his spoken English. Despite a sense of wariness, Mike and I nodded to each other in a spontaneous gesture of agreement. After all, we were trained military men and capable of looking after ourselves in the event of trouble. Trouble, though, seemed far from anyone's minds as we followed the Frenchman. In the middle distance we could see signs of the village's peaceful thirteenth century church, and nearby, an old dog, lying outside, lifted his head and gazed at us languidly. We did not feel in the least threatened.

The man now led us into his sweet shop. As we entered, he called out to his wife, then turned to us and said: 'Please...to meet my femme – my deux filles." Handshaking and smiles followed although conversation was difficult. Mike and I, still unsure why we'd been hi-jacked, must have looked puzzled. The Frenchman appeared to appreciate this for he bowed his head slightly before he went to the back of his shop. Within moments he returned clutching an old-fashioned watch. "Ma montre," he said, "she save my life!"

"Saved your life?"

"Mais oui...regardez..." When he held out the watch, which was of the type designed to be pinned to a jacket lapel, we could see at once that it was compressed almost into two halves.

"What happened?" I asked. He placed the watch up to his chest and we noticed that his eyes began to fill. "A German bullet..." was all that he said but it was obvious that the watch, by deflecting the bullet, had saved his life. It was obvious, too, that he'd probably been a member of the French resistance in World War Two. He'd been through tough, tumultuous times. One of his daughters placed an arm around his shoulders. The family gazed at us, then at each other, then at the watch – valueless yet so valuable. All of us sensed a moment of reflection and recollection to be treasured.

Not much more was said; words at that instant seemed less than adequate, especially in view of language barriers. Even so, when we indicated that we should leave in order to catch up with our colleagues, the family's warmth towards us lingered. It seemed that they felt glad and honoured to be able to tell their story to members of the British military. The feeling was heartening and poignant. The mother handed us a couple of tins of local speciality sweets: "Pour vos enfants," she said and after further handshakes all round, Mike and I left the shop.

As we walked away, perhaps our thoughts coincided for it was as if the past, coming so unexpectedly, had sharpened our intuition. We'd come face to face with uncomfortable memories, a time when everyone felt, perhaps, that they should have done more. In our own way, and without speeches or fuss, we'd been able to offer a small tribute to someone who'd fought against tyranny. His chance survival was something which he and his family could not forget. While we hastened to re-join our colleagues, we realised that this brief, unprompted incident had induced in us a sense of privilege at being in such a place and at meeting such people.

Canine supervision (from Malcolm Harvey)

HE HALF-TURNED his head, screwed one knuckle into his eye and his body shuddered. To say that Warrant Officer Malcolm Harvey was taken aback would be to understate the case. Admittedly the Perspex bubble-nose of the Army Air Corps AH-1 Gazelle helicopter that Malcolm was flying offered good, clear views appreciated by his passengers, and perhaps that encouraged what was about to happen. His passengers that day were two 'Red Cap' military policemen, one of them a dog handler, and Malcolm had been briefed to fly the men, including their police dog, to a particular spot as part of a local military exercise. Although animals were not normally carried in army helicopters, exception was made for the highly trained police dogs. As the AH-1 Gazelle, a five-seat helicopter used for light transport, scouting and light-attack duties, was an easy machine for passengers to board and disembark, at the passenger pick-up point the disciplined dog had jumped aboard quite happily before sitting down next to its handler.

Malcolm was about halfway through the short re-positioning flight when he sensed that something unusual was happening behind him. He wasn't entirely sure, but he gained the impression that the police dog was becoming restless. He knew that this was no obese Staffordshire bull terrier, or some tiresome Yorkie with an ingratiating smile, but a large and powerful Alsatian. Such a dog, he mused, could create havoc. Nevertheless, as a skilled and experienced pilot, his priority was to concentrate on a safe and expeditious flight, and anyway, he reasoned, even if the dog was becoming a bit restless, he had every confidence in the handler's ability to control the animal.

It was when an enormous, damp nose quietly rested itself on one of Malcolm's shoulders that he half-turned his head. I say half-turned for, in truth, Malcolm was too startled to turn his head any further than halfway. And when he noticed two large, brown Alsatian eyes staring at him, Malcolm's reaction was impulsive: he screwed one knuckle into his own eye as if to confirm that this was actually happening, and his body suffered an involuntary shudder. The dog itself, though, appeared unfazed. Gazing in turn at the Gazelle's instrument panel, at the flight controls, at the view outside, at Malcolm himself, the Alsatian took it all in. Even when Malcolm set up his approach to the briefed landing spot in a field, the Alsatian remained in place, oblivious of the statutory requirement to fasten a seat belt. And when Malcolm cleared his passengers to disembark, the dog did not seem a bit interested in the Gazelle's distinctive features, the single Turbomeca Astazou turbine engine, the unique fenestron tail which, as a first in the helicopter world, was used instead of a conventional tail rotor, or that the Gazelle, which was introduced to service in 1973, had been active in numerous conflicts around the world. But no, while the dog handler shrugged his shoulders and grinned at Malcolm, the Alsatian merely bounded off without so much as a backward glance as if to say: "Woof! Nice flight, young man. Well done."

Belvedere days (from David Lanigan)

VISITORS TO THE ROYAL Air Force Museum at Hendon in north-west London may be interested to view a Bristol Type 192 Belvedere helicopter on display. This machine, airframe number XG474, has been carefully prepared with immaculate, polished paint-work and kept in pristine condition as a good and rare example of the type. Operated by the Royal Air Force in the 1960s, the Belvedere was Britain's only tandem rotor helicopter to enter production and it was this type which Flight Lieutenant David Lanigan flew in the Far East when he joined 66 Squadron at Seletar, Singapore, in the spring of 1963. The squadron, which had reformed at RAF Odiham in 1961, had moved to Seletar the following year to support forces operating in Malaya for even though the Malayan Emergency had ended with the communists' surrender in 1960, renewed insurgency against the Malaysian government persisted.

When David arrived at Seletar as a young pilot aged twenty-four, he faced something of a culture shock. The average age of the squadron pilots was in the mid-forties and this, his first helicopter tour after the operational conversion course at Odiham, seemed a world away from the RAF's V-Force where he'd started his service career as a co-pilot on the Vickers Valiant bomber. The operational conversion course at Odiham had been an eye-opener. Both of the only two Belvederes available had remained unserviceable for the entire period of David's course, so he'd experienced no Belvedere flying, just a few start-ups and ground runs. As a consequence, he was woefully unprepared for operations when he arrived in the Far East where good results were expected. On joining the squadron he was issued with two Australian green flying suits and some basic maps of Borneo, the squadron's main area of operations. These maps featured coastlines, rivers and the border with Indonesia, but not a lot else. He therefore sat down with other pilots to copy on his maps the locations of border hill forts, settlements, individual long-houses, low hills, even different groups of trees which made helpful navigational aids.

As his flying began, David was glad that, unlike the single-pilot Whirlwind squadrons, the Belvedere crew consisted of three – two pilots and a crewman. In this way, by learning from the experienced pilots, the inadequacies of his Odiham operational conversion course could be rectified. He soon became familiar with some of the Belvedere 192's interesting and uncommon characteristics. For one thing, the helicopter had an unusually tall front undercarriage which meant that the main passenger door and the cargo door were some four feet above ground level. The engines were placed at either end of the cabin which, in the case of the front engine, caused difficult access from the cockpit. To resolve this, the manufacturers had provided a small passage past the front engine which, in turn, required an adjustment to the fuselage that appeared in the form of a peculiar bulge on the left side.

David learned that the first prototype Belvedere 192 was fitted with tandem wooden rotor blades which were synchronised through a shaft to prevent rotor collision. From the fifth prototype, the wooden rotors were replaced by all-metal four-bladed units, and he was told that this was the particular aircraft which, in

1960, had set a speed record of one hundred and thirty mph between Gatwick, near London, and Tripoli. And it was this speed and power which impressed David from his first sorties. In the event of an engine failure, the aircraft could operate on the remaining engine which was designed to run up automatically to double power. He discovered that the challenging jungle terrain of Borneo and the lack of roads meant that the Belvedere's ability to climb vertically out of a deep jungle clearing at maximum weight proved invaluable to the Indonesian and Commonwealth forces who conducted long patrols in the area.

David eventually served just over three years on 66 Squadron during which period he logged nine hundred and thirty-five Belvedere hours. By mid-March 1966 the Belvedere's days were numbered and as the leader of a formation flypast he flew XG474 on the last day before the squadron ceased flying operations. All the other squadron Belvederes were scrapped but XG474, while it currently resides in polished splendour at the Royal Air Force Museum, remains an apt reminder of the Belvedere's brief but important period of service.

Osprey experience (from Mark Service)

IT WAS A RARE indulgence. Shortly to retire in 2014 after some thirty years as a member of the Royal Air Force, Flight Sergeant Mark Service saw his opportunities to fly in the Bell Boeing CV-22 Osprey as fortuitous, even if arranged on a somewhat haphazard basis. This unorthodox tilt-rotor machine, fielded in the United States Marine Corps in 2007 and in the United States Air Force two years later, first flew in 1989 but Mark was told that the complexity of the world's first production tilt-rotor had involved many years of development. Designed to combine the functions of a conventional helicopter with the long-range, high-speed cruise performance of a turboprop aircraft, the concept of the Osprey was indeed novel. Powered by two Rolls-Royce AE 1107C engines, one on each wing tip together with a three-bladed prop-rotor and a transmission nacelle, Mark had been briefed that if one engine failed the other engine could power both prop-rotors through a common central gearbox. The Osprey, though, was not generally able to hover on a single engine and as the prop-rotors could not be feathered, Mark learned that if a prop-rotor gearbox failed, both engines had to be stopped before an emergency landing.

Mark had spent his service career in the RAF as a 'mover' whose duties included the planning and execution of the movement of personnel and cargo. While not classified as aircrew, he had flown nonetheless as a crew member on Boeing CH-47 Chinook helicopters and other types for which he received a form of flying pay and for which he was classed as 'support crew'. In this role he had befriended members of the USAF's 7th Special Operations Squadron based at Mildenhall in Suffolk. Equipped with the CV-22 Osprey, this squadron's mission involved long-range infiltration, ex-filtration and resupply of non-conventional special operations forces in hostile, sensitive or otherwise undesirable locations. The squadron scheduler would email Mark with details of planned flights for the following weeks and he'd recommend the more interesting flights which might include, for instance, low flying, in-flight refuelling and air-to-ground gunnery. Mark, who'd been given blanket clearance to fly with this squadron as much as he wished, would email back with his chosen flights.

One such flight, a night low-level training exercise, was selected by Mark who duly turned up at Mildenhall for the pre-flight briefing. The flight was planned to incorporate a transit down to Salisbury Plain where he'd be allowed to fire the aircraft's M240 machine gun against a ground target. Before the flight Mark was issued with a fair amount of paraphernalia which included a Gentex HGU-56/P flight helmet, night-vision goggles, gunner's belt, life preserver and a pair of flight gloves. When the crew of four (pilot, co-pilot, and two flight engineers/crew chiefs) walked out to the aircraft, Mark joined them. Soon, with the engines and the prop-rotors started, the captain was given clearance to taxi to the runway threshold during which procedure, Mark noted, the nacelles were set at an angle of seventy-five degrees. For the take-off itself he'd been warned to brace when the pilot called "power coming in" or "nacelles travelling". Sure enough, as he held on tightly to his seat he was aware that the Osprey seemed to shoot off like a rocket.

While the flight down to Salisbury Plain progressed, Mark was secured by a special long strap as he sat on the aircraft ramp and watched the familiar landmarks of Swindon, Wootton Basset and Lyneham pass by. He was conscious of the way that the pilots used the aircraft's advanced systems with terrain following and avoidance radar, and navigation systems that could operate in even the most adverse conditions. Approaching the gunnery area, the captain reduced airspeed and commenced a slow let-down before he conducted a clearing pass of the designated spot. It was during this manoeuvre that an electronically generated voice suddenly cried: "Fire warning! Left engine!" At once the captain ceased the descent and transitioned back to forward flight as the crew ran through emergency drills. "Okay," he said eventually, "I had this problem on another flight recently. It turned out to be a false alarm and I reckon the same thing has happened again. So rather than divert, we'll return to Mildenhall ASAP."

Back at Mildenhall, the captain was proved right when, after engineering inspections, a false alarm was confirmed. Meantime, Mark returned to the squadron operations set-up where the scheduler scanned through the list of planned flights. "Okay, Mark," he said, "to make up for that disappointment, I can offer you a day flight or a night flight tomorrow. Which would you prefer?"

"I'll go on both! How long's the interval between the two flights?"

"Zilch," grinned the scheduler, "apart, that is, from a rotors running refuel before the night flight. Still want to go on both?"

"Oh, yes," said Mark, "yes, please," for he knew that this was probably his last opportunity for an Osprey flight.

The pre-flight briefing for the day trip detailed a low-level mission with simulated troop insertions and extractions on the Otterburn range, a military training area covering over ninety square miles of Northumberland territory. Mark found the flight exhilarating as the large Osprey, with its length of just over fifty-seven feet and a capacity to carry twenty-four seated passengers or thirty-two floor-loaded troops, hurtled along at very low level with the pilot following the hills and valleys of the Southern Cheviots. At various landing sites, the pilot brought the machine to a hover as he skilfully manoeuvred to specific pick-up and drop-off spots. When all the pre-briefed locations had been covered, he said: "Okay, that's the last one. We'll return to Mildenhall now."

Back at Mildenhall, and while the rotors running refuel was in progress, Mark hastily changed to another aircraft which had been scheduled to act as leader of a two-ship Osprey formation. Soon, on completion of the refuelling, the formation took off to head north. As the aircraft climbed away from Mildenhall into gathering darkness, the Ospreys' green prop-rotor blade tip lights were switched on and Mark was fascinated to look out of the windows at the eerie green circles in the air produced by the lights. The captain assumed a course for Penrith before he turned starboard to head out over the North Sea by which stage Mark was standing between and slightly behind the pilots. Suddenly, the captain pointed left and high at an approaching aircraft which could be seen through night-vision goggles as it flashed past on a reciprocal heading. Mark was told that this machine was from the 67th Special Operations Squadron, an in-flight refueller – a MC-130J Commando II (a modified version of the Lockheed C-130 Hercules transport aircraft) – on a pre-briefed rendezvous. Slickly, swiftly, in the dark and in radio silence the Osprey captain now manoeuvred to follow the in-flight refueller as it turned due south. Before long, Mark saw two flight refuelling hoses reel out from the wing-mounted pods.

In the pitch-black conditions, the in-flight refueller was impossible to spot but as soon as he flipped down his flight helmet's night-vision goggles Mark was amazed to see the MC-130's tail so close that it seemed feasible to reach out and touch it. Initially approaching the hose streamed from the left wing, the pilot in his Osprey's right-hand seat pointed out that the engine exhaust showed up as a distracting bright green when viewed through night-vision goggles. He was cleared, therefore, to fly across to the other side where he made contact with the refuelling basket straight away. After a top-up of 4,000 lbs of fuel, he moved away from the MC-130 to allow the pilot of the other Osprey to manoeuvre into position for a refuel. This pilot, though, struggled to make contact with the basket. He eventually succeeded but the delay meant that the captain of Mark's aircraft had to return for a further 1,000 lbs of fuel. This pilot's polished, accurate flying, thought Mark, made the process appear deceptively easy.

With both Ospreys fuelled-up, the lead aircraft set off due south towards the military firing range at Donna Nook on the Lincolnshire coast. When there, Mark stood on the Osprey's ramp to observe the two crewmen aim at a ground target firing 7.62-mm live rounds from a M240 machine gun. At length, when one of them said: "Hey, Mark! Like to shoot the gun?" Mark grinned, gave a thumbs-up sign and moved into position. Meantime, the pilot gave a running commentary of the target's position relative to the Osprey so that when he declared: "Cleared hot!" Mark was ready. As he squeezed the M240's trigger, and as the gun's tracer rounds facilitated his adjustment to the fall of shot, Mark found that his rounds were quickly on target. After three passes, and with the M240's ammunition used up, the pilot announced that he'd head towards the military training facility at Sculthorpe in Norfolk for a simulated troop extraction after which he'd return to Mildenhall. By the time the Osprey touched down at Mildenhall, Mark had notched up ten hours of flying that day. His ears were ringing, his head was spinning, he felt exhausted but he wouldn't have changed it for the world.

Late mate (from Tony Stafford)

THE OFFSHORE SUPERVISOR came running up the steps. He entered the waiting room and cried: "You can board the chopper now!" at which half a dozen rig workers stood up and began to make their way towards the Westland Whirl-wind Series 3 helicopter parked on the platform's helideck. The men were met by the HLO (helicopter landing officer) who guided them into the Whirlwind's cabin where they sat down and strapped in. Most began to read and before long, as the pilot was evidently delayed, the air filled with the fumes of cigarette smoke, for this was during the days when smoking was permitted in helicopters.

The pilot's delay, however, was turning out to be longer than expected. Mut-terings started up amongst the passengers, especially those with train or airline connections to make. Suddenly, passengers lowered their newspapers and looked up. Eyes focused on a late arrival, a man with a dishevelled appearance who wore an old mackintosh. The man walked into the helicopter cabin, sat down and strapped in. Nobody seemed to recognise him, though that was not so unusual in this environment: people came and went. Some, like this fellow, looked like one of those technical types, a geologist or a specialist engineer that sometimes appeared on offshore platforms...bespectacled, Pythagoras-faced, charmingly dotty, completely divorced from Planet Earth.

"Everything okay, pal?" a Scotsman asked the newcomer.

"Aye," said the newcomer.

"Where you heading?"

"Dundee."

"You'll be lucky. Bloody pilot hasn't turned up. We've been waiting bloody ages."

"Oh," said the newcomer. Then: "Dammit. I canna afford to be late like this. I'll fly the thing myself!" He unstrapped, stood up and made for the cockpit which, in a Whirlwind helicopter was entered by climbing up a set of outside steps. Still dressed in an old mackintosh, the man sat down on the pilot's seat and began to go through the start-up drills. When he glanced up to say: "Relax everyone – just joking!" he had to yell above the din of the 76's engine. This went unheeded. For the half a dozen passengers had unstrapped from their seats and run off in alarm. It turned out that the mackintosh man had been the pilot all along. He was now left to ponder his next move and that of his boss at Bristow Helicopters, renowned to cry: "Too late, mate...you're fired!"

Vietnam legacy (from Chris Mutton)

IF THE VIETNAM War was renowned for unusual aspects, one of the more intriguing was the extensive and remarkable use of helicopters. This was a matter of much discussion when, in early 1975, Captain Chris Mutton of Britain's Army Air Corps was posted to the United States under a pilot exchange programme when he witnessed first hand the far-reaching effect on military thinking of this helicopter usage. He witnessed, too, the impact of the war on the American psyche, especially on the men and women who fought in Vietnam, and on the millions of US citizens who supported the war effort or who protested against it. Destined to fly the AH-1G Cobra attack helicopter, Chris found that the war was never far from conversations when he arrived at Fort Rucker, Alabama for his conversion training. For although direct United States military involvement had ended nearly two years earlier in the summer of 1973, fighting persisted and Americans took a keen interest in events – particularly as the culmination of hostilities approached, a day eventually marked on the last day of April 1975 when the North Vietnamese army captured Saigon.

At Fort Rucker, Chris's new-found colleagues seemed keen to talk about their experiences and the novel way in which helicopters had become key to US Army tactics. At induction briefings he was told that the Bell AH-1G Cobra and the Bell UH-1 Iroquois were closely related and that the latter, often referred to as the

'Huey', went through several upgrades during the course of the war. "You'll be given six hours of flight time on the Huey," he was told, "before you move on to the Cobra." Both aircraft types were equipped with two-bladed main and tail rotors and were powered by a single turboshaft engine. "The Huey was one of the most numerous helicopter types ever built," said the briefing officer, "for sure, an icon of the Vietnam War. These machines undertook troop transport, medical evacuation, ground attack, armed escort missions with rocket launchers, grenade launchers, and machine guns. They were called 'Frogs' or 'Hogs' if they carried rockets, but 'Slicks' for troop transport when weapons pods were not fitted."

Chris learnt that the theory of air cavalry, which had been applied successfully in practice in Vietnam, had meant that instead of long battles to hold positions, troops were carried by fleets of Hueys ranging across the country to fight the enemy at times and places of their own choice. "More than seven thousand Hueys served in Vietnam," said the briefing officer, "and of these nearly half were destroyed. Over a thousand Huey pilots were killed along with more than eleven hundred other crew members." The briefing officer shook his head: "it was a high price to pay."

When he began flying, Chris operated from Fort Rucker as the hub airfield with numerous satellite airfields each with a series of landing strips used by a multitude of training aircraft. With air traffic control kept to a minimum, students learnt the need for good lookout and flexibility. His instructor on the Huey was a clean-cut all-American football-star type, a man of few words who hacked rather than spoke past his unlit cigar which was in constant motion across his lips. "Gees, our women could do better than that," he'd said one time after a sortie when Chris had struggled with the Huey's lack of hydraulically assisted flight controls. Comments about the marine female pilots, Chris noted later, seemed to be directed at some of the no-nonsense characters he'd met who gave the distinct impression that any male misdemeanours were unlikely to be accepted in a spirit of benign forbearance.

After his six hours of Huey flying, when Chris moved on to the AH-1G Cobra, he found that most of his fellow students were hardened Vietnam veterans, usually with two or three helicopter tours behind them. "In Vietnam," Chris's new instructor briefed him, "the Cobra attack helicopters supported troops on the ground and escorted the transport Hueys. Sometimes the Cobras would team up with OH-6 light observation 'scout' helicopters that'd fly low and slow to root out enemy positions. If the OH-6 drew fire, the Cobra would attack the revealed positions." Chris's instructor went on to describe a dramatic case some seven years earlier in 1968 when a US fighter pilot, Captain Ronald Fogleman, was shot down. Fogleman ejected from his F-100 Super Sabre but was rescued by an army AH-1G Cobra which landed at the crash site. Fogleman then grabbed and clung on to the helicopter's deployed gun-panel door while he was flown to safety. "In the late 1960s and early 1970s," said the instructor, "Bell Helicopters built over a thousand AH-1Gs for the US Army. These aircraft flew more than a million operational hours in Vietnam."

For his first Cobra flight, Chris thought that the machine felt more like a fighter aircraft than a helicopter. He sat in the front seat, the air gunner's position, with side-positioned flight controls that offered a quarter of the power of the rear-seat pilot's controls. "If the back-seater passes out and slumps over the flight controls," said his instructor, "the controls in the front cockpit won't be adequate – the aircraft, in effect, will become uncontrollable." In flight, Chris found that the Cobra was agile although reluctant to pull out of a steep dive. Placed on top of the rear cockpit's coaming was a World War Two-type reflex sight with a spot of light ('pipper') projected onto a glass plate. When preparing to attack, the pilot aimed the pipper at a target while manoeuvring before the release of ordnance which could be rockets, flechettes, grenades, machine guns or a particularly potent weapon, the M61 Vulcan, that fired a Gatling-style rotary cannon. Developed specifically for the AH-1G Cobra and designated the M195, this weapon fired 20-mm rounds at a very high rate (typically six thousand rounds per minute). Weighty ammunition boxes attached to the skids of the Cobra (in this fit nicknamed the '20 Mike Mike bird') reduced the helicopter's performance. This was especially noticeable on take-off. When fired, however, Chris described the result as: "without doubt one of the most formidable weapons I have ever fired. The recoil was so violent that the canopy would pop open, and instruments would vibrate out of the cockpit panel to hang forlornly from their cables. The crew's tooth fillings would shake loose; eyeballs would refuse to synchronise." The effect on the ground was equally drastic: "a heavy armoured personnel carrier would be picked up as if a child's toy and thrown a distance of tens of metres. At night a twenty-metre flame beyond the cockpit would cause complete whiteout."

By the end of his course Chris had spent some months at Fort Rucker and when told that he'd passed, he grinned and nodded. His time there had proved demanding and now he was destined to join 7 Squadron 17 Air Cavalry at Fort Hood, Texas. "How'll you get yourself to Texas, Chris?" asked his instructor.

"I'll buy a second-hand car and drive there."

His instructor glanced at him suspiciously then just said: "Sure." Chris chuckled for he knew that he was an outsider, a foreigner. But he didn't mind. He did not smoke, chew tobacco, drink heavily or talk Vietnam. He was good at flying attack helicopters, though.

CHAPTER 7
RAPIER PROJECT

David Lanigan in the Falklands

WHEN THE RAPIER, a British surface-to-air missile system, entered service in 1972, some ten years elapsed before the system was fully exposed to a war scenario. Then the deterrence effect of the Rapiers, initially set up on the outskirts of Port San Carlos in the Falklands to provide air defence cover, allowed Harrier aircraft to be land-located for rapid reaction against Argentine air raids. Problems, though, soon became apparent. Siting difficulties, for example, meant that the missiles were prevented from operating efficiently, and from an engineering perspective the fragile nature of the launchers led to further difficulties, an issue exacerbated when the MV *Atlantic Conveyor* was sunk with almost all of the Rapier spares on board. Moreover, the intermittent unserviceability of the Rapier unit at Fitzroy was a factor that contributed to the success of the Argentine attack against the RFA *Sir Galahad* which destroyed the ship on 8 June 1982.

Early post-war reports suggested that Rapier missiles had been responsible for fourteen enemy 'kills' and six probables, although subsequent analysis indicated that this was highly optimistic. In truth, just one Argentine aircraft, a Dagger A of FAA Grupo 6 destroyed on 28 May 1982, could be confirmed as a Rapier kill, however two probables and two possibles were also attributed to Rapier. The Ministry of Defence had exaggerated the capabilities of the system and the powers that be realised that problems such as lack of range, the decision to omit a proximity fuse and other issues needed to be addressed urgently in order to update Rapier.

It was against this background that, two years after the conclusion of the Falklands conflict, Captain David Lanigan was involved with flying a S-61N helicopter to remote areas, including Rapier sites across the islands. Sent to the Falklands as part of a contract awarded to Bristow Helicopters, David and his colleagues were assigned to fly personnel and equipment as required by the military.

One day in mid-May 1984, David was tasked to fly to Kelly's Garden near Port San Carlos for a special mission involving Rapier. The weather that day seemed typical of an autumnal Falklands with haze that rested above the peaty stretches to a vanishing distance and where the land and the sky appeared welded together. Into this mournful gloom David took off from Stanley Airfield to head due west in his S-61N, flying low to avoid entering cloud. At the far end of Stanley Harbour where the ground rose, he flew above the remains of an Argentine Chinook helicopter which had crashed during the war and the wreckage had yet to be cleared. In the deteriorating visibility he was forced to follow fences which, fortuitously marked on aviation charts, provided one of the few navigational features as he approached a fog-bound Mount Longdon. It was a mere two years earlier, mused David, when Mount Longdon had been more than just meteorologically fog-bound and soldiers on both sides had faced the horrors of close combat in the fog of war.

Steering well clear of the mountain, David continued on a westerly course, occasionally reducing airspeed when thickening mist above the boggy terrain further restricted the local visibility. Luckily, when near to Kelly's Garden the visibility improved and he was marshalled to a landing spot by the water's edge, close to some parked Royal Air Force Chinook helicopters. As he closed down the S-61N, David noted how the water's surface shone from the glint of sporadic sunlight and only the gloom to the east retained its sombreness. Together with his co-pilot and crewman he walked towards the base set-up at Kelly's Garden (so named, apparently, by men of the Irish Guards) to be met by an officer in the rank of major. "There you are!" boomed the major, his 'I'm in charge' attitude encouraged by obsequious sergeants – all of them, perhaps, suspicious of civilians employed to carry out army duties.

"At your service," said David.

"We need you to fly to a Rapier site, lift the base unit and bring it here for maintenance, then fly out a replacement," said the major. "The plan is to remain fully operational throughout. Adjacent Rapier units will be firing at target drones all afternoon."

"Hmm," said David, "not sure that will be such a good idea." He went on to point out various hazards, not the least of which was interference with the intense concentration he needed when manoeuvring the heavy and expensive Rapier units into and out of confined revetments. The two discussed the use of men to help steady the units and the procedure if the helicopter suffered an engine failure forcing David to jettison the heavy load.

"This equipment is expensive, you know," said the major.

"So's the helicopter." A rough calculation valued the Rapier base unit at around one million pounds with the helicopter worth three times that amount. At this juncture the major agreed to halt the live firings for a period of one hour from 1400 hours.

So it was that, at the agreed hour, David flew the S-61N to a ridge line near Kelly's Garden where the Rapier unit to be lifted was installed in a deep pit with sandbagged walls. As part of the overall air defence set-up, other Rapier units had been judiciously placed along the ridge line. He headed towards a soldier who, with lifting cables in hand, was ready to clip the cables onto a short strop which hung beneath the helicopter's fuselage. David quickly rechecked the S-61N's fuel state: the machine had been refuelled to an exact amount – sufficient to cover the necessary distance but an expedient minimum in view of the ton-and-a-half weight that had to be lifted.

Tension rose as David brought the S-61N to a high hover, then manoeuvred carefully under the guidance of his crewman…"down ten…range fifty to overhead the load…maintain this speed…" With a westerly wind gusting at around thirty knots, David struggled against turbulence although the strength of the wind boosted the helicopter's available power. "Up five now…range twenty…ease your closing speed…" His experience paid dividends as David continued to move to the precise spot. "You're nearly directly above the load…steady…steady…overhead now…the load is being hooked on…the hook-up soldier is moving clear…standby… you're clear for a vertical climb…" David, after a final check that the cockpit instrument readings were satisfactory, raised the collective lever positively at which the helicopter appeared to groan slightly as the machine took the full weight of the load. Still directed by his crewman, he continued the vertical climb and as he lifted the load upwards, several soldiers on the ground guided the sides of the expensive Rapier base unit until it was clear of the revetment.

Eventually, as he reached a height of around fifty feet, David eased the cyclic stick forward to pick up airspeed as he headed back towards Kelly's Garden. The flight there took just five minutes after which he was again directed by his crewman to place the Rapier base unit at a required spot. The exercise was then repeated for the replacement unit. On return from this, he closed down the S-61N for refuelling during which an army captain, a tall and imposing figure, came up to speak with him: "Good show!" said the captain.

"Seemed to go okay," said David.

"Seems strange, though…" the captain hesitated. He stared at David as if he was some kind of *arriviste*. "The way civilians are taking on military jobs."

"I used to be a member of the military myself."

"Good man! Which service?"

"The Royal Air Force."

"Oh," a barely perceptible hint of disapproval now on the captain's face.

"Well the refuelling is nearly done here so I'd better get a move on. Good to have a chat though! Ta-ra," said David who hastened back to his S-61N which he swiftly started up and took off to head back to Stanley via a coastal route to the south of Wickham Heights.

With the by-now improved, if variable, visibility – over five miles but temporarily reducing to less than half a mile in some places – he could make out isolated settlements such as Darwin, Goose Green, Fitzroy, Bluff Cove and others, their corrugated-iron roofed houses and basic construction so characteristic of the Falklands. He reflected that the 'camp' folk (residents outside Stanley) usually seemed more than glad to greet visitors and ply them with home-made produce, often including a notorious plum wine which was doled out in generous quantities.

Conversation invariably centred on the war, the impact on individual settlers, the loss of over nine hundred lives on both sides including three Falkland Island women killed by so-called friendly fire when trying to shelter from shells during the Royal Naval bombardment of Stanley. The names of Mrs Susan Whitley, Mrs Doreen Bonner and Mrs Mary Goodwin were mentioned with contemplative sadness, for with a population of just two thousand or so souls, nearly everyone knew everyone else. There were personal accounts of the treatment of Stanley residents by the Argentine soldiers, including the fear felt following orders from an Argentine company commander shortly before the ceasefire was declared on 14 June 1982: 'take up positions in the houses and if a Kelper resists, shoot him.' But this order, hardly ideal in the battle for hearts and minds, had been ignored by the entire company.

As David flew past high ground made famous by the war – Mount Kent, Mount Harriet with the Two Sisters Ridge beyond – it was not long before he could turn left to fly back towards Mount Longdon again. Now in the better visibility, he could make out the remnants of the war's toughest battle: trenches, shell holes, abandoned equipment. This was where the British troops, facing both enemy resistance and friendly fire, became bogged down by assault rifles, mortars, machine-gun attacks, artillery fire, sniper fire and ambushes – but persisted with their advance despite it all. This was where Sergeant Ian McKay of 4 Platoon, B Company of the Third Battalion of the Parachute Regiment died in a grenade attack on an Argentine bunker, an action which earned him a posthumous Victoria Cross. This was where, after the battle, there were reports of screams heard as prisoners were shot and toppled into a pit to be buried. Senior officers had intervened but in the cauldron of emotions it had been decided not to take further action.

With Stanley now in sight, David was cleared by air traffic control to route south of Port Stanley which, together with a temporary port near the site of a new airfield under construction at Mount Pleasant, was crowded with container ships. In two years time this airfield would be ready and when opened it would be protected by Rapier units run by members of the Royal Air Force Regiment, a duty later assumed by the Royal Artillery. The upgraded Rapier 90, introduced ten years after the Falklands War, would be brought into service and further upgrades would follow. The new versions of Rapier, more efficient and more mobile than those David moved on that day in May 1984, would prove a key part of the air defence of the Falklands. And that, he reckoned looking back, was the way it should be.

CHAPTER 8
TRICKY TERRITORY

Richard Pike with Danish special forces

THE MAJOR'S PALE face betrayed emotion as he pondered the event. "Thank you," he mumbled, "I'm sorry…" he tried to continue but the words seemed to stick in his throat and he shook his head. His eyes, dark and troubled, stared at us. Perhaps, when he thought about the deficiency of his own actions, an unexpected sense of contrition added to his discomfiture. The major and his men, members of Denmark's special forces unit *Jaeger Corps,* or *Jaegerkorpset,* knew what was required of them and, in any case, they were experienced soldiers. Maybe, I thought later, a degree of complacency had crept into their mindset for these were tough, specialist troops, roughly the equivalent of the British Special Air Service (SAS), and perhaps they regarded themselves as less destructible than normal mortals. Then again, I mused, perhaps their training may have fostered such an attitude in which case, as one of my pilot colleagues put it, "a re-think, perchance, is needed".

As a helicopter pilot with 18 Squadron, I'd been sent, together with a number of colleagues, from RAF Gütersloh in Germany to the *Jaeger Corps'* base near Aalborg in northern Denmark for a week's detachment. It was mid-summer in 1980 and, flying in three Westland Wessex helicopters, our task was to train members of the unit in abseiling and parachute jumps from the helicopters. For the practical exercises our briefings had been thorough, although, on reflection, perhaps we should have taken more account of language barriers. Moreover, maybe we'd been a bit blinded by the *Jaeger Corps'* reputation for we'd heard that they were exceptional individuals – fighting fit, dedicated, determined, the crème de la crème. We'd been told, for example, that of the members of the Danish armed services, both men and women, who applied to join the *Jaeger Corps,* just ten per cent or so passed the acceptance procedures.

Perhaps it was inevitable, therefore, that the training course, which drilled recruits in a variety of specialised skills that included counter-terrorism, demolition, infiltration, sabotage, reconnaissance and parachuting, engendered a feeling of elitism. And perhaps this was felt even more by the successful candidates who, on completion of the course, were awarded the unit's maroon beret with a brass emblem depicting a hunter's bugle on a black felt liner, insignia that went back to the unit's origins as hunters and woodsmen. Their slogan, which roughly translated meant 'Rather to be, than to seem', was designed to reflect the idea that the soldiers' capabilities should not be widely recognised or boasted, that they'd be more effective if unknown. Despite this notion, however, maybe a sense of elitism was almost unavoidable.

It was a group of individuals with maroon berets that met us following the flight across Germany and Denmark on our way up to Aalborg. We closed down the helicopters before clambering outside where the *Jaeger Corps* major, all smiles, spoke in immaculate, if accented, English as he introduced members of his team. "Your squadron helped us last year, too," he beamed, "and hopefully this will become a regular commitment. But it seems that you're a busy squadron; we've had to wait our turn." We nodded and smiled at this remark. "We'll aim to fly tomorrow morning after briefings," went on the major, "and this afternoon we plan to show you around the unit." This, we knew, was a rare privilege. "Many of the techniques we employ here," said the major as we began to walk towards his unit's offices, "are based on your British SAS system. We're currently teaching recruits about resistance to interrogation. You should find this interesting – you'll know a bit about it from your own aircrew combat survival exercises." I glanced at my crewman, Mike, for the two of us had been paired-up recently during a combat survival exercise in Bavaria, southern Germany. In an organised escape and evasion event we'd managed to avoid capture and interrogation, although there were others on the course who'd been caught. The subsequent accounts of their experiences were at once intriguing and thought-provoking.

As part of the background training for that exercise, we'd been briefed on the various types of interrogator – the persistent bully, for example, followed by the kindly type, a contrast intended to confuse and lure a prisoner into co-operation. Then there was the forgetful guy, the mumbling trickster, the tiresome egotist, and various others. And since this was in 1980 when the Soviet Union was a formidable foe at the peak of its powers, we knew that we'd be likely to experience rough treatment if captured in the event of hostilities. During intelligence briefings we'd been told that if war broke out in Europe, massed Soviet tanks were likely to sweep across Germany. To counter this threat, NATO could be expected to mobilise some 30,000 tanks including the likes of Leopards, Chieftains and M-47 Pattons. The Soviet Union, however, could muster over twice that number including quantities of T-54s, T-55s, T-62s. Operating our Wessex helicopters close to the front line in fast moving situations made us prime targets and, if captured, the enemy would be anxious to extract current tactical information as rapidly as possible. As prisoners of war under interrogation, our duty was to avoid revealing information other than the standard response of name, rank, number, date of birth – the so-called big four. If asked to reveal, say, one's squadron and its location, the correct response was to repeat name, rank, number, date of birth or to say: "I cannot answer that question."

The interrogators, we were briefed, faced something of a paradox. A well-trained interrogator knew that a prisoner subjected to severe beatings soon became unreliable; excessive violence, therefore, was an inefficient tool. On the other hand, any useful information had to be extracted urgently before it became out-of-date. The conundrum was much discussed during our briefing sessions for a prisoner could not be expected to keep up the 'I cannot answer that question' routine interminably. But how long should he hold out? The prisoner, of course, had no inkling about the possible length of his interrogation. He was likely to be blindfolded or kept in a darkened room so that any sense of time soon became distorted. Isolated and weakened, his situation swiftly became lonely and confusing. The prisoner would know that if he did reveal information, he'd feel a sense of guilt and shame which could lead to a period of self-loathing. A good interrogator, of course, understood this well and used it to wheedle out the information he wanted.

That afternoon, when the major took us to observe the *Jaeger Corps* recruits' training unit, he emphasised that while he could show us the general set-up, we'd not be allowed to witness any 'live' interrogations. As we walked up to the specially arranged compound, we saw a few desolate-looking, blindfolded recruits awaiting their turn for interrogation. Made to face a wall in classic stress positions, each individual looked a sorry sight. With foreheads up against the wall and feet a dozen or so inches away from the wall's base, the 'prisoners' were made to stretch up on their toes, arms handcuffed behind their backs. The weight of the body, therefore, was largely supported by the forehead. We could see clearly that some of them were shaking, but not from cold for this was a warm summer's day and the sun shone brightly. If any of them tried to move, the supervising instructor yelled obscenities at them.

It seemed somehow inappropriate to loiter as observers of this forlorn scene and it was not long, therefore, before the major began to lead us away as he directed us towards a staff crew room. "The situation for our *Jaeger Corps* men and women will be different from yours as aircrew," he said as we walked. "For while an interrogator will be keen to extract short-term details from aircrew, he'll realise that aircrew probably have limited strategic information. On the basis that a prisoner cannot reveal what he doesn't know, I believe that aircrew will usually be briefed on the minimum needed for a particular mission. The interviewer will know this and will probably focus his efforts, therefore, on so-called 'tactical questioning'. However, if our *Jaeger Corps* members are caught in acts, say, of infiltration and sabotage, then their depth of knowledge might mean that they'll be subjected to weeks or even months of interrogation. This is known as 'detailed interviewing' and our training to cope with it is extensive.

The recruits' final selection test will include a resistance to interrogation exercise that lasts for thirty-six hours. It's a gruelling, harsh process and probably the toughest part of the selection system here. Many young hopefuls don't pass."

When we reached the crew room, the major beckoned us to enter and to sit down on chairs arranged around a table. Apart from the scrape of the chairs on a hard floor, there was an expectant silence while we waited for him to continue with his intriguing background brief. "There are various tricks designed to break down a prisoner's resistance," he went on eventually, "some of which are known to contravene international law. Methods used can include sleep deprivation, hooding, prolonged nakedness, sexual humiliation, loud music, alternate heat and cold, exploiting phobias, white noise, extended quiet spells in the hope that a frustrated prisoner will want to fill the silence. If such techniques are known and anticipated by a prisoner, it can help enormously with the ability to endure interrogation." From time to time the major gestured with his hands as if to clarify his accented speech. With both hands, swift and deft, he'd brush aside the air impatiently. Then, eyebrows raised, he'd stop talking and rest his elbows lightly on the table as if waiting for a response.

There was, indeed, a fair amount of response that afternoon with discussions which generated strong and sometimes unexpected reactions. However, it was the following morning, when it was our turn to conduct the briefings, that events took an even more unexpected turn. With about half a dozen *Jaeger Corps* members allocated to each Wessex, these were individuals, we were told, who'd passed the selection process and now, as part of their first year of training as probationers, they'd receive instruction in HAPO (high altitude parachute operations). Before start-up, and with the three Wessex lined up on a parking area, each crewman stood by the sliding entrance/exit door of his own machine to deliver briefings on required procedures. I watched the men allocated to Wessex XV731 which I was due to fly with Mike as crewman. One man, his expression worried and serious, swayed from side to side in mechanical, jerky movements. Another, whose face appeared almost shrunk inwards, kept his eyes half-closed as he concentrated on Mike's briefing. This man, I thought, looked a dogged type, one who'd cope well with the resistance to interrogation exercises. The soldier next to him was tall and gaunt, his prominent cheekbones and large hollow eyes revealing a determination to succeed despite daunting demands. Beside him stood a man with deep-set eyes who appeared silent and dour with much hardness in his features. He gave the impression that he was always on his guard against someone or something.

"You'll note," said Mike to his listeners, "that I've covered sharp edges with tape for your protection. Even so, please be careful – I'd hate you to be injured or for any of your equipment to be damaged. Parachuting from a helicopter can be very dangerous unless it's done correctly." He paused. "We'll practise abseiling first after which you'll don your gear for the parachute jumps." Mike then spoke about the hazards of the tail rotor and reminded the men of the minimum period of delay before the parachute ripcord was operated. "When we approach the drop area, I'll indicate that you should line up here," he pointed to a spot by the entrance/exit door on the helicopter's starboard side, "and be ready to jump when I give the signal." Eventually he concluded his briefing: "Remember that from an altitude of ten thousand feet your descent will take quite a while. Our aim is to position the helicopter so that your parachute landing will be on the airfield itself. However, we'll be operating close to the Fjord just south of the airfield so you should wear life jackets as a precaution."

With the briefings over, and as the *Jaeger Corps* men prepared themselves for take-off in the helicopters, there was a perceptible air of excited anticipation. We soon started up the three Wessex after which air traffic control cleared us to fly to three separate parts of the airfield for the abseiling exercises. When at my allocated area, I held a high hover while Mike helped with rope preparation as the abseilers readied themselves for a fast exit. I was no abseiling fiend myself, but earlier I'd been struck by talk about descenders, Munter hitches, carabiner wraps, low-stretch static ropes, anchors, cordellete, piton bar brakes and other equipment in a long lexicon of technical terms. The tactical heliborne insertion of soldiers, we were told, was usually done by abseiling although so-called fast-roping, a system which employed a thicker rope, was a possible, if more hazardous, alternative. But that day, as the abseiling theories were put into practice, the results were impressive. Indeed, I was amazed by the speed and efficiency of the troops as they left the helicopter then, on landing, deployed rapidly in well-rehearsed ground procedures.

After quite a few practice abseils, the *Jaeger Corps* men strapped themselves back into the seats of XV731 for the short flight to another part of the airfield. When there, all three helicopters were closed down for refuelling and the troops, meantime, donned their parachuting equipment including, as briefed, life jackets placed underneath the parachute harnesses. A single exception to this, however, was the major himself who, we were told, had exemption from the life jacket requirement, although the reason was not given. Soon, when the helicopters had been refuelled and when the men were ready, we re-started the engines and rotors after which we were cleared to take off and climb up to 10,000 feet, the maximum permitted altitude without an oxygen system. It was an unusual height for Wessex pilots who normally operated at very low level, and during the climb we maintained a loose echelon formation for which I held the number three position. With good views of the local landscape as we gained height, to the west I noted the sand dunes and the famous white beaches that lined the Bay of Denmark. Here, the sea ran shallow over the sands and for a time I could make out waves which were short and steep before turning back on themselves to curl into foam. Further out, great rollers were stirred up by a strong north-westerly wind across the sea's surface, and well to the west were signs of an approaching frontal system which was forecast to break up the recent spell of fine, anticyclonic conditions. We could see gulls that soared and dipped in the gusts and not too far away were clouds with dragging tails, black-edged and filled with rain and which threatened to scud across towards us.

I glanced at the aeronautical map upon my knee. The map with its frayed edges and worn surface seemed superfluous in a way for we'd climbed in an orbit above the airfield. However, I'd grown accustomed always to carrying a local map, furthermore I'd marked the map with an 'X' to indicate the narrow landing zone which was close to the fjord by the airfield boundary and which, the major had emphasised, was exactly where he wanted his parachutists to aim for. The helicopter pilots, therefore, had to judge a suitable parachuting start point which took account of the wind speed and direction. In the gusty, strengthening winds this was problematic and while the lead Wessex pilot (a very experienced helicopter man) manoeuvred for the optimum point, the other two held a position above and behind to observe. Eventually, with the lead pilot evidently satisfied, we could see that his parachutists were readying themselves. Suddenly, as the first man leapt, anxious moments ensued while the briefed number of seconds elapsed before his parachute blossomed open. Quite quickly after that, by which stage we could count half a dozen khaki-coloured parachutes drifting gracefully downwards, the lead Wessex pulled clear to allow the number two to manoeuvre for the next para-drop. This seemed to go as smoothly and efficiently as the first and soon we were watching another half-dozen parachutes drift down towards the landing zone.

Now it was our turn. As I manoeuvred to take up position, a cloud drifted across to pass over the scene like a dark hand before a face. It felt like an omen. In the cabin behind me I was aware of Mike giving instructions to the parachutists as they unstrapped from their seats to line up in a kneeling position ready to jump. I noticed that the first in line was the tall, gaunt man who I recognised from the earlier briefing. With both arms outstretched, he gripped the sides of the exit doorway. As he looked this way and that, he seemed impatient and edgy. I knew, however, that we needed to fly on a bit further because, compared to ground level, the wind at this height was inclined to veer to a more northerly direction. This was plain from the position of the first wave of parachutists now approaching the landing zone. "I'm turning starboard another ten degrees to allow for the wind effect," I said to Mike on the aircraft intercommunication system.

"Okay," he said, "the guys back here are ready when you give the word."

"We'll give it thirty seconds." I pressed the aircraft stopwatch and glanced back at Mike. With one hand firmly on the fellow's shoulder, he restrained the first man to jump. Looking ahead again, I glimpsed the sea to the west where the surface looked benign although this was deceptive, for the collision of the tides, the swirl of the waters could not be made out too well now that we'd settled at a height of 10,000 feet. I glanced at the stopwatch: "Fifteen seconds to go, Mike." A check around the cockpit showed everything to be in order: height, airspeed, heading, temperatures, pressures. "Five seconds...standby... four...three...two...one...clear to jump!" At once Mike released his grip on the first parachutist's shoulder. The man leant forward slightly then, in a deliberate and rehearsed technique, leapt out of the Wessex. Now the next in line took the first man's place and within moments he, too, leapt out of the helicopter. In what felt like practically no time at all, the *Jaeger Corps* men had jumped and we began to circle above them as we watched their parachutes blossom open.

It was at this juncture that we became aware of the first hint of trouble. Mike commented that the initial wave of parachutists appeared to be heading further south than planned. "The wind's proving stronger than expected," he said. Then the air traffic controller called the lead Wessex: "Zero One, we think that some parachutists may end up in the fjord." At this, the lead pilot immediately asked for clearance for a fast descent. "You're cleared," said the controller, and as the three machines hastened down, we prepared ourselves for any rescue work. We were painfully conscious, however, that we carried no rescue winches and that any rescue would involve fishing a survivor out of the water manually – hardly ideal. It was a strange sensation as we readied ourselves, a moment when time seemed to distort in the face of sudden danger. As we approached the drop zone, we flew the three helicopters in an orbital pattern, following the leader who maintained a position that avoided any interference with the final part of the parachutists' descent. Before long, it became evident that most of the men would reach land as intended, although two men would end up in the water. The lead Wessex and the number two therefore concentrated on a man each while I continued to hold an orbit to observe. When the first parachutist splashed into the water, the lead pilot positioned his Wessex to hold a very low hover nearby. Meanwhile, the crewman, who was secured by a special 'long' strap, leant out of the cabin door. The pilot started to inch his machine towards the survivor until the crewman, stretching out one hand, was able to make a grab for the man. The burly crewman then hauled the parachutist into the cabin without too much difficulty for this individual, buoyed up by a life jacket, had managed to discard his parachute.

The situation for the second parachutist, however, was less straightforward. This man splashed into the water but instead of coming back up, his head remained at or slightly below the surface. Clearly, he was struggling. "Look!" said Mike, "his life jacket's not inflated..." and suddenly we realised the awful truth: this was the major himself, the only man without a life jacket. The second helicopter now moved rapidly into position as, full of premonitory misgivings, I eased the third Wessex a little closer to offer any additional help if possible. I watched my fellow pilot fly ever lower, so low that the wheels of his machine became submerged beneath the water's surface. His crewman sat on the step by the cabin door while, leaning forward as far as he could, he began to use his aircrew knife to cut away the major's parachute. This, though, was a laborious, time-consuming task. The situation seemed to become increasingly urgent when we noticed that the major's efforts to keep his head above the water had started to weaken. "My God!" said Mike. "He's drowning!" We watched horrified and helpless while we saw the poor crewman work frantically to release the major from his deadly snare. At last, however, with most of the parachute cut away and by use of one of the remaining parachute lines attached to the major's torso, the crewman managed to haul him onto the cabin step. With one hand the major clung for dear life to the step while the crewman cut away the final pieces of parachute. Both men were now clearly exhausted; we saw them rest for a short period before the crewman was able finally to help the major move from the step into the cabin itself. And with that, the drama was over. We saw the cabin door close and we heard the pilot ask for clearance to fly directly to the base medical centre.

It was some hours later, when at a briefing for the next day's tasks, that we saw the major again. Engrossed in studying maps and diagrams, at first no-one seemed to notice when the door at the back of the briefing room was opened quietly. Then a sudden hush fell across the room as everyone turned to see the major standing in the doorway. We could see at once that his earlier aura of sanguine invincibility had altered. His thin face looked as white as a sheet, his hands were trembling, the carapace of confidence had crumpled. He looked embarrassed, furthermore it was apparent that his ribs hurt for with every inhalation he appeared to wince. At length he said stiffly, almost in a whisper: "Thank you." After a pause he went on: "I'm sorry..." he hesitated and shook his head "...no life jacket. Foolish. I'm very sorry." An awkward silence lingered as he stared at the pilot and crewman who had saved him. "The doctor has told me to use my stomach muscles to breathe," he continued eventually, "but I should be okay in a day or two. There's no doubt about it," he said, "I owe you guys a debt of gratitude."

"We only did our job," said the pilot while his crewman nodded modestly.

"That may be so," said the major, "but you saved my life in the process." And after that he turned to leave the room. As he did so, we remained silent and slightly shocked while we thought about the implications of his experience. With images in my mind of choppy waters and angry waves, I realised that for the rest of his life this *Jaeger Corps* major was likely to associate the clamour of a helicopter hovering overhead with the desperate, poignant moment of his rescue.

CHAPTER 9
PUSHP'S WAR

Background to war: In 1971 developing disputes between India and Pakistan erupted into a war that would last for thirteen days. Despite this short period, in the preliminaries and in the wake of war, tragic numbers of civilians were killed, genocide and other atrocities were on a scale almost too vast to comprehend and people in their millions fled from East Pakistan to India.

Complex circumstances lay behind this catastrophe which, at root, was caused by the deep divisions between the traditionally dominant West Pakistanis and the majority East Pakistanis.

Trouble escalated after elections in 1970, then in 1971 the Pakistani army initiated mass arrests of dissidents, conducted acts of ethnic cleansing against the Bengali population of East Pakistan (aimed particularly at the minority Hindus), and attempted to disarm East Pakistani soldiers and police.

As the situation worsened, in March 1971 Bengali political and military leaders declared the independence of Bangladesh. The East Pakistan-Indian border was opened for refugees who sought safe shelter in India, after which the consequent flood of millions of impoverished East Pakistanis started to place intolerable strains on India's already overburdened economy. India's leader, Prime Minister Indira Gandhi, who had expressed her government's support for the independence struggle of the people of East Pakistan, began to realise that armed action against West Pakistan would be more effective than continuing to accept endless lines of refugees.

Meantime, the mood in West Pakistan grew increasingly jingoistic against East Pakistan and India. An organised propaganda campaign resulted in stickers ('CRUSH INDIA') appearing in cars and elsewhere in West Pakistan. In November 1971 thousands of people led by West Pakistani politicians marched through Lahore and other places to demand that Pakistan 'crush India'. India responded with a build-up of military forces in border areas. Within the refugee camps, exiled East Pakistani army officers and members of Indian military intelligence started to recruit and train Mukti Bahini guerrillas.

On 23 November 1971 President Khan of Pakistan declared a state of emergency and warned his people to prepare for war. On Sunday 3 December 1971, in a series of late-afternoon pre-emptive strikes, the Pakistan Air Force (PAF) attacked eleven Indian Air Force air bases. That evening Prime Minister Gandhi made a radio broadcast in which she held that the Pakistani air strikes were an act of war against India. That same night the Indian Air Force responded with initial air strikes which expanded to larger retaliatory action the next morning and for the rest of the war.

The experiences of Flight Lieutenant Pushp Kumar Vaid VrC

FLIGHT LIEUTENANT Pushp Kumar Vaid of the Indian Air Force was a member of 110 Helicopter Unit which was located, together with 111 and 105 Helicopter Units, at Agartala Airport in north-east India. As the unit's senior flight commander, Pushp was in charge of organising a total of fourteen Mil Mi-4 Russian-made piston-engined helicopters.

Five days after the outbreak of war, all of these helicopters were ordered to fly early in the morning to a field some twenty miles from Agartala where, after landing, Pushp, his commanding officer and a number of others were briefed by an army general who outlined the day's plan. After the briefing, a helicopter reconnaissance flight allowed the general to point out a landing site, a large field of about twenty acres in size, where he wanted his troops to be flown that day. Situated in north-east Bangladesh, this landing site was near the town of Sylhet, a prominent Islamic spiritual centre which would become a focal point for Bengali revolutionaries during the war.

"Be prepared for operations from 0900 hours," said the general. The Mi-4s were refuelled and made ready for operations from that time, however a long wait ensued because the army was held up by enemy activity. As Pushp and his colleagues waited around apprehensively in the area's humid subtropical climate, they discussed the progress of the war and their part in it. The men had heard from intelligence briefings that, following the pre-emptive strike of five days ago, the Pakistan Air Force was on the defensive and evidently flying fewer and fewer sorties as the war progressed. The Indian Air Force, on the other hand, had flown many thousands of sorties and in Pushp's area of operations in the eastern sector, the small contingent of Pakistan Air Force had reportedly been destroyed. As a consequence, the planned flights that day (assuming, thought Pushp, that the army ever turned up) would be in an environment of air superiority. The Indian army, Pushp learned, had joined forces with the Mukti Bahini guerrillas to form the Mitro Bahini (Allied Forces), and unlike the conflict of six years earlier which had involved set-piece battles and slow advances, the strategy this time was to conduct swift, blitzkrieg-type attacks. A three-pronged assault of infantry divisions was planned with attached armoured units and close air support to converge rapidly on East Pakistan's capital city, Dacca (the spelling was changed to Dhaka in 1983). Pushp and his colleagues had been briefed that their task today would be part of this overall strategy.

Pushp was restless as he waited, maybe he wished the time away. His mind alternated between worrying about the flight's details and wondering when the troops would turn up. He and his colleagues paced back and forth, sharing the nervousness of the occasion. Some smoked cigarettes as they waited. Men clenched and unclenched their fists; the air grew heavy with tension. At one point a squadron of Indian Air Force fighter aircraft, heading north, flew overhead and from time to time a field telephone rang. All eyes would swing towards the operator, but news was sparse.

The morning passed, then from a hard, clear sky a wintry sun began to consume the shadows of the afternoon. Still they waited until, at around 1500 hours, khaki-clad troops appeared and the pilots knew that, at last, their task could commence. Programmed to be the first airborne, Pushp's Mi-4 was loaded up as rapidly as possible and when ready, he took off to head directly for the Sylhet landing site, a flight of around twenty minutes. At intervals of two to three minutes, the other Mi-4s followed so that by the time Pushp had dropped his first load and returned for the next, the last helicopter had just taken off to head for Sylhet.

This system meant that each helicopter had sufficient fuel for three flights before the need to refuel. By the time of the third flight, though, dusk was turning to dark and the fading light began to hinder flying operations. Furthermore, the Pakistan army had become aware of the helicopters and had started to surround the Sylhet landing site. On Pushp's third flight he suddenly saw what appeared to be hundreds of tracer rounds fired at his helicopter from all directions as he came in to land. At once he warned the other helicopter pilots of the danger and of the need to reduce time on the ground to a minimum. However, when all fourteen Mi-4s had completed their three flights and shut down for refuel, a check of the machines revealed that not one had been struck by a bullet.

At this point, with the time at around 1800 hours, the officer in charge of the Indian Air Force side of the operation, Group Captain Chanan Singh, decided that it would be too dangerous to continue. "We'll be like sitting targets on the ground at the Sylhet landing site," he decreed. "We'll start flying again first thing in the morning." This announcement, though, appalled the army hierarchy: in the afternoon's hurly-burly, troops and equipment had been loaded onto the Mi-4s at random. With no opportunity to plan who was going first and with what equipment, the army had assumed that flying operations would continue until everyone and everything had been delivered.

An intense conversation between an army brigadier and Group Captain Singh followed as both men strived to work out the best course of action. The hours passed, the pilots waited, the troops waited, everyone remained on tenterhooks. Nearly three hours elapsed before a decision was made. At approximately 2100 hours the worried-looking group captain emerged from his meeting and walked up to Pushp. "We've come to a compromise," said the group captain. "One helicopter will attempt a night mission and if it returns safely, the others will be sent in. I'd like you to muster a volunteer crew."

"I'll fly it, sir," said Pushp without hesitation, "I'll just go to the crew room and get a co-pilot." Pushp then went to the pilots' crew room and explained the situation. "I need a volunteer co-pilot," he said and was gratified when, to a man, every one of the forty pilots said that they'd be willing to fly. All of the men were aged under thirty and Pushp was moved by their courage. "Kanth, I'd like you to come with me," Pushp said as he nodded towards Flying Officer Kanth Reddy.

Pushp and Kanth now hastened to their Mi-4 and helped to load the helicopter with radios and essential equipment. Some soldiers were detailed to go, too, and both pilots were issued with .38 revolvers for personal protection. In addition, they each carried a lungi – a traditional garment worn around the waist – so that, if shot down, they could pretend to be Bengalis (even though neither man could speak Bengali). As part of the helicopter crew, a flight engineer was carried in order to manage all the ground handling while both pilots remained at the flight controls.

The time was 2200 hours when Pushp and Kanth took off. Blackout was in force and the complete darkness felt disorientating, especially as the only available navigation aid was the aircraft compass. Pushp and Kanth nonetheless flew on, their concentration acute. Their absorption meant that they had little time to think about the scenes below, a tragedy hidden within the veil of night – buildings bombed, homes ruined, great heaps of rubble, death and destruction on a massive scale.

The enormity of the war's implications pressed on minds around the world. Beneath the helicopter were refugees from towns and villages razed to the ground by the fighting. As people flooded south towards the border, the roads and tracks became clogged with vehicles, handcarts, bicycles, children's prams all filled with the treasured possessions of impoverished citizens. Indian troops and equipment required urgently at the front line struggled against the tidal flow of humanity. The soldiers became easy targets for snipers, exacerbating the congestion. For some there was doubt about where to go; the chain of command was stretched; confusion reigned.

But the interminable refugee lines, filthy and ragged, persisted. Exhausted, even past the point of caring, individuals were driven, no doubt, by an overpowering will to live. Small children, innocent and sweet, had died for nothing. Their parents still pushed onwards, their hearts paralysed by grief. Hard to imagine was the sense of desperation, of contempt, of helplessness and terror, of eyes wet with sadness. The situation, hardly assuaged by surrounding savagery, was intensified by the vast numbers all in similar circumstances.

Suddenly, Pushp and Kanth picked up the sound of an intermittent voice on the aircraft radio: "...do you read...?" Pushp recognised the voice: the air force liaison officer was calling on a hand-held radio.

"What's the situation on the ground?" asked Pushp. The radio reception was poor. "Say again?" yelled the liaison officer. Pushp repeated his question. The liaison officer, however, was unwilling to give details. Perhaps, thought Pushp, he was worried that the helicopter would turn back. The liaison officer went on to say that all was quiet and that a bonfire would be lit to indicate where the helicopter should land. The bonfire was lit quite quickly which caused the entire area to be illuminated as if a searchlight had been switched on. The effect was dramatic. Pushp and Kanth spotted the flames but they were not alone for the entire Pakistan army, so it seemed, promptly opened up with a barrage of weaponry. Pushp and Kanth still flew on, awed by the sight of hundreds, maybe thousands, of tracer rounds. Perhaps the enemy soldiers, lured by the brilliance of the flames, deafened by the sound of their own barrage, had failed to detect the camouflaged helicopter. Whatever the reason, as Pushp headed towards a position some distance from the bonfire, his perseverance was rewarded when he managed to carry out a successful landing.

Now all hell was let loose as the Mi-4 was unloaded. Pakistani soldiers continued to mount fierce, relentless attacks. Tracer bullets arched towards the helicopter; flashes of orange flame, sparkling like firecrackers, spurted out from areas overlooking the landing site. "Watch out...duck down..." cried Pushp to his co-pilot. Fearful that explosive rounds might pepper the fuselage and cockpit, he felt pitifully exposed; the whistle of bullets, projectiles and ricochets could be heard above the din of the helicopter. The whole sky appeared to change from night to day as the flashes from gunfire persisted. Distant rumbles suggested the use of heavy weaponry. The helicopter seemed to jolt and dance in the turmoil and, adding to the difficulties, choking dust began to contaminate the air. Each passing second felt more like an hour, even so Pushp, reckoning that the helicopter had not been on the ground for long, was astonished when he heard the flight engineer shout: "We can go..."

"Everything unloaded?" asked Pushp anxiously.

"Yes, yes...go!" The flight engineer's voice was full of fear.

This, Pushp knew, was not the time to prevaricate. Swiftly, surely, he raised the Mi-4's collective lever so that within moments he had taken off and turned towards base. "Check for bullet holes!" he said to the flight engineer.

The flight engineer now moved carefully through the helicopter using a torch to inspect the cabin. Glancing back, Pushp noticed the way that the flight engineer's eyes flashed through the grime of his face as he pointed the torch around the cabin. "I can't find any signs of bullet holes," he said eventually. "We've got one passenger, by the way," went on the flight engineer, "the soldier who lit the bonfire. He was hit in the thumb by a bullet."

"He was lucky not to have been killed."

While he flew back to base, Pushp spoke on the aircraft radio to advise the group captain that all the helicopters should be made ready to fly. "We can operate through the night," he said. Not long after this call Pushp landed at base to pick up the next load. With great urgency, troops and equipment rushed towards the Mi-4 and within a matter of minutes Pushp was able to take off once more to fly back to the Sylhet landing site. Remarkably, this flight, as with the previous one, proceeded without incident. During the third flight, however, by which time the other Mi-4s had begun to fly, Pushp and Kanth noticed on the return to base that the fuel gauge was reading zero. "Either we're out of fuel," said Pushp to his co-pilot, "or the bloody gauge is broken."

"The engine's still working – we're still flying!"

The two pilots, with fingers firmly crossed and (in Pushp's words) offering prayers to whoever's up there, resolved that they should fly on rather than land immediately. It was a good decision: when they landed at base, engineers discovered that a cable to the fuel gauge had been severed by a bullet. The cable was swiftly replaced after which Pushp and Kanth took off again and, together with the other Mi-4s, continued to fly through the night until the entire brigade had been dropped at the Sylhet landing site.

Just over a week later, Pakistan surrendered. Following the surrender, Pushp was asked to arrange for all the Mi-4s to be made ready to ferry journalists and VIPs to observe the signing of the surrender papers at Tejgaon Airfield, Dacca. In view of the large numbers involved, Group Captain Singh instructed that those pilots and flight attendants not needed to crew the ferry helicopters should be left behind. Pushp, however, ignored this instruction. He reasoned that these aircrew deserved to witness the momentous occasion having flown in situations of great risk for their country.

The helicopters landed at Tejgaon Airfield at 1615 hours. Large numbers of cars were lined up to take the Indian contingent to the grounds of a race course at Dacca where the signing would take place. During the drive, Pushp was moved to see so many Bangladeshi people wave and smile at the Indian contingent as the cars drove by. Many of the people had guns which they fired into the air in excitement. It was, Pushp said later, a great feeling – a bit like in the movies when the Allies entered Paris in World War Two.

The instrument of surrender was signed on 16 December 1971 at 1655 hours. After the signing, Air Marshal Hari Chand Dewan, head of the Indian Air Force Eastern Air Command, asked a Pakistani general why he had surrendered so quickly. "Because of the bombing," replied the general, "there was no safe place left in Dacca."

Citation

After the war, Pushp's name was sent forward for a Vir Chakra gallantry award which was approved within a few days with the following citation:

'During the operations against Pakistan in December 1971, Flight Lieutenant Pushp Kumar Vaid was serving with a helicopter unit deployed in the eastern sector. On one occasion it was decided to transport an infantry element to the sector by air. Flight Lieutenant Pushp Kumar Vaid, knowing full well that the helipad landing area was not lit and that he would be under heavy enemy fire on landing, volunteered to undertake this mission, and successfully completed the task. Subsequently, he flew thirty-four more hazardous missions deep inside the enemy lines. Throughout, Flight Lieutenant Pushp Kumar Vaid displayed gallantry, professional skill and devotion to duty of high order.'

[NB Under a system established by the president of India in 1950, the highest gallantry award was the Param Vir Chakra, the second highest the Maha Vir Chakra, the third highest the Vir Chakra.]

Aftermath

With the signing of the instrument of surrender, East Pakistan seceded to become the independent state of Bangladesh. Over 90,000 members of the Pakistani armed forces were taken as prisoners of war. It was calculated that more than two million civilians were killed in Bangladesh. Following the surrender, discipline within the Pakistani armed forces began to break down and many atrocities were reported, including the rape of hundreds of thousands of women. As a result of the conflict it was estimated that eight to ten million people fled in order to seek refuge in India.

Pakistani Major General Qureshi later wrote: 'We must accept the fact that, as a people, we had also contributed to the bifurcation of our own country. It was not a Niazi, or a Yahya, even a Mujob or a Bhutto, or their key assistants, who alone were the cause of our break-up but a corrupted system and a flawed social order that our own apathy had allowed to remain in place for years.'

In announcing the Pakistani surrender, Prime Minister Indira Ghandi declared in the Indian parliament: "Dacca is now the free capital of a free country. We hail the people of Bangladesh in their hour of triumph. All nations who value the human spirit will recognise it as a significant milestone in man's quest for liberty."

CHAPTER 10

HELI-MISCELLANY (2)

Australian antics (from Mike Lehan)

THE SITUATION WAS delicate, like walking on egg shells, and tension filled the cockpit. As part of his familiarisation training, Lieutenant Commander Mike Lehan of the Royal Australian Navy was required to land his helicopter on a narrow platform positioned just below Pigeon House Mountain in the southern coast region of New South Wales. He knew that the platform had restricted access but, as a new arrival at Nowra Naval Air Station, his briefing by the operations officer had been, well, brief: "No worries. Some other pilots have just landed there." As it turned out, however, these 'other pilots' were flying a Bell UH-1 Iroquois, otherwise known as 'Huey' – famous for combat operations in the Vietnam War – a machine with a narrow skidded undercarriage. But the Westland Wessex which Mike was flying had a wheeled, and much wider, undercarriage.

While Mike flew towards the platform, he and his observer spotted a number of walkers clambering up the mountain slopes. He'd been told that, on average, a walker would take three to four hours to climb and descend the mountain's two thousand three hundred and sixty feet. 'Quicker by helicopter,' he thought smugly. He gazed at the prominent remnants of the two-tier sandstone structure used, apparently, by Captain James Cook as a lead-in marker to Jervis Bay during his voyage of discovery along Australia's eastern coast in 1770.

When close to the landing platform, Mike decided that he should carry out a textbook approach: a high-level general reconnaissance followed by a low-level overshoot to check the site carefully before the landing itself. The weather that day was good, if not exactly perfect. The blue, blue sky was magnificent but the wind was fairly strong with gusts up to twenty-five knots. The gusts were particularly troublesome when Mike brought the Wessex to a hover by the platform's edge. Turbulent updrafts caused the helicopter to bounce around and the platform's limited size meant that he had to land with considerable circumspection. Guided by his observer, land he did, though, but just as he lowered the collective lever, a glance at the fuel gauges indicated trouble: the rear fuel gauge had started to cycle. From experience, he knew this to be an indication of air in the system or, worse still, a possible fuel leak.

Now Mike raised the collective lever again and, with maximum power applied, zoomed the helicopter up to a height of five thousand feet. As he levelled off, however, something strange started to happen: the Wessex was suddenly engulfed in mist. From the smell, the mist was clearly caused by fuel. A further check of the fuel gauges showed that the forward gauge was rapidly approaching zero while the rear gauge persisted to cycle wildly.

At once, Mike lowered the collective lever to enter autorotation while, simultaneously, he transmitted a Mayday call and headed for the bush terrain below. After a rapid descent, he had just sufficient fuel to carry out a powered landing before the Wessex ran out of fuel. Hastily evacuating the helicopter, Mike and his observer now had to wait for rescue which came in the form of the duty search and rescue Huey. "So what went wrong?" asked the Huey pilot after he'd rescued the two Wessex men. Mike shrugged as if to say: 'search me, Cobber', but instead he said: "Can you take us over the Pigeon House platform? Perhaps there's something there we didn't see."

The Huey pilot duly agreed and as he flew low and slow past the platform he pointed to a post which had been cemented into the centre of the landing area. "Hardly surprising you didn't spot that," he said, "it blends perfectly with surrounding granite rock."

Later, Mike learnt that the four-foot-high post had been placed by local Boy Scouts. The pole had penetrated the underside of the Wessex, then pushed upwards to cause a crack in the high pressure fuel pipe. The consequences, Mike reflected, could have been much worse if the pipe had severed. He felt, therefore, heartily grateful for the sturdy construction of the Westland Wessex.

Sixty-second escape (from Alan Boulden)

FLIGHT LIEUTENANT Alan Boulden clicked his tongue disapprovingly. He held the flight controls of his Agusta-Bell 205 helicopter which, with engine and rotors running, was parked on a precarious helipad in Oman. With narrowed eyes he gazed anxiously at a group of people standing nearby: all were in the process of deferential farewells before some of them boarded the helicopter. Far be it for him, he mused, to encourage anything other than the best of good manners, especially as one of the group was a senior British government official, but this was no time to dilly-dally.

Alan glanced up at the bright sun. As with the whole of the Persian Gulf, Oman was renowned for one of the hottest climates in the world with very little rainfall. An exception to this general rule, however, was Southern Oman where he was now. For it was here that the tropical-like climate in the Dhofar mountains near his base at the coastal town of Salalah, the provincial capital, meant seasonal rainfall from June to September, rainfall caused by monsoon winds from the Indian Ocean. He'd not been in Oman for long so he was still in the process of acclimatising to the extreme weather, although the weather conditions – and even this tiresome wait for his passengers – were not the only reasons for his angst. For this was just the second operational helicopter tour in his flying career, and his time here was turning out to be even more unusual than he'd been led to expect, indeed his experiences were proving to be...well, quite an eye-opener. He was a loan service pilot with the Sultan of Oman's Air Force (SOAF) and he still had much to learn in an environment that was at once uncommon, intriguing, hazardous.

For one thing, as he was employed to carry out duties in the fight against communist insurgents in the conflict known as the Dhofar Rebellion, Alan was in an active war zone with all of the implications. It was now September 1974 and he reflected that war here had been ongoing for a dozen or so years. He'd been briefed that when hostilities began in 1962 in the province of Dhofar by rebels against the Sultanate of Muscat and Oman, the country in the early 1960s was very underdeveloped with a leader, Sultan Said bin Taimur, who was an absolute ruler under British control. Alan learned about how, back then, the Sultan had banned almost all technological development and had relied on British support to maintain the rudimentary functions of the state – a state, therefore, which needed to be radically reformed and modernised to cope with the campaign. In 1970, after eight years of war, Sultan bin Taimur had been deposed by his son, Sultan Qaboos bin Said, who'd opened up the country with economic reforms and a policy of modernisation which included more spending on health, education and welfare. Sultan Qaboos had also outlawed slavery.

As part of these reforms, so Alan learnt, cash incentives were offered to rebels who changed sides, also training and re-equipment of the Sultan of Oman's Armed Forces (SAF) had helped to re-establish the Sultan's authority. Regular units of the SAF were expanded and re-equipped, and officers as well as NCO instructors from the British army and the Royal Marines were attached to the units. In addition, the Sultan of Oman's Air Force was enlarged with aircraft such as the BAC Strikemaster, Shorts Skyvan transport aircraft and eight Agusta-Bell 205 transport helicopters, one of which Alan now continued to hold at readiness while he mentally urged his passengers to board quickly. His passengers, though, still showed no inclination to hasten; their elaborate adieus appeared to go on and on. 'For goodness sake,' he thought irritably. The helipad was placed near a hilltop defence position, one of many dotted around Dhofar and manned by Omani soldiers led by British officers who, like Alan, were on loan service. These defensive positions formed a line aimed at holding back enemy assaults, nonetheless the positions were attacked regularly by communist rebels who infiltrated from neighbouring Yemen and who employed a variety of weapons

– one of which, a recoilless rifle grenade known as 'RCL', posed a particular danger and which, Alan reckoned, could strike them right here at any moment.

While he tried to force himself to be patient, Alan stared at nearby shrubs and grasses typical of southern Arabia. He spotted a lone bush that poked its way through the sun-dried surrounds. Perhaps bush, he pondered, was too grand a term for what amounted to a twig with a couple of stalks, although it was not, in general, necessarily symbolic of this, the most fertile part of Oman, where he'd seen coconut palms in plentiful numbers near his Salalah base and along the coastal plains that led up to the mountain range with its distinctive habitat.

But it was not habitat that was bothering him right now so much as the seemingly interminable handshaking and prolonged farewells. Particular attention was directed towards the important one – the British permanent under-secretary for defence (PUS) – who was here on a so-called fact-finding mission. No doubt the permanent under-secretary had been briefed extensively about this and that, including the action a couple of years ago which had involved helicopters operating with the British SAS (Special Air Service). Following that action, the end of the rebel cause appeared inevitable, though time would prove that another four years would elapse before the rebels were finally defeated in 1976. The permanent under-secretary would be interested, too, to hear first-hand accounts on the impact of the recent increase in troops from the Iranian Imperial Task Force. Alan was aware that the previous year, following Sultan Qaboos' diplomatic efforts, the Shah of Iran had sent helicopters and an Iranian army brigade of over a thousand troops to help in the fight against the rebels.

Suddenly Alan saw that an accompanying officer had started to make hand gestures to encourage the permanent under-secretary and his entourage to board the helicopter. The passengers bent low as they entered the rush of air stirred up by the Agusta-Bell 205's rotating blades. Once his passengers had strapped into their seats, Alan raised the helicopter's collective lever to apply maximum permitted pitch. Then, immediately after take-off, he turned the machine away from the helipad and flew close to the side of a wadi occupied by friendly forces.

It was only later that Alan learnt about the narrowness of his escape. A mere matter of seconds after take-off, the helipad was bombarded with RCL grenades, an event marked by a certificate sent to all involved and signed by the commander of the Dhofar brigade with the words:

> This is to certify that the bearer's unbelievable dining-out story is in fact quite true. On 8 September 1974 at 1524 hours SOAF helicopter 706 lifted off from the helipad of the FLAG position carrying PUS and party. At 1525 hours 6x 75-mm RCL fell on and around the helipad.
>
> Signed J B Akehurst, Brigadier
> Commander Dhofar Brigade

The brigadier's initial words, perhaps rightly, appeared to make light of the situation. In truth, however, Alan and his passengers may have come closer to meeting their creator, as the saying goes, than any of them would have wished.

Naval niceties (from Peter Donaldson)

IT SEEMED ODD, thought Sub-Lieutenant Peter Donaldson, that such a straight-forward point should cause an illustrious admiral to become flustered. The admiral, after all, had invited the group of young officers recently arrived on his flagship, the aircraft carrier HMS *Hermes*, to ask him questions and Peter's question – "What exactly do you do, sir? – was surely a reasonable one. But Admiral Sir Peter Ashmore, caught off-guard, appeared to flounder as he pondered the answer. Perhaps, thought Peter, the admiral was unclear about what, precisely, he DID do. Maybe a slight reddening of his cheeks, as well as Peter's, emphasised the moment's awkwardness. In any case, as nearby senior naval officers gazed aghast at the scene, it was shortly afterwards that the commanding officer explained that such questions should not be put to admirals and that young Peter would be well advised to keep his head down in future and to concentrate on his job as a pilot trained to fly the Westland Wessex helicopter.

Before this incident, Peter, who'd joined the *Hermes* off Aden in May 1967, had been briefed on the diverse roles that he and his colleagues would under-take on the ship. These included anti-submarine work using sonar, movement of personnel, and 'Vertreps' (vertical replenishment between ships). HMS *Hermes,* a conventional British carrier and the last of the Centaur class, typically carried at that time a dozen de Havilland Sea Vixens, seven Blackburn Bucca-neers, five Fairey Gannet aircraft and six Westland Wessex helicopters. When these aircraft were operating from the carrier, a Wessex helicopter would remain on standby in case a search and rescue task arose. However, currently overshadowing these and other peacetime duties was the prospect that the ship was likely to be in a war zone shortly as trouble brewed between Israel and her Arab neighbours.

Despite his junior naval rank, Peter was allocated his own cabin on board the *Hermes*, a cabin which, although too small to swing the proverbial cat, none-theless meant that he could play his electric organ keyboard, a skill for which his reputation grew amongst the crew. One day a Royal Marine bandsman invited Peter to join a rock group, an offer which Peter accepted gladly despite the disapproval of some senior officers. The group was popular on board and when in harbour the leader arranged nightclub bookings, including one in an establishment that, embarrassingly, turned out to be a brothel. When he learned about this, Peter's commanding officer summoned him: "This sort of behaviour, you know Donaldson, is not what we expect of an officer. Naval officers are not supposed to work in brothels."

"I was only playing my organ."

"You should keep your organ away from such places."

"We earned a bit of money."

"Money?" the commanding officer stared.

"Yes, sir. Ten per cent of the evening's take."

"Ten per cent? Is that all...I mean..."

"We thought that was pretty good, actually. Anyway," went on Peter, "the ship's coffers have seen the benefit."

"The ship's coffers?" the commanding officer gazed weakly at his sub-lieutenant.

"Charity begins at home and all that. And by the way I believe that it was one of the ship's senior officers that reported me."

"Yes, it was."

"The senior officer who was clearly enjoying himself in the establishment?"

"Well, I wouldn't know about that."

"I can assure you that he was."

"How do you mean?"

"He was with a group of senior colleagues. One in particular clearly appreciated our music. He was dancing on a table."

Swiftly dismissed, Peter heard no more on the subject although a few nights later the commanding officer's displeasure was evident again, if for rather different reasons. A group of helicopters had been briefed to conduct sonar sweeps to search for submarines, a laborious task which covered a large area. After an hour or more, as the night passed minute by slow minute without any signs of action, Peter's observer in the helicopter's crew of three started to mutter remarks about: "I am bored...really, really bored..." when Peter suddenly realised that his observer, disguising his voice, had pressed the radio transmit button during this rant. At once the commanding officer's voice was heard: "Aircraft transmitting – identify yourself!"

"I'm not that f***ing bored," came the reply, a comment which subsequently earned a general lecture on radio procedures when the sortie was debriefed after landing.

In any case, mused Peter later, proceedings needed to be lightened from time to time for the sake of good morale. This hypothesis, if ambitious, nonetheless was demonstrated one evening after a ship's 'pipe' had declared: "Do you hear there – flying for the day is complete." Normally a routine announcement, on this occasion the flight deck officer saw to his horror that a forklift truck was still parked on the flight deck in the path of a Sea Vixen about to land. This officer immediately barked orders, jumped around in excitement and waved his arms. Meanwhile a nearby pilot cried: "I'll move it!" and leapt aboard the forklift truck. However, despite the best of intentions, the pilot selected the wrong gear and the flight deck officer's alarm multiplied approximately tenfold when he saw both pilot and forklift truck reverse at speed over the carrier's side. Before he struck the sea's surface, the hapless hero parted company with the vehicle; the duty search and rescue Wessex crew fished him out of the water then deposited him into the hands of a medical team who established that, fortunately, he'd not been seriously injured. The next ship's pipe therefore announced: "Do you hear there – forklift truck flying for the day is complete."

A more sombre mood developed on board HMS *Hermes* when June 1967 approached and underlying hostility between Israel and Arab countries became increasingly tense. Israel reiterated its position that the closure of the straits of Tiran to its shipping would amount to a *casus belli,* but despite the warning Egypt's President Gamal Nasser announced that the straits would be closed to Israeli vessels and that Egypt would mobilise forces along the border with Israel. On 5 June 1967 Israel launched a series of air attacks against Egyptian airfields and the infamous Six Day War began. From the perspective of the crew of HMS *Hermes,* as the ship was now in a war zone its admiral was in charge of the entire Royal Naval presence in the Arabian Gulf.

It was early one morning in this anxious period that Peter was hastening towards his Wessex when, by chance, he met Admiral Ashmore rushing in the opposite direction. At once, Peter came to attention and saluted as one should. Then a curious thing happened. The admiral abruptly slowed his pace, stopped and took a few paces backwards. He glared at Peter and frowned although his expression changed to a grin when he declared: "*Now* you know what I do!" and promptly hurried off.

Feet on the ground (from Pushp Vaid)

THE ARMY GENERAL'S farewell tour included visits to a number of his Indian army bases in the Himalayas north of the city of Bareilly in the state of Uttar Pradesh. Flying the general in a Mil Mi-4 helicopter was Flight Lieutenant Pushp Vaid of the Indian Air Force. After take-off from a helipad at Joshimath, Pushp climbed up to an altitude of around nine thousand feet as he headed due south for the flight of twenty-five minutes or so to the army base at Ranikhet.

However, after ten minutes Pushp noticed that an unusual amount of smoke was emitting from the helicopter's exhaust, smoke which had seeped into the passenger cabin to cause looks of alarm amongst the general and his retinue.

The smoke began to increase to the point that Pushp and his co-pilot started to search anxiously for an open field so that, in the event of engine failure, they could autorotate the helicopter down for an emergency landing. Below, though, the terrain was mountainous and covered in thick jungle with very few open spaces. Pushp decided that landing from an autorotation would be impractical and that he should continue towards Ranikhet where he requested a priority straight-in approach and landing. Luckily this worked out satisfactorily and as quickly as possible after landing Pushp closed down the helicopter and helped to evacuate his passengers.

At this juncture Pushp was taken aback by the general's un-general-like reaction. "Thank you, thank you," cried the senior officer as he marched up to Pushp, "you've saved all of our lives!" Pushp shrugged his shoulders modestly. The general, though, was clearly in no mood for bashful behaviour for he grabbed Pushp and hugged him for what seemed like about five minutes. "Oh but you *have* saved us," went on the general eventually, "and what a wonderful feeling it is to have one's feet back on the ground!"

Sunlight and dark (from Richard Pike)

I COULD BARELY believe it. Having been briefed on procedures, warned of the hazards and told what to expect in this training exercise, still the shock of reality caught me off-guard. Outside, where the sun shone, people walked around bullishly indifferent to what was happening inside the building. But for those of us seated and strapped into a simulated helicopter cabin known as a dunker, minds were concentrated by the whine of an electric motor as the dunker device was lowered slowly, deliberately into the Royal Navy's special swimming pool at Portsmouth. The sensation was not pleasant. Those seated next to me looked as apprehensive as I felt when, gradually approaching the water, the upper part of our chests finally became submerged. It was not long before chins began to touch the water after which our faces were one moment above the surface, then briefly under water, above again, then ducked under, above once more before disappearing a final time: after a last gulp of air, there came the inevitable instant of complete submersion.

Compelled to endure inaction, we had to sit still while, as instructed, our orientation arms grimly gripped a section of fuselage. Eventually the orientation arm would show the direction of escape, but for the present I forced myself to focus on a slow release of breath while the dunker steadily sank lower. In a real situation there was a danger of decapitation until the helicopter rotors struck the water and stopped turning. We'd been briefed, therefore, that for a valid training exercise escape attempts should not be made until a bump was felt as the dunker touched the bottom of the pool. As precious time ticked by I was aware of underwater noises, peculiar irregular clangs and clatters. The distorted, hollow sounds induced a feeling of disorientation within me. There was light, yes, but a feeble semi-light which made seeing almost impossible, as if struggling through a cloudburst with eyes half-closed. The supervising safety diver was positioned just a couple of feet from where I sat yet I could not see him. My chest was painful, so were my sinuses. I longed to move upwards, to breathe air, to see and hear properly.

I could imagine the potential scenario if, instead of a regulated training environment, we'd been in a helicopter which had ditched during a storm. An immense sea might be black and cold and seething with giant waves which crashed down in pitiless, relentless surges. The air would be filled with spray and tall walls of water – so tall that they looked practically perpendicular – would collapse from a great height that threatened to overwhelm the survivors. In a heavy downpour, as the wind threw the rain this way and that, the sky would turn darker, day would look like night. Assessing one's prospects in the light of reason, it could be easy to give up, easy to allow a suffocating paralysis to consume the mind and body. But the will to live was strong. Thoughts of family, of friends, of prospects and plans, of the need to talk and the necessity to stay alive to be able to tell one's story had to overcome fatalistic notions. The urge to carry on living involved effort and such effort was surely paramount.

Still we had to wait and as we did so my mental processes swung wildly. In my head, ideas were fixed either on practical details like maintaining the position of the orientation arm, or transfixed by the unpleasantness of the situation. Second by second my available breath was vanishing. The consequent sense of panic could be self-feeding. It struck me that to be confined in a small space like this and with sight restricted to no more than a few inches, the mind was inclined to play tricks.

Seated nearby was the wife of one of the naval instructors. Earlier, amidst cheerful banter with quips about 'crabs' and 'fish-heads' and other comments characteristic of inter-service rivalry, she'd appeared confidently jaunty, encouraged, no doubt, by her husband's reassurance that the dunker experience was 'a piece of cake'. When we were strapping into the device, however, I noticed a rather more serious look on her face and then, as we were lowered into the pool, her expression developed into one of horror. The sight sent a shiver down my spine. I wondered how she was coping right now.

When I became aware that the person seated next to me had started to move and that it was my turn next, something unexpected occurred: I felt a reluctance to follow. As if this new sub-aqua world had taken control of my senses, a still, small voice in my head seemed to suggest that I should remain where I was, that life in this watery form of panopticon was not so bad after all. As he fought to follow his orientation arm I was just able to see well enough to notice that my neighbour's movement seemed slow and tentative, like trying to wade through treacle. The effect was mesmeric. If nature was preoccupied with balance, right now I felt no urge to upset an uncommon awareness of balance – a beneficial one which suggested that if I was patient, if I remained seated, if I strived not to struggle, nature would ensure that I was looked after.

A sharp tap on my arm brought me back to reality. Later, I learnt that the supervising safety diver had noticed my disinclination to move, that this was not so unusual in the dunker and that people sometimes needed to be spurred into action. Training now prodded the cogs of my mind back into life: unbuckle the seat straps with one hand; make sure that the orientation arm remained firmly in place; now wriggle free of the seat straps, push away from the seat itself and swim upwards as directed by the orientation arm. Within moments, as I popped up to the surface of the pool, I had the feeling that I'd been under water for ages, yet it was less than a minute.

The pool was scattered with the accoutrements of sea survival – a solar still, life jackets, a whistle, a Day-glo vest, a loose manual – and I experienced a sense of amazement by the way immediate perils had concluded so quickly. My rapid gasps for breath on reaching the surface started to slow down and with the return of a semblance of normality, my heart stopped knocking about in my chest. Apart from an instructor comforting his rather upset wife, I noticed that the other instructors appeared quite relaxed. One of them whistled a tune as he walked briskly along the side of the pool, another indicated where we should climb out of the water. While I clambered up the steps of the pool ladder I glanced outside to observe that life carried on as normal. It seemed incredible; a conundrum. People strolled and pointed and laughed and chatted. The freedom of fresh air was all around, just taken for granted. As if I'd woken from a bad dream, the darkness of a few moments ago had disappeared abruptly and now I stared in wonder at the mighty sunlight.

Cross-decking (from Alan Boulden)

AS ASCENSION ISLAND came into view it occurred to Flight Lieutenant Alan Boulden that matters were beginning to look quite serious. Up to that point he, and many others, were convinced that the politicians and the diplomats would have assembled themselves around a large circular table, banged a few heads together, agreed that a war between Argentina and the United Kingdom was probably not a good idea, and ordered the task force of more than one hundred ships to turn around and go home. The early sentiments of many were expressed by Admiral Sandy Woodward: "...all initially suspected that the operation was doomed."

Despite the anxieties, however, it was becoming evident that the progression of this task force was no mere bluff. Despatched from the United Kingdom on 5 April 1982 on the orders of the 'Iron Lady', Prime Minister Margaret Thatcher, it seemed that the task force, like the lady herself, was not for turning. The prime minister apparently had every intention of persisting with her promise made in the House of Commons two days previously: "The House meets this Saturday to respond to a situation of great gravity...the Falkland Islands and their dependencies remain British territory...it is the Government's objective to see that the islands are freed from occupation and are returned to British administration at the earliest possible moment..."

And in the words of an American columnist: "The British did not appear to be in a mood to be pushed around."

'So this is it,' thought Alan, 'war looms'. It was interesting, he reflected, that the first news of an Argentine invasion reached Britain from Argentine sources when a Ministry of Defence operative in London had a brief telex conversation with Governor Rex Hunt's telex operator. The latter confirmed that Argentine troops were on the island and in control. The transmission of that important news by such a means, mused Alan, emphasised the problems of dealing with very long distances, in this case nearly seven thousand nautical miles between London and Stanley. In addition to this, problems had been created by the hasty way in which the task force was assembled, a hastiness which meant that now, while he observed the Ascension Islands from the ship *Atlantic Conveyor,* Alan knew that as a Boeing Chinook pilot he'd be involved in so-called cross-decking flights – the transfer of equipment from one ship to another to ensure optimum 'tactical unloading' when the task force reached the war zone. This cross-decking, thought Alan, while a necessary part of war preparation, would have secondary effects as realities were underlined and tensions heightened.

The cross-decking soon commenced. Alan was ordered off the *Atlantic Conveyor* to join the merchant vessel CS *Iris,* a cable-layer requisitioned for government use through a scheme known as STUFT (an acronym for 'ship taken up for trade'). Under this scheme, diverse vessels were used in the Falklands War including tankers to convey potable water and fuel, freighters to transport food and munitions, and luxury liners converted to carry troops. It was estimated that these merchant ships eventually carried some one hundred thousand tons of freight, ninety-five aircraft, nine thousand personnel and four hundred thousand tons of fuel. As one wag put it: "Without those ships we would have been well and truly STUFT."

One of Alan's tasks was to move a Snowcat vehicle which, as part of the operation to retake South Georgia, had been earmarked for that place. The vehicle needed to be cross-decked to the CS *Iris* and for this Alan knew that highly accurate flying would be required: the design of the *Iris's* centre hold afforded little room for manoeuvre. He was briefed on the need to move judiciously to an exact position before the Snowcat, underslung beneath the helicopter, could be released. To help with this task, Alan decided to use the ship's masthead as a hover reference point. On top of the masthead he noted a stationary scanner. Flying with the skill and precision acquired over years, he inched the large helicopter gradually closer to the designated spot. His concentration, though, was abruptly interrupted when he saw that the scanner was no longer stationary.

The device, plainly not designed to cope with the powerful down-wash of a Chinook helicopter, was starting to rotate – indeed, not just any old rotation but at an accelerating rate. Round and round it went like an over-enthusiastic spin dryer. His eyes tried to follow the scanner's movements, but this made him feel dizzy. 'Don't stare at it!' he told himself. Soon the whole masthead began to oscillate violently and his hover reference point became a blur. Luckily, the oscillations ceased as rapidly as they'd begun when the scanner, still spinning like a top, shot off laterally and Alan's peripheral vision picked up a splash on the surface of the sea. Now devoid of a scanner, the masthead settled, his hover reference point became usable, his concentration returned and the Snowcat was delivered safely into the depths of the *Iris's* central hold.

After this, Alan carried out many more flights but at length, with the cross-decking complete, the task force resumed its voyage to the South Atlantic, although without Alan who was ordered to remain at Ascension which continued to act as a forward base. Sent to the Falklands at a later date, he nonetheless took a keen interest in the *Iris* as the war progressed. In due course he'd learn that the ship steamed over forty-five thousand nautical miles in seven months of active service, and was involved in over eight hundred helicopter operations. All of that without the benefit of a radar scanner.

Classic Cash (from David Lanigan)

AS HE WALKED through the streets of Stanley in the Falkland Islands, and with an interest in the historical background of the place, Captain David Lanigan, a pilot contracted through Bristow Helicopters to fly British military personnel and equipment, was struck by a sense of timelessness. In the scheme of things, he mused, it was not so long ago, indeed a mere one hundred and fifty years or so, that the capital was not at Stanley but at Port Louis, north of the present site. But the governor back then, His Excellency Major-General Richard Clement Moody, had evidently stroked his long beard reflectively and decided to up-sticks for a move to Stanley with its deeper anchorage at Stanley Harbour. 'Of all the miserable bog holes,' recorded one resident, 'I believe that Mr Moody has selected one of the worst for the site of this town.' David glanced around him. Nowadays the town offered shops, hotels and guest houses, three churches including a cathedral, a post office, a bank, a hospital, a police station and a prison with thirteen cells, to name just some of the facilities. Perhaps, thought David, that nineteenth century resident might now admit to a change of heart, and even the major-general himself might be delighted by the way his town had developed.

David hesitated for a moment. Lost in thought, he realised that he was lost in another way too. Admittedly he sought a somewhat unusual and tucked-away establishment, nevertheless as a professional helicopter pilot trained to navigate his Sikorsky S-61N accurately, to lose one's way when walking around a small town seemed a little...well, infra dig. However, he was anxious to exchange his sterling for local currency and he'd been directed to the office of Harold Rowlands, the islands' financial secretary. Happily, after a further experimental turn or two, it was not long before he came across the required building.

When he entered Rowlands' office, David was impressed by the warmness of his reception. With a mop of heavy blonde hair and a resemblance to a famous German composer, the financial secretary, so David had heard, had been dubbed 'Beethoven' by the Argentines during their invasion two years ago. David had heard, too, that the financial secretary had earned wide respect for his courage and resourcefulness at that unfortunate time. As the most senior administrator left when the governor, Rex Hunt, and other expatriate officials were deported to Uruguay by the invaders, Rowlands' position had proved more than a little fraught. David was told that when the invaders demanded that the financial secretary change the local currency from pounds to pesos, he refused and declared that he was "far too old to learn about all those noughts".

Just now, though, as David explained the reason for his visit, the financial secretary beamed and said: "You're in luck, dear boy. As it happens, I've just received a block of newly printed notes from London. Look at this..." the financial secretary placed a cardboard box on his desk. "Brand new, beautiful fivers," he went on, "here...have a couple. And here..." He delved into another cardboard box to produce two one pound notes. "Treat them as souvenirs! On the house, as they say."

"Well thank you. So kind! But I must pay my way, though," said David as he handed over the relevant amount in sterling.

"Actually, the last time someone asked me for Falklands currency was two years ago." The financial secretary pulled a face. "General Menéndez himself was standing there – standing right there where you are now."

"I heard about your aversion to lots of noughts."

The financial secretary grinned. "The exchange rate at the time was something like twelve thousand pesos to the pound. When I refused to mess about with the local currency, the general ordered me to print more Falkland pounds."

"Could you have done that?"

"No way – these notes are printed by De la Rue in London on behalf of the Falkland Islands commissioners of currency."

"What was his reaction?"

"He decided to leave. But as he did so he turned to me and said that when he needed more currency in Argentina he simply instructed the printing press in his barracks to run some off!"

David and the financial secretary continued to chat for Rowlands was interested to learn about David's flying to North Sea oil installations and his experiences as a search and rescue pilot. At length, though, David said that he had to leave: "Forgive me – I've probably taken up too much of your time."

"Before you go, would you like me to sign your banknotes?"

"Sign them? They're already signed!"

"Yes – signed by me. I'm the only person in the world legally entitled to endorse these notes." At this, the financial secretary pulled out a pen to add his autograph next to the printed version of his signature.

David kept the notes for many years. However, after the death of seventy-two-year-old Harold Theodore Rowlands CBE in May 2004, he decided to sell them through Spink and Son, the London auction house. The notes were sold for a price which included a nought or two added to their face value. The financial secretary, thought David, would have been quite pleased about that.

Army life (from Richard Pike)

BURIED IN THE HEART of Hampshire, Royal Air Force Odiham was 240 OCU's (operational conversion unit) base back in the 1970s, and the place where budding Westland Wessex helicopter pilots learnt necessary skills. As a student posted there in 1978, I listened keenly to introductory briefings which explained that the course syllabus would cover various aspects of Wessex flying such as operating in confined areas, night flying, underslung load tasks, sloping ground work and much practice of a manoeuvre known as the 'quickstop'. "For a good quickstop," said my instructor, Bob, "it's as if you have to grab the machine by the scruff of the neck and let it know who's boss." Bob was conscious that, as an ex-fighter pilot with a new medical category that precluded fast-jet flying, I was finding the support helicopter (SH) world to be something of a culture shock. He was at pains, therefore, to emphasise that even though this novel and gritty environment was far removed from that of a glossy fighter station with its neatly lined-up, shiny fighter aircraft, it was still a significant arm of the service with an important role to perform.

One day in June of that year, while we walked across grass towards our allotted Wessex for a training exercise, Bob noticed my glum expression as we went past green-painted vehicles, drab tents, camouflaged equipment and great quantities of anomalous paraphernalia spread out next to the tents. I could smell the crude, earthy odour that seemed such an inevitable part of camping and knew that this was not a good omen for, in truth, I did not enjoy camping. Nearby, an army radio operator with an antiquated headset grasped a World War Two-looking microphone to mumble a steady flow of dull messages in a slow, deliberate voice.

At this juncture, as we walked beyond the radio operator, I spotted a section of soldiers who appeared to be wandering about as if in a perpetual daze. Nearby, a detachment of Royal Air Force Regiment men grunted and cursed as they hastened to re-site a Rapier airfield defence system in preparation, I assumed, for a planned field exercise. One man suddenly stood up, raised a finger in the air as if about to deliver a speech on advanced revolutionary theory in the context of opportunist-socialism, though in the end he said nothing. Another man kept wiping his face with his sleeve but usually succeeded only in replacing one muddy streak with another. A flight sergeant squinted through binoculars as he muttered something about the hidden ground between the Rapier unit, the airfield perimeter and the area beyond.

"You'll have to get used to all of this," beamed Bob, nodding his head, "things may seem a bit strange at first but you'll soon adapt. We all do!"

When, at last, we reached our camouflaged Wessex, I set about the pre-flight and start-up routines. As I did so, I remembered from briefings that the Wessex, which had entered service over fifteen years ago in 1961, was one of the RAF's most successful general-purpose helicopters. Based on the Sikorsky H-34 but developed and built under license by Westland Helicopters, I'd learnt that the machine was one of the first helicopters in the world to be produced in large numbers (nearly four hundred were built) using gas turbine engines instead of the original Sikorsky piston-engined powerplant. I'd been told that the twin-engined helicopter I was about to fly was different from the Royal Navy versions which were usually single-engined. With a capacity to carry sixteen troops and two pilots, the machine had a range of around three hundred miles and a maximum speed of one hundred and fifteen knots. The Wessex, I'd been assured, had earned a reputation for versatility and rugged reliability.

"When you do the external checks," said Bob, "pay particular attention to the engines' single air intake. We're generally okay here in a training situation, but loose debris can be a problem when operating in the field, even with the protective mesh." As I performed the external checks that day, our Wessex, if not exactly as shiny and dashing as a pampered fighter aircraft, was nonetheless quite a pleasing sight. I stood back to admire the length of over sixty-five feet, the height of nearly sixteen feet, and the dapper khaki-coloured paintwork. Despite deep-seated doubts, I was determined to try to convince myself that helicopter flying would prove to be just as fascinating and enjoyable as flying fighters, a hope which, over time, would indeed turn out to be true.

Before long, with the start-up checks completed and the Wessex happily 'turning and burning' we were cleared by air traffic control to take off then head towards the small grass airfield at Upavon near Salisbury Plain. When there, Bob told me to practise all the things one is supposed to practise in a helicopter such as spot turns, sideways flying, backwards flying, even the odd curtsey until eventually Bob said: "I have control", and explained that he'd demonstrate the procedure for a quickstop. Now he backed the Wessex into one corner of the airfield and paused. He held the machine in a low hover and quickly reminded me of the points he'd made in our pre-flight briefing. Tension rose. "Right," said Bob eventually, "follow me through", by which he meant place my hands lightly on the flight controls. Then, as he said: "Here goes!" he commenced instructional patter while he lowered the helicopter's nose and simultaneously applied collective pitch to check the descent. The airspeed increased...twenty knots...thirty knots...forty knots but we needed ninety knots and the airfield boundary was looming. "Standby!" he cried just as the Wessex reached ninety knots: "Quickstop now!" at which he hauled back the cyclic stick and lowered the collective lever fully. The helicopter's nose reared up and I could feel a series of positive yet finely controlled cyclic inputs as, in the hands of an experienced pilot, the machine almost shuddered to a halt without any height loss or gain.

"Okay," said Bob on completion of the manoeuvre, "what did you think of that, mister fighter pilot?"

"It was...different!"

"Right then! Your turn next. Remember what we said about judicious control for the final part of the manoeuvre, especially if the wind is behind us." This comment referred to a hazard peculiar to helicopters known as vortex ring when the machine, by entering its own downwash, suffered severe loss of lift. By raising the collective lever the pilot would merely feed the vortex motion without generating additional lift. In briefings Bob had emphasised that a badly handled quickstop could lead to vortex ring: "If the machine suddenly starts to vibrate violently," he'd said, "remember to lower the collective lever at once and turn into wind."

We now spent a fair amount of time careering around Upavon Airfield perfecting my quickstop techniques which certainly needed quite a bit of perfecting. At length, however, we were quickstopped-out and Bob told me to head back to Odiham. When we'd landed and shut down there he chatted about the flight while we walked to the engineering line hut to sign the technical log.

"You're typical of a former fixed-wing pilot converting to helicopters," said Bob, as ever irritatingly reasonable, "but don't worry. We'll soon re-wire your brain. It won't take long."

"Thanks," I said, "I'm probably due for a good brainwash."

"Whether it's the brain or any other part of the anatomy," said Bob, "washing is not necessarily our strong point here. You're entering a place of muck and mud. Take heart, though. The SH world may be basic, we may lack glitz and glamour, we may even be seen as philistines but underneath, deep down in the DNA, we're all right."

"I joined up as a pilot, not to become an infantryman."

"Nonsense!" said Bob, grinning. "You're just the chap! Not so sure about those snazzy aviator-style sunglasses, though."

"Should I paint them green?"

"I think you should," he said, "after all, you're in the army now."

CHAPTER 11
DIVERS' DELIVERANCE

Peter Donaldson's bright sparks

WHEN, IN 1929, an American physicist called Robert J Van de Graaff invented an electrostatic generator device, he may, as a man of vision, have predicted the gadget's use as a means to sterilise food, or to accelerate protons for nuclear physics experiments, or even for the production of energetic X-ray beams in nuclear medicine. Surely, though, never in his wildest dreams could he have foreseen the strange circumstances in which a helicopter would become part of a giant Van de Graaff machine.

It was in late October 1977 when Captain Peter Donaldson, a senior pilot with Bristow Helicopters, was flying a S-61N helicopter, G-BAKB, from Bergen in Norway, where he'd been operating for a few days, back to his home base at Sumburgh in the Shetland Islands. This re-positioning flight was via the Belford Dolphin, a semi-submersible drill rig used at that time as an accommodation rig for personnel involved with the construction of the Thistle Alpha platform. With some distance to run, Peter suddenly received an urgent radio message: a diving support vessel needed some bags of chemicals for divers who were in difficulty. Something had gone wrong during the standard decompression process and high winds were thwarting attempts by the diving support vessel to receive the chemicals by crane. "That's understood," said Peter, "how can we help?"

"Do you have a winch?"

"Yes," said Peter, "and I have a winchman." This, as it turned out, was entirely fortuitous because winch crews were not normally carried on passenger flights. However, Peter had on board his engineer from the Bergen detachment, a man who he'd helped to train recently in the particular art of helicopter winching.

As the Belford Dolphin had supplies of the necessary chemicals, arrangements were hurriedly made for them to be packaged into suitable units for winching by helicopter. While this was organised, it was not long before Peter was flying G-BAKB on final approach to the rig. "The wind's currently gusting over sixty knots, captain," said the radio operator. Peter glanced at his co-pilot: both men knew that their operating limit was sixty knots.

"Are the divers still in trouble, or have things stabilised?"

"Not too stable, apparently, cap. The diving support vessel has reported only about one hour's life support left for those divers."

Peter was now left with no doubts that he was confronting a life-or-death situation. Persisting, therefore, with his approach to the Belford Dolphin, he had to cope with the rig's pitching up and down and side to side in the stormy conditions. As an experienced and skilful pilot, though, Peter landed successfully after which a deck hand from the Belford Dolphin bent low while, safety rope in hand, he struggled against the wind to reach the S-61N's air-stair door. The passengers were then allowed to disembark one at a time, gripping the safety rope firmly as they made for shelter. Nature's challenges, thought Peter, could be at once thrilling and terrifying but continuous exposure to such conditions could be exhausting, not only to the body but to the mind as well. Indeed, in some circumstances it was necessary for personnel to have to crawl around on hands and knees while holding on for dear life to the heavy rope permanently attached to the surface of the helideck. On that day, however, such extreme measures proved unnecessary and soon, with the passengers safely disembarked and the chemicals loaded, Peter was given the all-clear to take off and head for the diving support vessel.

During the take-off, Peter noted that his cockpit airspeed indicator registered seventy knots. Then, for the short transit of about five miles to the diving support vessel, he could see that the sea's surface was being blown about by the gales, a bizarre phenomenon which gave the impression of flying in high speed fog. Moreover, another potential problem began to worry him: the danger of static electricity. "Has your deck crewman got an earthing stick?" he asked the radio operator.

"Yes, captain."

"Good. Tell him not to touch the winch cable until it's been earthed."

With the vessel eventually in sight, Peter began to manoeuvre to a position aft of the bridge. He noted that, with the elements in charge, conditions were getting rapidly worse. As the ship moved about in the giant waves, he watched with a mix of fascination and alarm as crests of waves exploded against the hull. He peered into the storm but could see little apart from rain and the marauding waves of dark ocean. From the crest of a wave one moment, a mountain would seemingly collapse to leave a great emptiness as the ship plunged down into the next trough. He watched as spray pelted down to end up on the helideck. For the unfortunate deck crewman whose duties forced him outside, his oilskins provided a measure of protection although Peter imagined that the man would wince when raw seas bit against his fingers and hands, against his ears and cheeks. With the wind's howl rising to a shriek, Peter knew that jets of water as solid as streamers would lash against the man's oilskins before heading for scuppers. The ship's crew would feel shuddering beneath their feet as the vessel struggled to tackle the conditions and the air would be filled with many kinds of odd noises as the structure creaked and groaned in protest.

Peter, however, had to persist with his task, storm or no storm. The engineer-cum-winchman now opened the helicopter's cargo door and talked Peter into a suitable position to start winching. "Okay," said Peter, "let's do it!"

"Roger. Attaching the first load to the hook."

By now Peter had chosen a reference point on the vessel to assist his station-keeping. His concentration was intense as he said: "Confirm you've started to winch out?" Most unusually, though, there was no response. An ominous silence lingered until the winchman spoke again: "Sorry about that, captain," he sounded breathless, "bit of a problem back here. All's fine now – I'll explain later." And it was later when the winchman revealed that the instant he stuck his head outside to reach for the winch, his headset had been blown away by the wind. With no spare 'bone dome' helmet available, the winchman, resourceful as ever, grabbed another headset then clamped it firmly to his head with a trouser belt. "Hold that position...steady...now move right two and back one... steady...steady..." with a continuous flow of instructions he guided Peter while the packages were lowered towards the deck.

However, when the load was about halfway down he heard the winchman make some remark which was drowned out by crackling noises in Peter's headset. Despite the noise interference, after a moment or two he managed to pick up fragments of patter – "...huge sparks, captain...electrical sparks...they're flying around everywhere..."

"Flying from where?"

"...flying off the winch wire..."

Good grief, thought Peter, what next? "Is the crewman clear?" he asked.

"...yes, captain...the deck looks clear now...looks like he's retreated for shelter..."

Afterwards, when debriefing the flight, Peter and his crew deduced that storm-blown salt crystals had brushed against the helicopter's rotor blades to cause a build-up of static electricity which then jumped to earth or sea through the closest point (in this case the winch wire). The resultant sparks meant that the helicopter was acting, in effect, as part of a giant Van de Graaff electrostatic generator. The deck crewman's retreat to shelter was prudent: a strike by one of the electrical discharges could have proved as fatal as a direct lightning strike. But eventually, with the load on the deck and thus safely earthed, the sparks ceased and the crewman could emerge from his place of refuge to unhook the chemicals before waving a thumbs-up signal to the helicopter winchman: 'ready for the next load'.

The task's hazards, however, were not quite over yet. As the hook was winched up Peter was startled to see waves begin to break not just around but above the ship's bridge. The vessel climbed then plunged again as white foam caught by the wind was whipped along the surface. The waves raged, frothed, boiled and reached up in riotous profusion. Confined to a wild and worrying world Peter had to battle against ferocious levels of turbulence as well as rain that was hurled against the S-61N's windscreen like a river rushing towards a boulder. He had to apply, then reduce, then re-apply large amounts of power to cope with the ship's violent movement.

While he struggled on, Peter was briefly aware that his cockpit airspeed indicator showed a reading which he preferred not to think about. Meantime, with eyes half-closed against the elements his winchman continued with the task until he announced with relief: "Chemicals all delivered, captain. Hook recovered – closing the cargo door – you're clear to depart!" Peter immediately turned away, bade farewell to the diving support vessel's radio operator, set heading for the Shetland Islands and checked-in with the Brent Alpha: "Request you take our radio watch, please Brent."

"No problem, captain," said a relaxed-sounding radio operator, "I can do that for you."

Peter, along with his fellow crew members, now began to breathe more easily. As the flight progressed and as they chatted about the task, at one stage the Brent Alpha's radio operator interjected: "I've got an updated weather report, captain. A gust of ninety knots has just been recorded. Were you winching in that?" "Err yes, not much choice I'm afraid!"

Luckily the wind speed started to ease as Peter flew towards the Shetland Islands until a relatively pleasant sixty knots was reported for the final approach and landing at Sumburgh.

After landing, Peter taxied to his company's dispersal area then kept the engines and rotors turning. This was routine to allow his winchman to run out the winch cable and hose off salt deposits with fresh water. The procedure, though, was interrupted when the winchman suddenly signalled to close down at once. "What's up?" asked Peter on completion of the shut-down drills.

"Look," said the winchman pointing at the cable, "it's burnt through. It'll have to be scrapped!"

"What would Robert Van de Graaff have to say about that?" quipped Peter.

"He'd probably say that it was worth the effort."

"How do you mean?"

"We've just had a message," said the winchman. "The oil company telephoned to say that the chemicals reached the divers – but only just in time."

"And?"

"And all of them were saved."

CHAPTER 12

SEA SORE

Alan Boulden's training turmoil

Streaked in foam and spray, the sea's surface looked chaotic. The waves went in one direction while the sea swell appeared to rumble through from a different angle. Though not particularly steep-faced, the swells, driven by a strong wind, possessed hidden power and it was this which caused a problem for Flight Lieutenant Alan Boulden and his crew during a search and rescue training session one day.

Such sessions, which typically made use of an old oil drum, involved a specific winching circuit which had evolved over time: a climb into wind from a hover, followed by a turn downwind before another turn onto finals and let down to the target. Parameters of speed, height, angle of bank and other factors were flown accurately to ensure an efficient rescue and the winch operator's patter helped to guide the pilot throughout the proceedings. After a successful training circuit, the oil drum, having been 'rescued' by a grapnel attached to the end of the rescue hoist's cable, would be thrown back into the water before a further attempt. As an experienced operator, Alan had flown hundreds of these circuits and on the day in question he had the support of a winch operator and a winchman who were both experienced too.

One problem with the use of an oil drum, however, was the lack of training value for the winchman. While the pilot and the winch operator could perfect their techniques, the winchman was left with not a lot to do and, after all, this was the man who would be lowered down to face the music, as they say, in order to complete an effective rescue. Instead of an old oil drum, therefore, the crews were always keen to find human volunteers who'd be lowered into the sea to sit patiently in a dinghy while waiting to be rescued several times over.

Fortunately for Alan, who was based at RAF Brawdy in Wales, he had the benefit of a fairly regular volunteer, a plucky young airwoman who worked in the safety equipment section at Brawdy and who evidently enjoyed opportunities for some fresh air and excitement away from the office. So it was that for the day in question the young airwoman donned an immersion suit before she boarded the Sea King helicopter ready for the flight to a stipulated training area. Since she was clearly interested, and as he performed the pre-flight external

Top: Sikorsky S-61s at Aberdeen Heliport on a clear day. (Richard Pike)

Middle: Passengers boarding an S-61 at Aberdeen Heliport. (Richard Pike)

Bottom: A Sikorsky S-61 registered G-BPWB of HM Coastguard rescue. (Mark Service)

Top: Bell Jetranger 5N-AHN on-board the offshore supply tanker
Niso – shortly before going for a swim. (Peter Donaldson)

Bottom: Bell Jetranger 5N-AHM on a passenger pick-up from
a beach in the Niger Delta. (Peter Donaldson)

Top: Flying an underslung 105-mm gun on exercise in Malaya. (David Lanigan)

Bottom: A Wessex helicopter on a flow station in Nigeria. A typical landing place at the time. (Peter Donaldson)

Top: An example of a V-22 Osprey taken at the Royal International Air Tattoo in 2012. (Peter Gronemann)

Bottom: Mark Service with a CV-22 after his flight with USAF's 7th Special Operations Squadron. (Mark Service)

Top: Sikorsky S-61N at RAF Stanley and happy pilot. (David Lanigan)

Bottom: Ships at anchor in Stanley Harbour. (David Lanigan)

Top: Sikorsky S-61N shut down in the 'country' in the Falklands. (David Lanigan)

Bottom: View of RAF Stanley and Stanley Habour. (David Lanigan)

Top: The president of India Mr Giri awarding the Vir Chakra to Pushp Vaid after the end of the Indo-Pakistan war of 1971. (Pushp Vaid)

Bottom: On exercise in Malaya. (David Lanigan)

Top: Bell 205 D-HAFR of Agrarluft Helilift photographed at a public event in West Germany. (Mark Service)

Middle: Unidentified UH-1 Huey of A Company, 5th Battalion, 159th Aviation Regiment, US army at a deployed location during the First Gulf War. (Mark Service)

Bottom: Unidentified UH-1 Huey of the German army at the Alpine Corps Training Centre high up in the Bavarian Mountains. (Mark Service)

checks, Alan pointed out various aspects about the Sea King, a version of the United States Sikorsky S-61 helicopter which was built under licence by West-land Helicopters. "Unlike the American version, we have Rolls-Royce engines," he said. "Depending on your point of view," said Alan, "this may or may not give you a sense of reassurance." After consideration, no doubt, of the relative merits of twin Rolls-Royce Gnome H1400-2 turboshafts versus the original United States General Electric T58 engines she merely nodded her head.

The proceedings followed a pattern with which, after several flights, she was reasonably familiar and before long she was happily ensconced in the yellow-liv-eried Sea King while Alan completed the start-up checks. When airborne, and as he headed for the coast, he made radio contact with a member of the local coastguard station who'd positioned himself on cliffs overlooking the bay where the winching would take place. This was an unusual arrangement for normally the practice survivor would be monitored by personnel in a safety boat but on that day no safety boat was available.

The first part of the exercise went as briefed. The young airwoman 'survivor' and an aircrew rubber dinghy were lowered into the water, she gave a thumbs-up sign after which the winchman gave a standard signal to indicate: 'clear up and around'. This was the cue for the winch operator to commence a running com-mentary of the survivor's relative position by use of a clock code. The visibility was less than perfect that day but still sufficiently good to continue with the planned exercise. The wind, though, remained strong – near gale force – and it was this which led to the initial problem. While the gusty conditions filled the air with spray which made the dinghy harder for the crew to see, just as the Sea King reached a position approximately halfway along the downwind leg the crew realised that they had misjudged the wind direction. The men decided, therefore, to change the orientation of the circuit.

Soon established in the new oval-shaped circuit, the crew members antici-pated the winch operator's next call: "Target at half-past three", at which stage Alan should have replied: "Turning on." Instead, however, the winch operator cried: "Lost sight of target!"

A horrified moment of silence ensued. Barely able to believe such a call, in his head Alan swiftly went through options. 'No problem, no problem,' he assured himself, 'I'll just turn now to head into the wind and the rubber dinghy should be in front of us.' He hastily explained this to the other crew members and all searched ahead anxiously when, quite quickly, the Sea King rolled out into the wind as briefed. No-one, however, managed to spot the rubber dinghy and eventually the winch operator had to repeat his call: "Still lost sight of target." As captain of the aircraft, Alan knew that he should come up with another plan rapidly. "We'll carry out a further full circuit," he said, "and this time we'll extend the downwind leg."

While flying this circuit Alan could imagine the young airwoman settled inside her rubber dinghy and he knew that blasts of wind and saltwater would be giving her an uncomfortable ride. With, perhaps, over-anxious conjecture, he pictured the way that the waves might be pounding against the dinghy which would roll into troughs between the swells. As the water's flow washed from side to side she could be rocked in an unpleasant, disorientating motion. On reaching the crest of a wave, the small rubber dinghy might suddenly topple forward before it began to glide down the face of the swell like a surfer rushing towards a shoreline. For a heart-stopping moment the dinghy might remain at the base of the deepest troughs until the oncoming swell bounced it back up again. He feared that she could be speculating apprehensively: what if the dinghy did not come back up? What if a rogue wave swamped the dinghy before it had a chance to rise to the surface? And where was the helicopter anyway? It seemed to be way out of position. Had the crew lost sight of her?

At about this stage Alan decided that, despite the inevitable embarrassment, he should admit to the coastguard that he and his crew had lost visual contact with the survivor and could he therefore ask the look-out to give directions. The answer, when it came, made Alan's heart sink. It was not the look-out himself who replied but the coastguard controller: "Sorry, captain. No can do. The look-out has been called away to assist with a local incident."

Gazing gloomily at the grim, grey sea, dark thoughts persisted to race through Alan's mind. He thought about the way that the dinghy's ongoing seaworthiness would be tested. Any warmth would be swiftly stripped away. He thought of the young airwoman probing around the dinghy which she'd been trained to pack and check. He knew that she'd search for the various survival aids including a heliograph, sea-sickness tablets, an instruction manual, bailing equipment, a solar still (that ingenious contraption designed to produce fresh water from sea water), day/night pyrotechnics and a smoke flare. It would surely be ironic, he thought, if she was compelled to make use of these aids for real.

As an experienced search and rescue man who had carried out numerous rescues in the past, some in the trickiest of conditions, Alan was used to remaining calm, composed, and dispassionate. But this situation felt altogether different. The survivor was a volunteer, someone he knew, a member of the team, one of 'us' – all of which made everything seem more personal, more complex, harder to bear. Perhaps, though, the time was approaching when he should swallow any sense of pride, call for backup and ask the controller to order the launch of the coastguard lifeboat. It seemed particularly inappropriate to summons help from the rescue service – after all, he and his crew were the rescue service – but he was beginning to see no alternative.

Suddenly, however, a call from the winch operator, excitement in his voice, disrupted Alan's despondent meanderings: "I think I see something."

The winch operator, secured by a long strap, was leaning out of the open cargo door as he gazed hard in a particular direction. "You know what…" he went on eventually, "we've been looking in the wrong place. The rubber dinghy seems to have drifted upwind."

"Upwind?!" exclaimed Alan. "That's crazy! How could it be upwind?"

"Perhaps the tidal flow has affected the dinghy's movement."

"Ah!" said Alan as the proverbial penny promptly dropped. "We forgot to check the tide tables," he added sheepishly. Turning towards the direction given by the winch operator, Alan soon saw for himself what the eagle-eyed winch operator had detected and with considerable relief Alan manoeuvred to a position to winch up the long lost survivor who, when hauled aboard dripping wet, revealed that she had been unaware of the developing drama.

"I saw you in the distance," she said later, "and I heard the sounds of the helicopter clattering in the background. But I reckoned that you were trying out a new system or just larking about or something."

"I'm afraid it was more to do with the conditions than anything else," said Alan. "There's a powerful spring tide running at the moment – anything up to three or four knots – and the strong wind caused us problems. I was concerned that the waves might have been swamping the rubber dinghy."

"Oh no," she said, "it really wasn't as bad as all that. I wasn't worried or anything. Like everyone else, I have complete faith in the search and rescue crews."

Alan now felt even worse. Although reluctant to over-state the case to his willing volunteer, nonetheless he knew that the incident had shaken him up quite badly. He was mindful that this had been a training exercise, one which should have been more or less straightforward and an exercise which, while not exactly routine, was still one he'd practised many times. It bothered him that an experienced and highly professional crew had managed to get into a situation where matters had appeared to go awry so readily and so rapidly. "Occasionally things go wrong," he said, a remark at which the young airwoman merely looked at him as if to say: 'But not very often.'

Alan sighed. Perhaps he should arrange a get-together with his colleagues to expound on the hazards of endangerment of good people who volunteered, and it should be understood that what had happened to him was the sort of thing that could happen to anyone. Maybe he thought he should compose an exposition on the need to improve the training environment with sentiments about the way that customary British reserve inhibited the potential of…of… On the other hand, he reflected, and not wishing to labour the point, maybe he should just be a bit more circumspect in future when assessing the power of wind, wave and tide.

CHAPTER 13
BLIZZARD BABY

Chris Mutton's mid-winter callout

THE TIME MUST have slipped past four in the morning when the telephone rang. Doctor David Hawson, who was asleep at home, wearily lifted the receiver to take the call. "She's gone into labour, doctor," said the anxious voice of the young father, "and I'm calling from a neighbour's house – our phone has been cut off."

"Okay Tom," said Doctor Hawson, shaking off drowsiness, "we'll arrange an ambulance to take her to hospital."

"Have you looked outside?"

At once, Doctor Hawson drew back his bedroom curtains to see a remarkable sight: snow, driven by strong winds, was piled high around his country cottage; just a few hours earlier the ground had been snow-covered, but nothing like this. As a local general practitioner who lived near the village of Monymusk in rural Aberdeenshire, the doctor was used to harsh weather conditions, but these were clearly exceptional. "Stay calm," he said to the father, "I'll make some phone calls." He knew that his patient's pregnancy problems meant that, if at all possible, she should have the baby delivered in hospital. The doctor now rang the Aberdeen Royal Infirmary: "We'll need a snowplough to clear the way for an ambulance," he said, "my patient lives in the remote Mains of Shiels farmhouse."

"Terribly sorry, doctor," came the reply, "even the largest snowplough is stuck fast and can't move. It's really bad out there. We'll get on to the helicopter boys to see if they can help."

Desperate times, thought the doctor, needed desperate measures. He rang his neighbour and friend, a young farmer who owned a powerful tractor. "Can you attach a snowplough to your tractor, John?"

"Yes, David. There's a snowplough already attached to the back."

"I'll join you shortly," said the doctor and it was not long before the two men met up to scramble hurriedly into the tractor's cab. Without delay, and at times driving the tractor backwards to tackle monstrous snow drifts blocking Aberdeenshire's roads on that night in January 1984, they set off for the Mains of Shiels farmhouse, a distance of around eight miles.

Meantime, Captain Christopher Mutton of British Airways Helicopters had just returned from a task in the Peterhead area where he'd helped to evacuate workers from a semi-submersible rig, the Ali Baba. He was about to go home when he was summoned by the company's duty operations officer: "Chris! We've received a call from Aberdeen Royal Infirmary. There's a pregnant lady with medical complications who needs to go to the hospital."

"Where does she live?" asked Chris.

"Near Sauchen. Evidently she's stuck way out in the boondocks and with all this snow the ambulance can't get to her."

A few moments of silence ensued. Chris was well aware of the hazardous weather conditions – conditions which had caused the Ali Baba to be wrenched from its moorings by fifty miles per hour gales and twenty-foot waves, then dragged across Peterhead Harbour. As he lived reasonably close to Aberdeen Airport, he was one of the few members of staff who'd made it to the airport through the snow drifts. The weather's been so bad of late, he mused, that even the liveliest imagination might struggle to picture it ever being fine again. However, snow or shine, he knew that with the benefit of fifteen years as an army officer, nine as a military helicopter pilot, he was as well placed as anyone to deal with the challenge.

"Is Aberdeen Airport now fully manned-up?" asked Chris.

"Unfortunately not," said the operations officer. "Air traffic control is operating, but with a reduced number of staff. And their navigational services are limited."

"So what about medical support for the flight?"

"A senior registrar and a community midwife are on their way here as we speak. They'll fly with you and tend to the patient if you manage to get through."

At this point, Chris reassembled the co-pilot and crewman who'd flown with him on the Ali Baba rescue task. Huddled together for a briefing, Chris said: "I know it's been a long day, but this is an emergency situation. It might be touch and go but I believe that we should be able to get through." He glanced at them. "One of our main problems will be navigating to the exact spot in such poor visibility."

"Will there be any radar cover?" asked the co-pilot.

"There'll be minimal service to the west of the airport," said Chris. "We've no Decca maps of that area, but we do have Ordnance Survey maps – one-in-fifty-thousand scale."

While Chris and his crew talked about the operational issues, the company engineers had their own problems for the force of the wind and the slippery surfaces made it hard to find a suitable spot to park and start up the helicopter. Eventually they succeeded, though, and it was not too long before Chris, his co-pilot and crewman together with the two members of medical staff were able to board the helicopter ready for their unusual mission. Soon, having started the engines and safely engaged the rotors of S-61N G-BEID, Chris spoke to the controller in air traffic control (the only controller who'd made it into work) who authorised a vertical take-off manoeuvre. Without further ado, therefore, Chris raised the collective lever to lift G-BEID clear of the hangars and other airfield obstructions before he turned onto a south-westerly heading towards the suburban area of Westhill, due west of Aberdeen city. In the poor visibility he was forced to fly 'low and slow' and a further danger, the mass of electricity pylons and cables, added to his difficulties. Lights from the city and from local villages helped with navigation although he had to be wary: viewed from certain angles, the selfsame lights could deceive and disorientate.

Chris remained in radio contact with the controller who was initially able to monitor the helicopter's position on radar as the flight progressed. "We've just passed Westhill," said Chris, "I'm turning due west to follow the main road."

"That's confirmed," said the controller, "I've got you on radar. The road you're following is the A944 towards Dunecht."

"Good-oh," said Chris, "but the road is hard to make out because of the snow drifts."

"Understood," said the controller, "just continue due west. I can still see you on radar, though the signal is getting weak."

"Okay. We've got the Loch of Skene coming up on the port side."

"Affirmative," said the controller, "but I'm beginning to lose your radar return now."

"Understood."

"Can you still see the A944?"

"Affirmative. I'm following the road due west."

It was at this stage that the controller revealed that he lived in the local area and therefore knew the roads well. As if guiding a car on a cross-country journey, he was able to give detailed instructions: "Beyond the Loch of Skene and Dunecht you'll come to the village of Ordhead which is where I live. A short distance after Ordhead there's a road going off to the left – the B993." Members of the Automobile Association, thought Chris, would be proud of this air traffic controller, especially when Chris was able to announce: "We've just flown past Ordhead, I'm turning left to follow the B993."

"Fly due south for about one mile then standby for a left turn to the Mains of Shiels property," said the controller in his last radio message for at this distance from the airport, and at such low altitude, communication was now lost.

And so it was that a combination of local knowledge, initiative and single-minded persistence meant that Chris and his crew were by that juncture close to the Mains of Shiels. This was an area, however, with a number of remote, individual properties...but which was the right one? The crew had been briefed that the landing spot would be marked with lights, though no lights could be identified in the poor conditions. Despite this, they flew on determinedly. Dawn had yet to break and the helicopter's powerful searchlights were needed to pierce the gloom of that dark and dismal January morning. G-BEID came closer and closer to the required spot until, suddenly, a single light could be seen sparkling from the area ahead. The visibility was such that Chris saw the light, then lost it, then saw it again. It appeared to come from open country and, behind the light, the pilots could glimpse an old-fashioned house. And they spotted something else: tramping through deep snow drifts was a lone figure who turned around to wave at the helicopter. Later, Chris and his crew discovered that this was Doctor Hawson who'd decided to walk the last part of the journey to reach his patient for even the powerful tractor had been defeated by snow drifts. It was a courageous and dedicated act; the blizzard would claim four lives across the country that night.

Suddenly, the co-pilot pointed: "That light ahead...it's someone signalling."

"I see it, Duncan," said Chris, "we'll land nearby." He knew that to land a large helicopter in deep, powdery snow was a risky business, although he was encouraged by one factor: downwash produced by the helicopter's rotor blades was whipped away by the fifty miles per hour winds thereby alleviating the hazard of whiteout through snow re-circulation. Thus, by judicious and skilful flying, Chris managed to land G-BEID close to the man with a lamp. When satisfied that it was safe to despatch his crewman, Chris said to him: "Jump out, Peter, and confirm that we're in the right place." The crewman, however, returned quite quickly to say: "We're in the wrong place! This farmer thought that we were in trouble so he decided to indicate a safe area to land."

"Did he point out the right place?"

"Yes, we've just overflown the property. It's downwind – about five hundred yards behind us."

"The wind's too strong to turn around, so can you give directions if I fly backwards?"

At this, the crewman, secured by a long strap, leant out of the gap created by the open cargo door then, aided by the light of a powerful torch, began a running commentary: "...you're clear to lift and move slowly back...there's an up-slope behind us...increase your height..." In this way, as the helicopter crabbed cautiously backwards, the Mains of Shiels farmhouse started to emerge gradually from the gloom. "...I can see some figures behind us...they're gesturing where to land..."

The landing spot, when it was reached by the S-61N, turned out to be a small triangle of field between a barn on one side and fir trees on the other two sides. As soon as he'd landed and was sure that it would be safe to allow the doctor and midwife to leave the helicopter, Chris said to his crewman: "Okay, Peter, the medics can go now. Tell them that we'll remain in this spot with rotors running until they return."

A long wait now ensued while the medical team attended to their patient. Meanwhile, the two pilots discussed their options for the return flight. "To go back the way we came in," said Chris, "would mean flying downwind in gusts that will cause severe snow re-circulation and whiteout."

"Our other option is to climb to safety altitude," said the co-pilot, "but this could lead to icing problems." After further deliberation, the two agreed that on balance their best choice was to climb to the area's safety altitude of three thousand five hundred feet at which height they'd be able to speak again with the air traffic controller.

When, at length, the medical team returned together with their patient, she had to be assisted carefully into the helicopter. Then, as swiftly as practicable, the crewman ensured that all three were safely ensconced in the cabin before he said: "All secure in the back, captain. You're clear to lift!"

"Roger," said Chris, "standby...I'm going for a vertical lift..." At this, he raised the collective lever to power vertically upwards followed by a transition to forward flight as he continued the climb to safety altitude. While he climbed up, radio reception was soon restored so that Chris was able to relay his plan of action to the air traffic controller. "No roads to follow up here," he quipped, "just a lot of cloud."

"I see you on radar," said the controller, "but you're clear of other air traffic. On your present heading you'll overfly the Bridge of Don."

"Roger. At the Bridge of Don we'll plan to coast offshore then let down over the sea. When below cloud, we'll head directly for the hospital." Chris knew that the plan involved a number of uncertainties, however the conditions were such that his options remained limited and tenuous. "We'll just have to play things by ear," he said to his co-pilot. He was aware that, among other issues, the turbulence that buffeted the helicopter in the strong winds made life very uncomfortable for the patient as well as for the medical staff. To add to the tangled mix of related factors, he was conscious of the possibility that the baby may be born in the helicopter with all of the attendant risks.

The crew, though, struggled on as the S-61N, thrown repeatedly upwards, downwards, sideways in the fierce gusts, leapt and lurched alarmingly. Chris decided to turn off the helicopter's searchlights for the beams of light showed up snow driven in horizontal sheets like marauding waves that blinded and confused. Nature's show, he thought, presented a paradoxical blend of ferocity and magnificence. Eventually, as he flew above the Bridge of Don before crossing the coast, he prepared for a descent over the sea. Monitoring the S-61N's internal radar system he ensured clearance from obstructions ahead. He went down to fifteen hundred feet initially, a height which coincided with a range of five miles offshore, then he turned through one hundred and eighty degrees to head back towards the Bridge of Don as he continued the descent. In his mind he could picture the sea's commotion below, a scene of waves that surged and raged with white foam caught by the wind to fuse with the snow showers that shot across the surface.

The helicopter was down to two hundred feet above the sea when the pilots made visual contact with the surface. Still flying back towards the Bridge of Don, they eventually spotted the mouth of the River Don where Chris, as he followed the line of the river inland, was compelled by the weather conditions to remain at very low level (which regretfully prompted a complaint from the chairman of the local housing association, a fellow pilot from the same company, who cited the crew of G-BEID for a low-flying offence). At the Woodside area of Old Aberdeen, Chris turned due south towards the heli-landing pad at the Aberdeen Royal Infirmary where the hospital staff, fully alerted, whisked away the patient and her medical team. An hour or so later, a baby boy was delivered safely. The boy was called Henry and the epic nature of his blizzard birth was duly recognised in press reports:

"When the helicopter took off," said Henry's father, "and disappeared in the snow, I wondered if I would see her again. Flying conditions were bloody awful."

"The helicopter crew," said Henry's mother, "saved me and the baby's life...it was a complete whiteout and very rough when I was getting into the helicopter... it was my first experience in a helicopter and it was marvellous."

CHAPTER 14
PIPER ALPHA

A night to remember: The two pilots heard a loud bang. While the business of North Sea oil and gas extraction persisted with its twenty-four-hour routine, they were familiar with the background hum, the occasional clatters and crashes that reverberated through the structure of the multi-support vessel (MSV) *Tharos* which was, in effect, a giant building site. That bang, though...that was something else. "We'd better check the aircraft," said one of the pilots as he clambered out of his bunk. The other Sikorsky S-76 pilot hastily followed suit. The two shared a cabin on board the *Tharos* for it was their job to fly regular shuttles between installations in the area. These shuttles were usually flown by a single pilot and one of them, who'd arrived earlier in the day to begin a two-week period of duty starting on 6 July 1988, was scheduled for tomorrow's early morning flight. He'd climbed into his bunk shortly before 10 p.m. hoping for a good night's rest before that early start.

Now, as the two hurried along corridors, they headed for the *Tharos*' helideck where they'd satisfy themselves that their S-76 was okay. When close to the helideck they were joined by one of their company engineers who'd been similarly alerted by the loud and unusual bang. As soon as they walked outside one of them cried: "Look...!" and the three men gazed at the Piper Alpha platform positioned alongside the *Tharos*. A small but intense fire was evident part-way up the west side of the Piper Alpha – a fire that showed no signs of dying out.

"We'd better get airborne," the pilots agreed, "we might be needed there."

At once the three of them hastened to detach rotor blade tie-down ropes, remove engine blanks and carry out other pre-flight essentials. Within minutes, the helicopter (tail letter 'Yankee Bravo') was ready and the offshore installation manager (OIM) radioed permission for the flight to proceed. Plainly there was no time to lose. As the pilot lifted the machine clear of the *Tharos*, he aimed for a position downwind of the Piper Alpha from where he planned to line up Yankee Bravo for a landing on the installation's helideck. By now, though, the helideck was blanketed by thick, choking smoke. With a feeling of dread, the pilots realised that they'd be unable to offer help. In a remarkably short space of time the fire had taken hold. A landing would not be possible. The pilots' task, therefore, became one of sending situation reports.

Fanned by a westerly breeze, the fire and smoke persisted although at one point one of the pilots thought that he could make out the helideck. He manoeuvred the S-76 for another try at landing but, as before, this proved impossible. He therefore asked for clearance to divert to the nearby Claymore platform to refuel. In the fading half-light of dusk on that July night, the twenty-mile distance between the Piper Alpha and the Claymore was illuminated as if by an enormous firework.

On the return flight from Claymore, the pilots received a radio message: some Piper Alpha crew members had been seen to climb the derrick: was there any chance of a rescue attempt? What level of desperation, they wondered, would drive men to climb the derrick? With a tangle of tired, disconnected thoughts they stared groggily at the giant firework ahead whose brilliance and energy belied the suffering within. The intensity of the light seemed to pierce the brain like a dagger through the eye. The pandemonium of events, the way that night was turned to day, the danger and uncertainty...all conspired to overwhelm the senses. When they reached the Piper Alpha, no derrick was visible.

At about this stage the *Tharos* itself became endangered. The Piper Alpha fire had started to belch out strange balls of incandescent gas which, like spectral beings, appeared to 'walk' slowly across the sea. The *Tharos'* OIM realised that the inferno threatened to engulf his vessel. He therefore ordered a pull-back, a move which probably saved the vessel as well as making the helideck usable by Yankee Bravo and the rescue Sea King which had arrived at the scene. The winch-equipped Sea King began to pluck survivors from the water to transfer them to the intensive care medical facility on board the *Tharos*. The pilots of Yankee Bravo, meantime, received instructions to divert to a semi-submersible oil rig about twenty miles away where they were to shut down for the rest of the night.

The next morning, after, no doubt, some fitful, dream-filled sleep, the two S-76 pilots were ordered to return to the *Tharos* for the start of a day destined to bring little consolation. From the *Tharos* they gazed at the sad, fragmented remnants of Piper Alpha which continued to emit haphazard flames from what was left of the central structure. Occasional clouds of black smoke drifted across to cause some helicopter engines, deprived of oxygen, to cough perilously on take-off from *Tharos*. As the day progressed, the pilots were required to assist with the melancholy process of flying corpses to a temporary mortuary at Aberdeen Airport. Normally used to park snow-clearing equipment, the hangar was now central to a role not originally envisaged. As a mark of respect, the S-76 was limited to carrying three victims at a time, each one strapped across seats. On arrival at Aberdeen Airport, the S-76 and other crews were briefed to ask for clearance to land at 'Snowbase' where the 'cargo' was rapidly removed before the pilots were cleared by air traffic control to return offshore.

It was not long before the volume of numbers caused a shortage of body bags, a problem alleviated by a passing United States Navy ship. The captain sent one of the ship's own helicopters to deliver extra body bags, and he offered to help in any other way possible. The captain was thanked and told that, regretfully, there was no other way in which to help.

Meanwhile the *Tharos* continued to act like a giant fire-engine with powerful water jets permanently directed at the charred remains of Piper Alpha. For a further three or so weeks the remains of Piper Alpha continued to throw out flames before a team led by Mr Paul Neil 'Red' Adair, the legendary American oil well firefighter, finally managed to extinguish them. Then, in mid-October, a derrick barge, the *DB102,* headed from Rotterdam to lift the Piper Alpha's accommodation modules from the seabed. The *DB102,* a mammoth vessel equipped with two cranes with a capacity of six thousand tons each, had teams on standby who faced daunting tasks when the Piper Alpha site was reached. Starting at midnight, the teams took some twenty hours to recover an accommodation module known as ERQ (east replacement quarters) from the seabed. The subsequent search through all four storeys of the ERQ, which included the Piper Alpha's galley where the majority of bodies lay, was the responsibility of Grampian Police. The policemen had to work through blackened, sodden and malodorous debris which was stacked several feet high. With twenty officers divided into four groups of five, the harrowing processes were eased (at least, that was the intention) by giving each group three days off after a day of duty. It was estimated that about one hundred personnel had taken refuge in the galley, largely in the belief that helicopters would rescue them, and of these the policemen found the bodies of eighty-seven victims.

As there were serious concerns about the psychological impact on these policemen and others, a doctor at Aberdeen University's mental health department was asked to offer advice on how best to manage the situation. Ten years later the same doctor tried to track down Piper Alpha survivors. Approximately half of them agreed to co-operate with his study into the long-term psychological and social effects of the disaster. Most of the men reported symptoms of post-traumatic stress disorder with psychological and behavioural difficulties. In a cruel twist, a number said that they'd experienced unexpected obstacles when trying to find further employment because some companies regarded them as Jonahs – bringers of bad luck and therefore not welcome on other offshore installations.

There were positive aspects too. The good doctor recorded that some of the men were stronger than before Piper Alpha. Inner strengths became evident; individuals learned things about themselves; values and relationships changed for the better. "There was a lot of heroism that took place," said the doctor in a comment that may have offered a degree of comfort to some.

Richard Pike remembers the horror

A DAWN START for me on the morning of 7 July 1988 heralded an interesting flight to the Claymore/*Tharos*/Piper Alpha complex. Just four days previously I'd flown a similar route, and as I drove to work on empty roads on that fine summer morning it was with a sense of appreciation at living in a great place, an ideal one, I felt, in which to bring up our young family. Behind me the Bennachie range of hills provided a brilliant backdrop to the general scene of warm summer colours all of which stimulated a sense of well-being, an appreciation of being at one with the world – what was not to like?

The answer came quite quickly and in an unexpected form: "We've just received information," announced the voice on my car radio, "that the fire on the North Sea Piper Alpha platform reported earlier is still not under control. The Piper Alpha is situated about one hundred and seventy miles north-east of Aberdeen and there have been reports of casualties arriving by helicopter at the Aberdeen Royal Infirmary."

At once my mind began to race as I tried to work out the implications for my flight. Hastily, I completed the journey to Aberdeen Airport and by chance met up with another pilot in the Bristow Helicopter's car park. Neither of us knew anything about the Piper Alpha situation other than the brief reports we'd heard on the radio. Together we hurried into the company building then paced upstairs to make our way towards the flight planning room. Even before entering the room we were aware that something was amiss. In the room itself, an excited buzz of conversation created a dramatic and chilling atmosphere as some of the rescue crews who'd recently returned from the Piper Alpha gave their accounts. I walked up to a colleague of mine, a fellow Sikorsky S-61N pilot, and nodded. His haggard look as he glanced up made my blood run cold. "There was a fast rescue craft in the area," he said, "the guys didn't stand a chance. They were...just...liquidated."

It was a long time before all that took place that night was pieced together. In the public inquiry that followed Piper Alpha, Lord Cullen observed that the installation had been inspected by the Department of Energy just a month before the disaster. He stated that the findings were: "superficial to the point of being of little use as a test of safety on the platform."

Other things we learned included the point that the Piper Alpha's designers had made no allowance for the destruction of the control room and that the installation's organisation had disintegrated soon after the transmission of a third and last Mayday call, a call made in a panic-stricken voice: "Mayday... Mayday...we're abandoning the radio room...we're abandoning the radio room... we can't take any more...we're on fire..." In the minutes before this call, men who'd been watching a film in the installation's cinema had commented on the excessive noise from the gas flare outside, a noise described as a 'deep roaring sound'. Beneath the Piper Alpha a diver was working at a depth of fifty feet. His colleague had just finished the decompression process and awaited instructions from his supervisor. While he waited, he stared with others at the exceptional gas flare which looked enormous until it died momentarily before resuming with a thunderous roar. Within the accommodation block, a number of personnel listened to the radio or watched the television in anticipation of the ten o'clock news. Some claimed to have heard the ten o'clock time signal, others said that they'd not heard the tones because the programme had been abruptly interrupted by a high-pitched scream, an eerie sound described by survivors in various ways – some thought that scaffolders were 'acting the goat', a group in a workshop tea room discussed the 'loud screech', one man likened the sound to 'somebody strangling a woman'.

From a nearby vessel, the master described the next moments: "Well, I actually saw the explosion, I did not hear it. I actually saw it before I registered anything else. What I saw I can only explain as like the starting of a gas burner or a water heater. It seemed to go along the bottom of the platform like a very light blue explosion or ignition more than anything else, then contracting again before a further explosion which came from a certain point which I believe to be below the crane pedestal and slightly to the left."

The explosion flung the two men in the Piper Alpha control room across the floor causing them injury. Equipment and tables were hurled about and there was a chaos of debris with telephones, computer equipment and furniture littering the area. Smoke began to drift into the control room and vision was further hampered when the main lighting failed. The diver submerged beneath the platform reported later that he'd experienced a simultaneous flash and bang followed ten seconds after that by a second flash and bang. Immediate efforts to recover him were hampered by fires although he was eventually retrieved. This man survived the disaster and went on to help with the rescue of others during the night.

In the accommodation block, personnel were catapulted from their beds. The cinema rapidly emptied as folk ran to their cabins to don survival suits. Meanwhile, the OIM rushed to the control room where he instructed the radio operator to send out a Mayday call. The OIM left the control room only to return within a few moments, apparently in a state of sudden panic. He said that the access was on fire and full of smoke. He discussed with the radio operator (who went on to survive the disaster by jumping from the helideck into the sea) the possibility of leaving the area via an escape hatch. The OIM then left the control room again and managed to make his way to the galley situated within the fire-proofed accommodation block directly below the helideck.

Following the control room abandonment, no attempt was made to use loudspeakers or to order an evacuation. Personnel tried to head for lifeboat stations in accordance with training and stipulated emergency procedures, but the intensity of the fire thwarted such efforts. Instead, many of the men moved to the galley where they awaited further instructions. Instructions, though, which never came. A survivor described how the OIM stood on a table in the centre of the galley trying to take some kind of command. This, though, proved virtually impossible due to hysteria, commotion and heckling. One man yelled at the OIM that he was supposed to be in command and to get them out of there. The OIM told the man to calm down. Tragically, the OIM was not numbered amongst the sixty-one souls who survived the disaster.

When the smoke in the galley area started to intensify and when the emergency lighting failed, a state of general panic set in. Men were forced to crawl along the floor at low level with wet towels as face masks. The smoke curled its way into the corners of the room, up to the roof, down to the floor, into every chink and crevice of retreat until it began to incapacitate people both physically and in their thought processes. Some individuals dipped their towels into a fish tank, some poured juice from the fruit machine over their heads. One man was heard to shout: "Is there anyone here from Bawdon drilling?" – evidently thinking that if he was about to die, he wanted to be near someone he knew. Numbers of individuals apparently made no attempt to leave the accommodation area in spite of the clear and urgent need to do so. One survivor, a rigger, gave the following account to the Cullen Inquiry: "I just said to myself – get yourself off. I got my pal Francis and I got him as far as the reception area but he would not go down the stairs because he says: 'We've done our muster job, they'll send choppers in'. I said to Francis: 'I've tried to speak to the lead production operator but he cannot talk to me, Francis. We'll have to get off.' But Francis would not go and he just slumped down. Anybody that knows the rig and the reception next to the bond, he slumped down there. That was as far as I could get him."

Various reasons have been suggested for this mentality which seemed to affect so many: poor leadership; a dearth of information; lack of ideas about what to do next; dogged belief in helicopter rescue. Helicopters, though, were unable to land because of the fire and smoke that persisted to surge across the helideck.

Shortly before 11 p.m. a major gas line ruptured. The resultant explosion shot huge flames into the air to a height of over three hundred feet above the Piper Alpha. When the MSV *Tharos,* which up to that point had held its position to spray powerful water jets at the fire, was forced to draw back the heat by that stage had begun to melt machinery and steelwork on the *Tharos* itself. By now those left alive in the Piper Alpha either desperately sought shelter within the scorched, smoke-filled accommodation block, or tried to leap into the sea from different deck levels including the helideck which was one hundred and seventy-five feet above the surface. One of those who opted to leap from the helideck recorded his experience later:

'It must have been an hour I'd been going around the platform trying to get off. I was quite fatalistic by that time. The platform was beginning to break up. I could hear the gratings breaking. The noise was an eerie creaking and grinding as if the welding was melting. Supports gave way and the area we were on actually tilted. Everyone just shook hands and we were saying that was it, this is the end. I thought, I've got to do something, keep trying to get away from this. I came out of the tool store and that's when I could see clear air. The crane operator had dropped pipes onto the deck and they were creating a bridge to walk along. I could see this guy at the end of these pipes. He'd been walking along the pipes and he jumped off into the sea and I thought – I'm going the same way, that's where I'll go. The deck was very hot. It was hot to touch. I could feel it through my feet. It was definitely melting. I had my life jacket on and I had my survival suit on and I stood looking down. I could not see if there were any obstructions, but I did as you should do – hand across your life jacket, hand over your nose to stop the water going too far up, and I went to jump. As I was doing so someone from behind said that his feet were on fire and he gave me a shove. In I went, head over heels, and I remember thinking, I'm getting away from the flames but I'm going to break my neck hitting the water now. I don't remember hitting the water but I came up on my back marvelling at how warm the water was. I came across a partition floating, and I paddled away from the platform. I was thinking, thank God I'm away from that inferno, away from the smoke. I think the smoke was as bad as the heat.'

The loss of one hundred and sixty-seven souls on that abhorrent night had far-reaching implications. The disaster exposed a complacency which appeared to have crept into the activities of the North Sea oil industry in general, activities, including helicopter operations, which would be profoundly influenced in the future.

As for me, my flight that morning was cancelled; the area was already inundated with helicopter traffic. However, some two weeks later I was scheduled for a flight to the *Tharos* to take personnel and equipment, some of which was needed by 'Red' Adair. Flying towards the vessel, which was still positioned next to the remains of the Piper Alpha, it was soon evident that even then the area was overshadowed by clouds of smoke and fumes. The *Tharos* crews still pumped powerful jets of water at the broken remnants of Piper Alpha and after landing on the deck, when I left my seat in the Sikorsky S-61N cockpit to supervise the unloading of the passengers and freight, I was struck by the sad, world-weary expressions on the faces of the deck crew. The men seemed to go about their duties like automatons. I noticed that a temporary bridge had been set up as a link between the *Tharos* and the Piper Alpha, and I spotted 'Red'

Adair with members of his team huddled around a particular spot on the Piper Alpha from where flames continued to emerge.

It was on the flight back to Aberdeen that a brief radio conversation with the air traffic controller seemed to crystallise the whole sorry saga. "Confirm that you're inbound from the *Tharos?*" asked the controller. Yes, we were. "Is the Piper Alpha still on fire?" Yes, it was. Then, after a pause: "I guess," said the controller, "there'll be flames there forever and ever." I glanced at my co-pilot, Geoff. We both nodded as if to say, 'Amen'.

Author's note: some quotations in this chapter have been reproduced by kind permission of the BBC.

CHAPTER 15
JUNGLE TURN

Tony Stafford in the Far East

"THE ELONGATED LAND-MASS of the island of Sumatra, the world's sixth largest island, has a number of interesting aspects," Captain Tony Stafford and his colleagues were told at a briefing in Singapore, "which include several active volcanoes, lowlands with swamps, complex river systems, and an oil and gas industry that claims to be one of the oldest in the world."

It was the early 1970s and this briefing went on to cover various facets including information on the south-western portion of the Sumatran Basin where a section of the Batang Hari River, the island's longest river, wound its way through Jambi City. The city itself was an urban sprawl that was between zero and sixty metres above sea level and which was thus vulnerable to severe flooding. "Despite this risk, a hangar on one side of the river will be used as your base for the two Westland Wessex 60 helicopters." These helicopters, owned by Bristow Helicopters, were planned to be operated by a team of company personnel which included Tony. "Your task will be to fly men and equipment needed to build oil drilling sites slap, bang in the middle of the central Sumatran jungle which, in turn, is positioned more or less slap, bang in the middle of the equator."

The task, therefore, was a daunting one in view of Sumatra's tropical climate with its hot, humid conditions which could prove less than ideal for operating helicopters. This was especially the case in the rainy season from October to March when an average of twenty rainy days a month could be expected. Then it was that vast cumulonimbus clouds would signal the approach of a tropical storm, and local observers realised the need to seek shelter urgently. As the wind picked up to blow fiercely and the clouds piled together to race low over the area, the rain would soon follow and when it came, it sometimes began with gusty showers, pauses and downpours. Quite swiftly the smaller drops would swell into heavier ones with a steady beat to produce rain that was hard to see through and which converted midday light into evening. When great tropical cyclones thrashed trees into a frenzy, a deafening roar, stunning in its intensity, would rise as graceful fronds of palms were clawed loose and sent flying like huge misshapen birds. Meanwhile, puddles formed which swelled into small lakes that started to pour their contents into the Batang Hari River whose muddy waters whirled along the bank sides, slipped up the banks, spilled over into the fields, into the streets, into the busy highway network. Fortunately, during the two years that Tony spent in the area, the helicopter hangar escaped this onslaught, although he experienced other hazards, including an incident in mid-March 1972 that ended in a crash landing from which he and his two local assistants were lucky to escape.

Despite the potential flooding problems, the Batang Hari River proved useful for the oil rig construction process as materials could be floated to a point close to the planned rig site before onward conveyance by the Wessex 60s. For this, loads would be carried in a special sling attached to a hook underneath the helicopter. As the maximum permitted weight of each load was four thousand six hundred pounds, every part of the oil rig had to be dismantled to that figure or below. "As a rough calculation," said Tony when he discussed plans with his colleagues, "I reckon that approximately one thousand seven hundred individual loads will have to be carried!"

"At least that amount – probably more."

"How do you mean?"

"There'll be drilling pipes, consumables and personnel to move around. With all of that, we'll probably have to fly about three thousand separate flights."

"That'll mean flying virtually continuously for ten hours a day!"

And so it turned out, although before the helicopters could begin, a team of tough local rig workers led by a wiry ex-Foreign Legion Frenchman had to struggle by foot into the depths of the jungle. There, they laboured to clear a site large enough for a Wessex 60 to hover and for an oil rig to be constructed. An area of dense forest had to be beaten back to form a compound encircled by more forest the giant trees of which were a challenge to fell although Tony, and probably some of his colleagues, felt regret at the destruction of part of nature's untouched environment. Working towards a selected site the rig men had to cope with heat and humidity that pressed relentlessly on the skin.

Progress could be hampered by a strange jungle darkness with a curious, ghostly light that broke through the canopy of leaves to produce a shimmering, eerie effect. Attacked by mosquitoes, leeches, stinging ants, the rig workers could feel unnerved by the wild sounds of jungle animals concealed in the dense under-growth. The men had to hope and pray that scorpions and snakes, perhaps even large and venomous pit-vipers, were not amongst the animal life. The abrupt screech of a parrot, the sudden jump of a Sumatran gibbon or a Sumatran orang-utan, the ominous movement of a cat-like binturong with sharp meat-eating teeth, as well as multitudinous other jungle sounds assaulted the senses in a weird and haphazard symphony. Movement was hampered by branches that brushed against the skin, scrub that sprang up under the feet after each step. Headway could seem painfully slow in the vexatious, suffocating environment.

At length, though, the rig men battled their way through, the first site was cleared and flying operations could commence. This first site, at a distance of thirty-two kilometres from the river rendezvous point, was further than originally advised which meant the need to carry extra fuel. Outbound loads from the river to the oil rig site therefore proved especially demanding and sometimes the Wessex 60's twin de Havilland Gnome turboshaft engines struggled to provide sufficient power. Although the Wessex 60 was designed for two-pilot operations, a single-pilot routine was worked out with two and a half hours of flying followed by a similar period of rest. After two weeks of this sequence the pilots were flown to Singapore for a week of rest and recreation.

One time, Tony was tasked to fly up-river so that a reconnaissance team could explore another potential oil rig site. He landed and shut down the Wessex 60 close to a small village and waited for an hour or two while the reconnaissance team members discussed things with the local headman. While he waited, Tony noticed a man emerge from the village into the bright sunshine. The man stood quite still, keeping his distance, screwing up his eyes in the sunshine as he listened and watched warily. It was hard to guess the man's age but he seemed quite old. Before long, someone else sidled up to stand beside the old man, followed by another then another. Eventually a crowd of villagers stood there gazing in open-mouthed wonder at Tony and the others, and at the helicopter; especially at the helicopter. It was obvious that not one of them had ever seen such a thing before and clearly they were terribly afraid that the machine might attack them.

In due course, however, one of the villagers developed sufficient inquisitiveness and sufficient courage to creep closer to the Wessex 60. Suddenly, in an act of breathtaking boldness, he dashed forward, touched the side of the machine then ran away. Now others, similarly emboldened, followed suit. After a time it seemed that the whole village wanted to take part in the exercise as individuals moved up, touched, and retreated rapidly before the machine had a chance to bite. At length, as the boldness strengthened, villagers lingered a little longer after touching and in the end individuals started to rub their whole bodies along the fuselage as if magic would flow into them. The villagers' number swelled to about fifty at which juncture Tony and his colleagues needed to coax the villagers to a safe distance to prevent damage to the helicopter.

Not long after this incident, Tony was tasked to fly some drums of fuel to a fuel dump next to an oil rig site. The drums were carried in a net slung beneath the Wessex 60, and in the helicopter's cabin he carried a couple of local lads employed to help with the unloading procedure. This particular helicopter had been the subject of recent discussion between the engineering team and the pilots for the latter were aware of an unusual vibration felt through the rudder pedals. The engineers had inspected the machine but found nothing wrong. "Perhaps it's a bit of dust that's affecting some of the flight controls," said one of the engineers. "The dust could cause a little roughness but nothing dangerous."

It was as Tony brought the Wessex 60 to a hover above the fuel dump, and just as he was about to lower his load, that the helicopter, abruptly and violently, began an undemanded turn. The machine continued to turn and to wallow horribly as it lurched back and forth. Round and round it went like a mad thing; each sickening gyration was more violent than the previous one as the rotations accelerated. Tony was unable to climb away, but he couldn't land either – at least, not without crashing onto one hundred and fifty drums of highly flammable kerosene. Nursing the flight controls as best he could he tried to ease away from the kerosene dump. The whine and clatter from the helicopter's engines and gearbox grew louder and he was aware that, thankfully, the men working at the rig site had scattered. But still the machine, spinning like a top, blundered around perilously close to the kerosene. Jungle trees appeared to chase each other wildly, racing dizzily faster and faster, as did the bright sun above which flicked past the Wessex 60's windshield at an alarming rate. Tony felt suddenly very tired and very hot; with perspiration running down his face he still strived to move sideways until eventually, after some twenty-five revolutions, he realised that he'd made progress: the helicopter was no longer directly above the kerosene dump.

The ground was close now, as were the jungle trees. Tony glanced down to check the surface which was strewn with logs and other jungle debris – hardly ideal for landing. But he had to land; there was no other choice; the idea of persisting in a perpetual spin was absurd. With a dreadful sense of foreboding he prepared himself for the inevitable. He took a deep breath then, heart in mouth, pushed the collective lever down to lower the helicopter onto the ground. As he did so, he heard a series of crashes when the Wessex 60's main rotor blades struck nearby trees. He was shaken savagely by the impact which caused the machine's airframe to develop a vicious judder. Then a sudden *cr-r-r-umph* reverberated across the area as the helicopter struck the ground.

The engines and gearbox decelerated rapidly to create an ugly graunching sound followed by moments of stunned silence. In these moments Tony was aware that his arms and legs, the muscles in his whole body had been pushed and pulled by the force of the landing. He could see a tree that was leaning forward, damaged by one of the Wessex 60's flailing rotor blades. The helicopter had landed on the remains of other trees – heavy branches and trunks felled by the riggers – but the machine, remarkably, had stayed upright, probably held there by the underslung load which he'd tried unsuccessfully to jettison.

Numbed into a state of shock by the violence of the event, Tony sat still – very still. An immediate, strange sense of quiet lingered until he became aware of figures racing towards him, some swearing in French as they clawed grimly through wreckage to reach him. His tongue felt thickened and his head ached, otherwise he was not conscious of further injury. As the group of tough French riggers reached the cockpit, hands began to work frantically to release him, ever conscious of the danger of fire. The men seemed to be just shapes, menacing and huge, dressed in rough clothing but perhaps he was on the margins of consciousness. He realised that they were struggling against his seat harness, still locked to his body, so he pointed at the locking buckle. "Merde..." yelled one of the riggers who now managed to yank Tony free, though in the process he was probably responsible for inflicting Tony's only serious injury, a couple of fractured ribs.

"What about the two lads in the cabin?" Tony asked urgently as the riggers lifted him clear of the helicopter cockpit.

"Oui...oui...ce'st bon...we rescue."

As he was dragged free of the wreckage, Tony noticed the way that bits of adjacent tree had been devoured by the Wessex 60's four main rotor blades. The blades themselves hung limply around the remains of the wreckage and the tail section of the helicopter was separated from the main fuselage. His thoughts as he gazed at the machine may have been along the lines of 'flipping marvellous' although it might not have been the word 'flipping'. Maybe there was a feeling of slight madness in the air. Whatever the case, he knew that he was grateful to have survived, and he knew, too, that the accident had not been his fault; the maintenance error at the root of the accident, an incorrectly fitted bonding strip, would be revealed in due course. For now, though, all that he really knew was that he was just glad to be alive.

CHAPTER 16
FOWL FACTOR

Christopher Mutton's royal challenge

THE ROYAL CASTLE in Aberdeenshire was about to be opened up again. A low wind murmured through the corridors as staff in their numbers hastened to spruce the place up. Supervisors, secretaries, gardeners, chefs, cleaners, French-polishers, ghillies, ghoulies, goodness-knows-what raced here and there to prepare for an imminent, eminent royal arrival. All were aware that the castle known as Balmoral was required to live up to its good name, a name which, if equated to the likes of the mythical Taj Mahal or some fantastic Greek or Egyptian edifice might be overstating the case a bit, nonetheless met expectations as a fine example of Victoriana. The castle's use as a royal retreat was the brainchild of the young royal couple who were two years into their marriage when, in 1842, they first went to Scotland. Six years later, when Queen Victoria visited Balmoral she commented that she found the house 'small but pretty' and in her diary she recorded that: 'All seemed to breathe freedom and peace, and to make one forget the world and its sad turmoils'. The favourable impression must have persisted for, in the autumn of 1852, her husband Prince Albert formally took possession of the by-then extended property which had cost him £32,000.

Future royal generations, in taking on the Balmoral commitment, had added to the estate as a consequence of which a working estate with grouse moors, forestry, farmland, deer herds, highland cattle and ponies eventually extended to an area of approximately fifty thousand acres. Because all of this was without security fencing, members of the press and the public could roam freely about the estate with its many hunting lodges and log cabins. From the perspective of security this presented problems for the authorities. In the mid-1980s, therefore, in preparation for a forthcoming royal visit, Grampian Police contacted British Airways Helicopters. The company was offered a contract to provide helicopter support to insert so-called SWAT teams (special weapons and tactics – a largely American term) and, if necessary, to evacuate members of the royal family by helicopter. Additionally, as the company's air safety officer, Captain Chris Mutton, a former military helicopter pilot and therefore an apposite choice, was tasked to pinpoint the buildings around the estate and to survey suitable helicopter landing sites. A comprehensive booklet of these sites would be produced as well as a local Decca map.

Proceedings proceeded, contracts were signed, all was agreed and on the day that Chris drove to Balmoral for a meeting there, a preconception or two passed through his mind. One of these was that the Factor of Balmoral might turn out to be a quintessential Colonel Blimp, a prediction which turned out to be more or less true. "Just remember, chaps," said the colonel grandly as he conducted a briefing, "that the queen values the free roaming aspect of her country retreat here and does not appreciate overarching security." The colonel stared at those before him as if, one and all, they were ludicrously anomalous. His very presence appeared to announce: 'Take note of me and beware for I am a bulldog in disguise. I am most ferocious. Disobey me at your peril.'

"Then how are we supposed to protect her?" one of the policemen, not easily intimidated, asked politely.

There was a pause. The quixotic colonel glared with eyes as black as the brows above them. He cleared his throat. "I'm sure you'll do your best."

"Indeed we will but you haven't answered my question."

"If things get bad," said the colonel irritably, "we plan to evacuate royal members by helicopter."

"How long will it take for the helicopter to get to Balmoral?"

"That's one facet that Captain Mutton here from British Airways Helicopters will be investigating."

"And where will the helicopter land?"

"He's going to look at that too."

"How many people will this helicopter be able to carry?'

"He'll report on that as well..."

And so on and so forth for the briefing rambled on for quite a while but when, eventually, this and other issues had been covered, the colonel said: "Before you all disappear there's an important point that I want you to remember. Near one of the log cabins on the estate there's a resident capercaillie, a large bird which is the queen's pride and joy. It was gifted to her and on no account are any of you to disturb the bird or to interfere with it in any way."

At this, Chris, the policemen and others began to shuffle out of the briefing room for a site inspection. There were diverse categories of policeman present including officers from the local Grampian Police force, officers from London's Metropolitan Police, security operatives from the Ministry of Public Works and last, but by no means least, an inspector and a sergeant who were members of the elite Royalty Protection Branch under the direct command of assistant commissioner 'A' of the Metropolitan Police. The inspector wore a new, slightly shiny Giorgio Armani suit with clean, tailored lines as was fashionable at the time, while his sergeant, similarly attired, enjoyed the additional benefit of a navy-coloured honeycomb-jacquard silk tie. The local bobbies, on the other hand, wore unfashionable police-issue jackets and wellington boots.

Under the watchful eye of the colonel, the policemen and Chris made for two Land Rover vehicles, one earmarked for the fashionable brigade and one for the rest. Chris opted to join the latter, the lead vehicle as the local bobbies were well acquainted with the ins and outs of the Balmoral estate. While they bumped along rough tracks and muddy surfaces, Chris noted down various sites which could be used for landing a helicopter safely. Meantime, his travelling companions chatted away about this and that. "Aye, aye," said one of the bobbies, "that Armani gear should look good with the heather as a backdrop."

"Och aye," said his colleague, "and surely the tie will help."

"All these fops and bootlickers you find in royal establishments," interjected the driver, "the lieutenants, sub-lieutenants, lord lieutenants, right reverends, wrong reverends – the list is endless and all they want to do is toady up to royalty. They're a waste of space if you ask me."

"Good vehicle, this," said Chris in a tactful attempt to change the subject.

"More than can be said for the one behind us," said the driver.

"What's wrong with it?"

"It's an ancient Series 111 and hardly up to the Rolls-Royce standard that that lot are used to." By this stage they'd noticed that the Series 111 seemed to be struggling to keep up. "We'll just press on a bit and leave them to their own devices," said the driver grinning, "there's a log cabin ahead, we'll aim for that and wait for them there." At this he applied advanced driving skills as he accelerated away along the rough tracks of Balmoral. The conversation turned, appropriately, to a discussion on the pros and cons of different marks of Land Rover. The Series 111, it was agreed, made a reasonable workhorse "but it's dated now," said the driver, clearly an enthusiast. "If the memory serves, the first Series 111 was built in 1971 and five years later the one millionth Land Rover rolled off the production line – probably that one behind us now. Load of rubbish, in my opinion."

"Nice and shiny, though," said Chris, "just like our helicopters!"

"All that royal bull...but what's happening within? How do the guts of your helicopter compare with the quality of this Land Rover 90 with its coil springs, permanent four-wheel drive, two-speed transfer gearbox with lockable differential? It's altogether..." Suddenly the driver slammed on his brakes: "Look!" he cried as the Land Rover jerked to a halt. All those in the vehicle now craned their necks to see to their astonishment an enormous, aggressive bird dancing about as it blocked the track. "Wretched thing jumped out in front of me," said the driver.

"We'd better watch out," cried one of the bobbies, "that's a capercaillie! Stupid bird probably thinks we're threatening its territory." The bird, indeed, was evidently in no mood to move and wished instead to teach those in the superior model 90 Land Rover a thing or two about capercaillies, especially the point that, as a ground-living forest bird, it was renowned for a number of admirable attributes, in particular the most remarkable and spectacular mating display. With little choice but to remain as observers, the policemen together with Chris now stared transfixed at the display which began before them, a procedure which had probably started much earlier when the cock took up position on a lookout tree. The men watched as the capercaillie postured himself with raised and fanned tail feathers, erect neck, beak pointed skywards, wings held out and drooped to impress any nearby females and/or frighten off any competitors. The bird made a series of weird double-click noises, like the sound of dropping a ping-pong ball, which accelerated into a popping similar to a cork coming out of a bottle. The hullabaloo continued until, as if satisfied that he'd made his point, the capercaillie hopped to one side of the track, bowed and scampered off.

"Aye," said one of the bobbies as the Land Rover driver resumed his journey to the log cabin, "that's no helicopter but Her Majesty's pride and joy, no doubt about it. The thing's been around for years so they say." All fell silent for a while when they thought about this, and as the journey progressed it was not long before the log cabin came into sight. The Land Rover driver pulled up alongside and when the men stepped out of the vehicle, they appreciated the benefit of wellington boots to slosh through sludge as they walked towards the log cabin. "Aahh!" cried one of the bobbies as he poked his head inside, "it stinks in there." Sure enough, the others pulled faces of distaste when they sniffed the strange smell in the cabin, a blend of bacterial sickly-sweet, industrial chemical and the unpleasant odour of animal urine. Not just urine, either. "I'm staying outside," said one of the bobbies. "Me too," said his colleague at which everyone present nodded in agreement at the plan.

"I'm hungry," said one of the bobbies after a while, "what's for din-dins?"

"Barbecued pheasant for the peasants," said his colleague, a quip which was about to bring a rejoinder when the driver pointed and said: "Look – here come the others at last."

When the shiny Land Rover Series 111 pulled up alongside the superior model 90, those inside tumbled out in an unexpected state of disarray. "What happened to you lot?" asked the superior model 90 driver. An uncomfortable hush ensued as all waited for the elitist Royal Protection Branch inspector to make an announcement. The inspector, however, seemed in no frame of mind to make an announcement. The uncomfortable hush persisted. The inspector's pale face looked distraught. His Armani suit was mud-splattered, as was that of his sergeant. Both men's shiny, leathery, wafery-thin pointy shoes were layered in grass and slime. Their hands were covered in a mix of mud and feathers. Even the navy-coloured honeycomb-jacquard silk tie looked a mess. "OMG! OMG!" the inspector eventually started up in a whispery kind of voice, "I was the driver and what have I done? What the hell have I done? What am I going to do?"

"Well what *have* you done?" asked one of the local bobbies.

"I was just trying to catch you up. This vehicle is crap, by the way. I was going a bit too fast, perhaps, when this enormous bloody great bird jumped out in front of us."

"What happened then?"

"I flattened the damn thing!"

"You've *squished* Her Majesty's capercaillie?"

"Well...yes!"

"That's a hanging offence – aye! What have you done with the body?"

"We've pushed it down a foxhole. Luckily we found one quite a long way from the scene of the...of the...squishing."

"This gets worse and worse – aye, aye!"

"What am I supposed to tell that bloody colonel fellow?"

"Come, come," said one of the local bobbies mimicking a London accent, "consider the grit of your English forebears!"

The patronymic, though, did not appear to go down too well with the inspector. "It's all very well for you," he said grumpily, "what *am* I supposed to tell the bastard?"

"Never mind about the colonel," said the bobby soothingly. "Just make yourself scarce when we get back to the castle and leave him to us."

And so it was that when the two vehicles returned to the castle, those in the superior model 90 Land Rover braced themselves to deal with the Balmoral Factor while the others disappeared discreetly to swab down their Armani suits with expensive cologne. Meanwhile, it was not long before the Balmoral Factor charged up. "I've heard terrible rumours." He bit his lip theatrically and stared at the men. His expression was one of numb despair.

"Rumours?" said one of the local bobbies. "We haven't heard any rumours."

"Rumours about the capercaillie?"

"What capercaillie?"

"The one I briefed you about!"

"Och aye, that one. What about it?"

"I hear that something dreadful might have happened to the bird."

"Oh aye?"

"Well? Has it or has it not been...been..."

"Aye, aye," said the policeman in a matter-of-fact manner, "all I can say is that the bird was in the rudest of health when we last saw it."

His statement in a literal sense was, of course, true. Also true was the subsequent police get-together in a local hostelry to which Chris was invited. "I think we've gathered useful information for helicopter operations, inspector," he said. "And by the bye," he added with a grin, "I believe that we can thank canny locals for saving your hide." At this, the elite inspector nodded in response.

One of the local bobbies then pointed at the London suits: "If you can afford that expensive Armani stuff," he declared, "then you can afford to buy our drinks!" The two officers from the Royal Protection Branch, to give them due credit, conceded this point with grace and soon all present were invited to raise their glasses. "I have a toast, gentlemen," said the Armani-clad inspector. "Here's to you and here's to a right royal caper!"

"I think he means caper-caillie," muttered one of the local bobbies under his breath at which those who'd overheard the remark tried not to burst into fits of laughter.

CHAPTER 17

HELI-MISCELLANY (3)

Stop thief! (from Alan Boulden)

THE TELEPHONE CALL from the controller at the Rescue Co-ordination Centre, which came at around 3.30 in the morning, caused Flight Lieutenant Alan Boulden to wake with a start. He fumbled for the receiver then muttered a curt: "Hello?"

"Sorry to wake you," said the controller's voice, "but you're needed urgently."

"Okay. What's happened?" Alan's half-closed eyes began to open fully.

"There's been a mishap in London, on the River Thames. A pleasure boat called the *Marchioness* has sunk following a collision. There are many casualties."

"How many casualties?"

"We've received an estimate of over fifty at this stage. We'd like you to scramble and fly to the scene to offer assistance."

Alan, who was the captain of a Royal Air Force Westland Sea King rescue helicopter, now woke the rest of the crew and, while everyone dressed hastily, in his mind went through the implications of this drastic scenario. Normally based at RAF Brawdy in the western reaches of Wales, his crew members together with a team of supporting engineers were currently in Jersey for a training exercise with the local lifeboat crew. But now, with his team dressed, ready and anxious to proceed, everyone else in their Jersey hotel remained fast asleep. Alan was unable to find any night staff on duty. He did, however, manage to telephone for a couple of taxis although when they drove up to the airport, it was closed. Also closed was the air traffic control tower. Worst of all, the hangar containing the Sea King helicopter was closed and locked.

"Leave this to me!" cried one of the engineers, a burly fellow who quickly scrutinised likely-looking windows, checked side doors and the great sliding doors at the front. It was not long before he was heard to cry "Eureka!" A scrabbling sound inside the hangar confirmed that he had gained access so that he could unlock the sliding doors from the inside then push them open. But now they faced the problem of moving the helicopter out of the hangar without a towing tractor. The solution? Push by hand! 'And what,' pondered Alan, 'about filing the obligatory flight plan?' 'No chance of that', he thought. Soon, therefore, with the Sea King positioned safely outside the hangar (after a fair amount of push and shove) he fired up the engines and rotors to fly at maximum speed towards the River Thames.

When halfway there he received a message that the Sea King was not required after all. Tragically, fifty-one souls had drowned, there was nothing more that the helicopter could do. He was to divert to the airfield at Manston in Kent to await further tasking.

Dawn was breaking as they reached the vicinity of Manston and it suddenly occurred to Alan that he and his crew had crept away from Jersey in the dead of night in the most unconventional way. Surely, he mused, it was a good method in which to steal a Sea King helicopter for he and his colleagues had failed to arouse even the smallest hint of a cry, "Stop thief!"

Height of madness (from Pushp Vaid)

THE MIL MI-4 HELICOPTER, which helped to lay the foundations of the Soviet army aviation, was what might be described as a minimalist machine. It was used by a number of air forces around the world, including the Indian Air Force, and in the late 1960s, Flight Lieutenant Pushp Vaid, a member of that air force, gained unusual experience as an Mi-4 pilot. One time, based for a month at Keylong in the Himalayas some seventy-five miles from the border with Tibet, Pushp's task was to help in the search for a Soviet-designed Antonov An-12 transport aircraft which had crashed in the mountains.

Operating the Mi-4 from a helipad some eleven thousand feet above sea level, Pushp and his colleagues faced particular challenges, especially as the helicopter had no hover capability at such high altitudes. When flying at five hundred feet above the ground, this often translated into an altitude of twenty thousand feet above sea level. That meant the need for oxygen for the crew who, ever conscious of the dangers of anoxia, regularly checked each other for anoxic symptoms – lack of focus, poor co-ordination of movement, dizziness, headache, profuse perspiration, false sense of euphoria, impaired vision and various other dire medical features.

To add to their difficulties, the three-man crew were supplied with just one bottle of oxygen which they had to share. A typical sortie, therefore, involved passing the oxygen bottle from one man to the next as each took a few puffs. Inevitably, this could lead to a degree of hilarity. The trick was to gauge the cause of the hilarity – deadly anoxia or harmless mirth? The mission was com-pleted without mishap so mirth was assumed to have been the cause of the hilarity. However, as Pushp readily admitted later: "What we got up to was... well, it was sheer madness! We must have been mad!"

Afghanistan (from Mark Service)

THE EARLY DAYS of British action in Afghanistan involved some eight hundred and fifty members of the Royal Air Force sent there in the autumn of 2001. As part of this, Sergeant Mark Service was posted to RAF Kandahar for a four-month detachment as a 'mover' whose duties encompassed the planning and execution of the movement of personnel and cargo. Accommodated in a vast tented camp, when Mark first arrived he would gaze in wonder at detritus from the Soviet-Afghan War. This war between insurgent groups known as the *mujahideen* fighting the Soviet army and the Democratic Republic of Afghanistan, had lasted for nine years and had cost estimated figures of hundreds of thousands of Afghan lives lost as well as causing millions of Afghans to flee the country as refugees. Even though a dozen years had elapsed since the war's end in 1989, Mark was astonished that little appeared to have been done to clear up armoured personnel carriers, helicopters, aircraft and a multitude of different military vehicles, all of which had been bulldozed into a huge pile in the centre of the camp as if in preparation for some incredible Guy Fawkes bonfire event.

Near Mark's tent were soldiers from Company 'F' of the 131st Aviation Regiment of the United States Army who made their presence known which, from Mark's point of view, was fortunate for he soon befriended these men who operated Boeing CH-47 Chinook helicopters. When invited to fly with them, Mark jumped at the chance. One day, when offered one such opportunity, he attended a pre-flight briefing for a two-ship Chinook mission tasked to re-supply United States Special Forces' bases situated in the mountains. For the duration of the flight, Mark sat in a purpose-built jump seat placed between and slightly behind the two pilots. Both pilots shared the same first name as Mark so that when one of the crewmen on board shouted: "Hey, Mark!" all three would respond.

After take-off, the Chinook captain remained at low level as he followed the lead Chinook towards the Registan Desert, otherwise known as the Red Desert. The contrast was stark between the light brown sands surrounding Kandahar and the dark red of the Registan area with the boundary between the two deserts marked by a river bed. For a period, the Chinooks were flown at very low level following the line of this river bed before the lead Chinook turned towards the heart of the Red Desert. The desert sands looked to Mark almost close enough to touch while the ground rushed past as if in a speeded-up movie. Sparsely populated by nomadic tribes, Mark had been told that about three years earlier some one hundred thousand nomads from this area had been displaced by an exceptionally severe drought. And just now he saw few signs of desert life as the captain, weaving between small red sand dunes about fifty to one hundred feet high, held a loose trail formation on the lead Chinook which headed towards the planned drop-off points in the mountains.

Before long, while the two Chinooks began to climb as they approached higher ground, the stifling heat of Kandahar started to dissipate. Eventually cruising amongst the mountains, Mark enjoyed spectacular scenery with scattered forestry at lower levels, vast areas of rock and stone higher up until the tallest peaks, some of which were snow covered as they reached altitudes of over twenty-four thousand feet, glistened in the sun. As the helicopters continued towards the first drop-off point, Mark spotted the crewman of the lead Chinook waving one hand while, from his position manning a M60 general-purpose 7.62-mm machine gun on the aircraft ramp, he looked back at his colleagues in the helicopter that still followed in a trail formation.

When the first drop-off point came into view, Mark noted the judicious way in which this special forces base camp had been set up. Both Chinooks were flown to specific points where, after landing, hectic activity ensued as pallets of ammunition, bottled water, fuel and rations were offloaded. With about half of the total load delivered, the Chinooks then took off to head for the second special forces base camp to convey the remaining pallets. This camp was as carefully concealed as the first one, and while bearded special forces troops helped with unloading the helicopters, Mark sensed the strong spirit of determination displayed by these highly trained men following the 9/11 attacks. He knew that less than a month after 9/11, the United States, aided by the United Kingdom, Canada and other countries including several from the NATO alliance, had initiated military action against Taliban and Al-Qaeda camps. He knew, too, that the CIA's elite Special Activities Division had been the first US forces to enter Afghanistan to prepare for the arrival of the special operations forces such as those he now observed.

For Mark, a sobering reminder of this resolve was underlined when he saw two blindfolded and handcuffed Taliban prisoners, their heads bowed as they were led out to the Chinook. The activities of the Taliban, the subject of such international outrage, had included the brutal repression of women highlighted recently by Laura Bush, the American First Lady, in a radio address. Mark had heard that, in areas controlled by the Taliban, girls were forced to abandon their studies at schools and colleges after an edict that forbade the education of women. Those who wished to leave home to go shopping had to wear the burka, a traditional dress that covered the entire body apart from a small screen by the eyes, and had to be accompanied by a male relative. Individuals who appeared to disobey were publicly flogged. Mark and other crew members were no doubt conscious of these and other abuses for it was with a sombre atmosphere on board that the Chinook captain flew directly back to Kandahar where the fate of the two Taliban prisoners would be decided by the US authorities. The bedraggled prisoners, thought Mark, seemed symptomatic of a turbulent country with a long history of violence which was unlikely, he reckoned, to be settled any time soon.

Top: Off the coast of West Falkland Chinook HC2 'Y' prepares to lift a 20-foot ISO container from the deck of the MV *Saint Brandan*. This was an almost daily occurrence as underslung loads were lifted to and from the mountain-top radar sites at Mount Alice and Byron Heights and various other locations around the Falkland Islands. (RAF via Mark Service)

Bottom: Chinook HC1 ZA713 at Al Jubail Port in hastily applied camouflage to support 7 Squadron Special Forces Flight operations behind enemy lines.

Top: Joint formation photograph to mark the introduction of the Chinook HC2 to 18 Squadron at RAF Gütersloh. All four helicopter types operated by 18 at that time are represented. Gazelle XW902 'H' was used for daylight reconnaissance of the night NVG routes, Puma XW226 'BY', Chinook HC1 ZA670 'BG' and an unknown Chinook HC2. (RAF Gütersloh Photographic Section)

Bottom: Chinook HC1 ZD980 'BJ' in special 75th Anniversary markings outside the 18 Squadron hangar, RAF Gütersloh, 4 May 1990. (Mark Service)

Top: The Piper Alpha structure
still burning two weeks after the
horrible disaster on 6 July 1988.
This photograph was taken by
the author. (Richard Pike)

Middle and Bottom: A closer view
of the fire at Piper Alpha.
(Richard Pike)

Top: A Wessex from RAF Gütersloh flying over German countryside. (Richard Pike)

Middle: A Wessex 60 surrounded by jungle debris following a crash in Sumatra. (Tony Stafford)

Bottom: The extent of the damage to the Wessex 60 is evident in this photograph. Note how the tail section has come away from the main fuselage. (Tony Stafford)

Top: Chinook HC1 lifting Meteor 504 to the Danish Air Force Museum.
(RAF Gütersloh Photographic Section)

Top: A crowd of Albanian Kosovo children with the author (centre to the right). Taken during the delivery of flour rations around Kosovo as part of the UN World Food Programme. (Richard Pike)

Middle: Sikorsky S-61N in UN colours over Serb base at Knin. (David Lanigan)

Bottom: An S-61N from the UN World Food Programme flying over Central Kosovo. (Richard Pike)

Top: An unidentified Sea King HC4 during the First Gulf War. (Mark Service)

Bottom: Chinook HC2 'F' at the tactical load park at RAF Odiham during the final phase of the landing point commander course. The instructor (blue helmet cover) and students prepare to hook up a triple-rigged 20-foot ISO container. (RAF Odiham Photographic Section)

Top: Driver John Baillie and SAC Mark Service of the Joint Helicopter Support Unit (Falkland Islands Detachment) with 78 Squadron Sea King XZ592, RAF Mount Pleasant 1988. (Mark Service)

Bottom: Sea King HC4 ZD477 'A' at Al Jubail Port during the First Gulf War, note 'Invasion Stripes'. (Mark Service)

Falklands voyage (from Dave Lowry)

WHEN THE CUNARD-OWNED roll-on/roll-off container ship *Atlantic Conveyor* was struck by two Argentine Exocet missiles on 25 May 1982, the loss of six Westland Wessex helicopters and all but one of the five Boeing Chinook helicopters on board meant that British troops had to march, or 'yomp', across treacherous Falkland territory in order to re-capture the islands' capital of Stanley. Following seventy-four days of conflict, the Argentine surrender on 14 June that year occurred after the loss of six hundred and forty-nine Argentine military personnel, two hundred and fifty-five British military personnel and three Falkland Islanders. The large number of casualties doubtless added to the war's strong impact on both countries with patriotic sentiments and general emotions running high.

So it was that, even though the war was over, the need for security was not. Especial emphasis was placed on air defence and as part of this, Flight Lieutenant Dave Lowry, a Royal Air Force fighter controller, was tasked in the autumn of 1982 to accompany radar equipment due to be shipped down to the Falklands in the Royal Fleet Auxiliary ship *L3027 Sir Geraint*. As an ex-Royal Navy man, Dave was an appropriate choice for the long sea voyage. In addition to the radar equipment, on board was a Chinook helicopter with its ten-ton lifting capability – the only practical way of setting up radar sites on remote hilltops in the Falklands.

In late-October 1982 Dave arrived in Southampton where he met the master of the *Sir Geraint,* Captain Overbury, who invited him together with a Royal Air Force colleague to dinner one evening. It did not take long for Captain Overbury to extract the information that Dave had various naval qualifications including watch-keeping, ship handling and coastal navigation.

"Looks like we're going to be a bit short-staffed for this voyage," said the captain. "If you're willing, I'd like you to help out on the bridge – help the first mate with his duties."

"Why not?" said Dave. "A three-week voyage and nothing else to do. Yes, I'll be glad to help!"

As things turned out, the three-week period extended to about two months and after just a couple of watches under the vigilant eye of the first mate, Dave was handed a bulky instruction manual and told to go to his cabin to 'swot up'. "You'll have a theory test tomorrow," he was told. The test, when it came, was conducted by the first mate over a drink or two in the ship's officers' saloon. "Well done," said the first mate on conclusion of the test, "you've passed! But don't have any more to drink. You're on watch first thing in the morning!"

"Ohh...okay...but what is my status?"

"Consider yourself to be 'fourth mate'."

And in this way a Royal Air Force fighter controller – a flight lieutenant holding, simultaneously, the rank of fourth mate – found himself on watch the following morning with a Chinese quartermaster and a Chinese bosun's mate. Dave's position, he reckoned, might well have been unique in the annals of the merchant marine.

While the *Sir Geraint* made progress towards Ascension Island, Dave's confidence grew as the days passed and he developed a good working relationship with other crew members while he settled in to his unorthodox position. As with many United Kingdom merchant ships, the *Sir Geraint* was manned by British officers with a Chinese crew and the latter, who struggled to remember any of the officers' names, referred to him only as 'fourth mate'. On board were soldiers from the Royal Hampshire Regiment and when, eventually, the ship reached Ascension Island, these men disembarked before the *Sir Geraint* was dispatched to the Falklands with no further passengers. Not long after departure, however, the ship's master received a message to return in order to pick up some Gurkha soldiers.

Arriving back at Ascension Island, the crew learnt that to save time the Gurkhas would be transferred to the ship at night by helicopter. This turned out to be a harrowing experience for all involved, including the fourth mate who observed the operation with trepidation. Most of the Gurkha men had not seen the sea before, let alone been on board a ship. In the noise and excitement of the helicopter transfer, the crew worried that the young Gurkhas, drilled to obey orders without question, would dash clear of the helicopter as trained, only to run straight over the ship's side into the Atlantic Ocean. In the commotion of that evening, the fourth mate witnessed surreal scenes. People ran blindly across the ship's deck which, apart from the flashing of the helicopters' strobe lights and the focused brilliance of the ship's floodlights, was surrounded by the darkest dark of night. A potentially disastrous situation was saved largely thanks to the ship's warrant officer, a big, no-nonsense Scotsman, who grabbed numbers of the small Gurkhas by the scruff of the neck to send them in a safe direction before they ended up overboard.

At length, with all of the Gurkhas accounted for, the voyage south could resume. With a maximum speed of seventeen knots, progress was slow and it was towards the end of the year, therefore, when the *Sir Geraint* approached a misty Port Stanley harbour. Before entering the harbour, though, the ship was scrutinised by a Lockheed C-130 Hercules aircraft which overflew low and slow, followed by further investigation by a Royal Navy Type 12M Leander-class frigate.

Eventually cleared to proceed, it was on a warm, calm evening that the *Sir Geraint* sailed slowly through the narrow entrance of the harbour to drop anchor. However, as was typical of the variable weather experienced in the Falklands, conditions the next day were so rough that the ship's boats were unable to operate. Perhaps this gave Dave opportunities to deal with the enormous pile of mail which had accrued during the voyage – mail which included letters from his two daughters who, in their first years of school, were prolific letter writers and who expected every question to be answered in detail.

After discussion it was decided that the Chinook should be unloaded as a priority but that the unloading should be performed adjacent to the Chinook detachment site at San Carlos. As swiftly as possible, therefore, the *Sir Geraint* set sail for San Carlos Water, a name delivered from obscurity the previous May when Argentine aircraft had attacked ships with British troops trying to land on those hazardous shores. Dave recalled that in the ensuing battle, problems with the Argentine bombs' fuses had meant that over a dozen had failed to detonate. In the chilling words of Marshal of the Royal Air Force Lord Craig: "Six better fuses and we would have lost."

All of this, though, was in the past and now Dave had to concentrate on the delicate task of supervising removal of the Chinook from the deck of the *Sir Geraint*. Operating with very little clearances, another Chinook manoeuvred above the deck. Uneasy glances reflected an air of growing suspense as crew members stared at the proceedings, but in the end the pilot's skilful flying meant that little damage was caused other than a few minor dents.

On completion of the unloading at San Carlos Water, Dave's association with the *Sir Geraint* ended although, without doubt, he had left his mark with the ship's crew. This became evident a week or two later when he happened to be in Stanley. Walking through the town's streets he heard some voices cry out: "Fourth mate...fourth mate...!" At once he turned around to see a group of worried Chinese sailors run up to him. "Fourth mate...we lost...we no find ship..." At this the former fourth mate, greeting his erstwhile crewmen as if long lost friends, led them, like the Pied Piper of Hamelin, through the streets of Stanley to the jetty where a ship's boat was waiting.

As he waved farewell to his Chinese friends, Dave became aware of the distinctive 'wokka' sound made by a Chinook helicopter. He glanced up to see a Chinook flying overhead and he wondered if it was 'his' machine, the one with the tail letter 'BZ' which had been transported on the *Sir Geraint*. He suddenly realised that he felt a particular affinity for this machine. After all, they had come a long way together.

Fire! (from Malcolm 'Mac' McDougall)

CAPTAIN 'MAC' McDOUGALL, as the co-pilot flying a British International Helicopters (BIH) S-61N G-BEID in July 1988, was the first to notice something unusual. The flight from the Safe Felicia oil rig to Sumburgh in the Shetland

Islands had proceeded normally up to that point, and he was unsure if he'd heard or felt something, nonetheless he experienced a strange sensation that all was not well. He glanced at the aircraft commander, Captain Ian Sutherland, and said: "I thought I heard..."

As the two pilots scanned the cockpit instruments they felt quite relaxed at first for the gauges indicated that both engines were matched and functioning normally. No trouble in that department, they thought. Then a fire warning light for the number two engine suddenly illuminated. The cockpit gauges, however, still showed that both engines continued to work normally. The pilots discussed the possibility that the fire warning could be spurious – an electrical malfunction, perhaps. At this point Mac glanced over his right shoulder to check the cabin. As he looked back he saw white smoke swirling down from the roof. "We're on fire, Ian!" he cried.

At once the pilots carried out stipulated drills and Mac turned starboard towards the nearest land. During this turn, and some thirty seconds after completion of the drill for the first emergency, the other engine's fire warning light illuminated. As with the initial case, the cockpit gauges still showed normal readings. The pilots now agreed that, despite the fire warning, they should not shut down this engine which, while running, would allow them to carry out a controlled landing on the sea. At that stage, Ian Sutherland, as the aircraft captain, took over the flight controls. By now an acrid smell of burning had started to waft through to the cockpit from the cabin – a smell which Mac likened to that emitted by faulty electrical equipment and which, even after many years, would continue to haunt him. He opened his cockpit window, gripped his headset in the slipstream, and looked back along the outside of the fuselage. What he saw stunned him – so much so that he experienced stress-related memory-loss for it was only later, when listening to his own voice replayed on G-BEID's recovered cockpit voice recorder (CVR), that he heard his words: "...we are seriously on fire!"

As the two pilots began to prepare for ditching, both suffered emotional seesaws and their thoughts raced when they realised the degree of danger. Any sense of time became oddly distorted: each second seemed more like an hour. Their paramount fear, that the fire would suddenly disable the flight controls, played on both of their minds while they went through the drills...transmit a Mayday radio call...re-check the emergency list...brief the passengers. Mac pulled off his shoes and threw them behind him; he extracted his immersion suit, shook it out and laid it fully extended beside him. "We should select the gear down," said Ian as he operated the undercarriage lever.

"No!" said Mac, raising the undercarriage again, "I've practised water landings in the past. The gear should be up!" Without argument, Ian accepted this. He asked Mac to inflate the sponson floatation bags by which time the S-61N was down to an altitude below one hundred feet. Soon, with an airspeed of about sixty-seven knots – slightly faster than ideal – the final countdown began...fifty feet...nose coming back...forty feet...small amount of cross-wind noted...thirty feet...the sea swell looks significant but manageable...twenty feet...nose coming back a bit more... ten feet... the helicopter is about to...SPLASH...Mac saw a wall of sea water spill up over the forward windscreen as the nose dug in. The helicopter, however, recovered quite quickly to settle into a stable rolling motion on the sea's surface.

"Jettison the rear port door!" Ian now ordered his co-pilot. Mac, though, endured a further psychological block and, as later revealed on the CVR, Ian had to direct his co-pilot's finger to the relevant switch. After this, Mac left his cockpit seat, hastily donned his survival suit and stepped into the cabin. The passengers, he noted, all looked very tense as they sat at the edge of their seats. "Please remain seated while I launch the life raft," he cried – worried that some may start to panic and impede the emergency disembarkation drills. Fortunately this didn't happen and, when summoned, the men filed in a disciplined manner to the helicopter's forward door then jumped into the dinghy. Beyond the third row of passenger seats, however, a wall of thick smoke had formed. Mac attempted to run through this but after a few paces he had to stagger back. Spluttering and choking he shook his head at which Ian yelled: "I'll have a go!" for as aircraft captain he was desperate to help his passengers at the rear of the aircraft. However, he, too, was swiftly forced back. With no choice but to leave these passengers to launch and manage the rear life raft without crew assistance, Ian joined the passengers now ensconced in the front life raft.

Before leaping into this life raft himself, Mac hesitated in the doorway. Leaning forwards, he gazed up at the engine area where the fire appeared to have subsided temporarily, although soon it would resume with a vengeance. This gave him a moment to reflect on final procedures – take the first aid kit, pick up the aircraft documents and torch – when a panic-stricken shriek from one of the passengers was followed by an urgent hand signal from Ian to jump into the dinghy. Mac duly jumped and the dinghy was cast off to be paddled a hundred yards or so from G-BEID. The survivors now watched in awe as the helicopter was gradually consumed by the fire. They heard a mighty crash when the heavy main gearbox fell to the floor. In three distinct explosions, the fuel tanks emitted white balls of sparks when they disintegrated. The sixty-two-feet-diameter main rotor blades were reduced to nothing as they melted and crumbled like wax. It was not long before the tail section alone was recognisable.

At about this stage, survivors in the rear dinghy came into view as they paddled round from the helicopter's port side. Relieved by the sight, Ian confirmed after a quick head-count that all of the passengers were safe. He was told that the electrical jettison mechanism for the rear door had failed so one of the men had pushed out a window then dived into the sea to operate the outside manual-release system. Just now, though, the two dinghies were lashed together after which the twenty-one survivors settled down to wait for rescue. In the surreal situation perhaps they pondered that, in some ways, they were lucky for the sea temperature at fifteen degrees was unseasonably warm, the sea state caused no problems and a BIH S-61N helicopter circling overhead provided a reassuring presence. The pilots may have offered, on reflection, quiet thanks that limited visibility had influenced their decision not to continue towards land for a few more miles: the burning hulk of G-BEID now confirmed that failure of the flight controls before touchdown had indeed been imminent.

After some twenty minutes, when the coastguard S-61N helicopter operated by Bristow Helicopters reached the scene, the crew of four, including Captain Richard Pike as co-pilot, quickly assessed the situation and decided that the survivors should be winched up two at a time. Ian, as G-BEID's captain, wanted to be last up but as the only man without a survival suit he'd started to shiver with cold. The winchman therefore decided to take him up straight away and to leave Mac for last. When dangling on the end of the winch wire, Mac's final glance at G-BEID revealed the machine at an ungainly angle with smoke still pouring from the hulk, an image that would remain with him for a long time. Eventually, after the coastguard helicopter had left, G-BEID slipped below the waves and sank to the seabed.

A week after the accident, Ian and Mac entered a darkened room at the Air Accidents Investigation Branch at Farnborough where the cause of the fire, disintegration of a bearing within the engine, was explained. When they listened to the CVR tape with all of the mechanical sounds and conversations accurately reproduced, the reminders were sufficiently harrowing for them to ask for time out before the debrief was resumed. Both pilots suffered emotional traumas and sleepless nights which, in Mac's case, did not ease for at least two years. Perhaps one of the most surprising aspects was the revelation that the interval between Mac's initial sense that something was wrong to the aircraft's ditching in the sea was just three minutes and eight seconds. Time, assuredly, played tricks on that fateful July day.

Wild Falklands (from Malcolm Harvey)

"BEWARE OF THE ELEPHANT seals," Captain Malcolm Harvey was warned, "they're bad-tempered, belligerent and huge. Some of them weigh over three tons and can be up to six metres long, about a third of the length of your S-61N helicopter!"

Malcolm, who was about to fly a squad of soldiers stationed in the Falkland Islands for a day's rest and recreation, nodded wisely. He planned to take the men to Saunders Island where he'd close down the helicopter and join them while they enjoyed observing the famous wildlife.

Before long, together with his co-pilot and crewman, he started up the S-61N, obtained clearance from air traffic control then took off from Stanley Airfield to fly in a westerly direction. Just a few miles after take-off he overflew Mount Longdon, the site of fierce fighting two years earlier during the Falklands War. As an ex-army pilot, Malcolm had read how the Third Battalion of the Parachute Regiment, led by Lieutenant Colonel Hew Pike, had stormed Mount Longdon to face strong resistance from defending Argentine forces led by Major Carlos Carrizo Salvadores. In dire, hand-to-hand struggles, over fifty men from both sides were killed.

Beyond Mount Longdon, Malcolm flew low over the peaty Falklands terrain which was devoid of roads although settlements were connected by rough, random tracks. To the north, smoke curled upwards from underground peat fires thought to have been started by lightning strikes. The fires smouldered away unchecked for fire-fighting efforts were thwarted by the lack of cost-effective access. As he flew along, Malcolm was impressed by a sense of freedom; beyond life within the settlements, the absence of civilisation was remarkable. Wildlife roamed openly and the local topography looked positively Jurassic, including long stretches of boulders, some up to four kilometres long and several hundred metres wide, which had tumbled down hillsides and were known by Falklanders as 'stone runs'.

When the S-61N approached Falkland Sound, the sea strait that separated East and West Falkland, Malcolm and his co-pilot recalled that a Harrier pilot had been shot down here during the war. Despite serious injuries, the Royal Air Force man, Flight Lieutenant Jeff Glover of Number 1 (F) Squadron, had managed to swim to the surface where he was eventually dragged at gunpoint from the sea by Argentine soldiers in a rowing boat. Taken to Argentina, he became the only British serviceman to be held as a prisoner of war. "The episode was witnessed by locals," said Malcolm, "who apparently watched in helpless horror from Port Howard Settlement which – look! – is over there to our left." He pointed with one finger as he went on: "And ahead we should make out Hill Cove Settlement with Saunders Island beyond."

As this far-flung corner of north-west Falklands came into view, they could see that Saunders Island, the fourth largest in the archipelago and run as a sheep farm, was dominated by Mount Richards at fifteen hundred feet high. Malcolm knew that a potentially tricky issue for pilots was the fickleness of winds inclined to gust fitfully through the island's complex of three peninsulas linked by narrow necks. He headed for a small landing strip on the south-eastern corner of Saunders Island where, after landing and shut-down, he cleared the soldiers to disembark. As the men set off to walk the short distance to settlement houses,

Malcolm and the other crew members worked to secure the S-61N. While they did so, tussock birds hopped in and out of the helicopter's cabin. Noted for their tameness, the birds unashamedly searched for scraps of food while the crew carried out necessary duties. When completed, the three men walked to join the soldiers who by then were in conversation with local residents, including a young woman who agreed to act as a guide to accompany the party to observe the sea lions and other wildlife.

When the group set off, Malcolm reflected that, as settlement folk led lonely and insular lives, they were usually glad to welcome visitors and to have opportunities to describe living conditions on the Falklands. Soon, as the group made for a beach known to be inhabited by sea lions, the guide began to explain some of the particular difficulties that affected Saunders Island. "We're inundated with feral cats, rats, mice and rabbits," she said, "then there's a problem with coastal erosion and we're troubled, too, by spear thistle."

"The national flower of Scotland?" said Malcolm.

"Break into song if you wish," quipped the guide, "but national flower or not, it was introduced here accidentally and now we're struggling to contain it." She indicated at this juncture that the group should slow down. "We'll see some penguins just beyond that sand dune – Gentoo, Southern Rockhopper, Macaroni – there are lots of varieties here. Walk slowly so we don't disturb them."

At the top of the dune, where members of the group stopped to stare at the wild scene across the sandy bay before them, they watched prodigious numbers of penguins as well as terns, striated caracaras, southern petrels, snowy sheath-bills, steamer ducks and many others, most of them squabbling loudly. When the penguins waddled towards the shoreline, sneaky skuas chanced their luck at stealing an unguarded egg or chick. In the sea itself, occasional pods of dolphins leapt through the surf. One specific area of beach seemed to be favoured by the elephant seals, and it was towards there that the group eventually started to walk. "Take it easy," said the guide as she drew near to the great creatures, "though they seem calm today." The ungainly elephant seals remained flopped onto their bellies where they looked like giant grubs. "Tell you what..." went on the guide as she signalled to the others to remain still, "I'll just see..." and stealthily she continued to move forwards alone. Turning for a moment, she looked back at the group then, to gasps of amazement, began to climb onto the monster's monstrous back. "OMG!" cried onlookers, "what the..." and cameras clicked away to capture the crazy scene. In a gesture that seemed to defy the animal's reputation for destructive rampage, she waved cheerily and grinned for the photo shoot.

Merry Christmas (from Richard Pike)

IT WAS NEARLY Christmas Day and, as snug as a bug in a rug, I was in a dream-filled sleep at home when the station alert siren suddenly sounded. A half-moon hung in the sky and the stars shone brilliantly on that cold, pre-dawn morning when I woke with a start. Hastily getting dressed, I then kissed my poor, confused wife and family farewell before brushing past a newly decorated Christmas tree to dash out from our married quarter at the Royal Air Force base at Gütersloh in the Nordrhein-Westfalen region of Germany. Perhaps I should say West Germany for this was in the late 1970s, the Cold War days were as cold as ever and ten long years were due to go by before the iniquitous Iron Curtain collapsed and the Berlin Wall crumbled to dust, like the regime responsible for it all.

When I reached the squadron set-up, hectic activity was underway and as one of the squadron's Westland Wessex pilots (18 Squadron), I had specific tasks to carry out as, along with colleagues, we all prepared for a field exercise close to the East/West German border. The frequency of these exercises seemed relentless and that night, with festive anticipation in the air, everyone appeared more than usually edgy. Even the squadron boss, a wing commander known for his unbounded enthusiasm and ambition, looked a little piqued. Nonetheless, a well-rehearsed system ensured that the squadron, divided into five flights, was soon ready to proceed. Ahead of the helicopters, Land Rovers, four-ton trucks, refuellers and other specialised vehicles drove off in the direction of pre-briefed map references where the five flights ('A' to 'D' and HQ) would establish separate bases.

Some hours elapsed while this was underway but at length a message was received that our 'D' Flight advance party was ready for the helicopters. The engineers, drivers, cooks and others had established a base in a farm close to the border, and the farmer and his family, we'd been assured, were friendly and happy to accept our presence. Now, therefore, the flight's aircrew began to walk out to their allocated Wessex – four of them neatly lined up on the squadron's dispersal area. In company with my crewman for the exercise, a shrewd and practical Irishman called Frank (a senior non-commissioned officer with the rank of master air load-master [MALM]), I carried my bone dome as well as a bulky rucksack packed with paraphernalia including maps, spare clothing, a sleeping bag and a gas mask – all the essentials for our next 'home'. During the helicopter's start-up routines, however, I received a message on the aircraft radio: "Change of plan: you're to fly directly to Tin City then rejoin your flight after tasking there. Acknowledge."

Clouds dappled the December sky and the frozen German landscape looked bleak as we flew towards Tin City, a unit established by the army to train troops in specific techniques including riot control. A mix of flat farmland, large forested areas, the Teutoburger Wald range and other hills moved steadily past as I flew the Wessex at low level so that it was not long before the first signs of Tin City loomed. Set in open countryside, this was no city but a haphazard arrangement of buildings surrounded by a high wall of corrugated iron. When I'd landed the Wessex and closed down the machine, an army captain emerged from one of the buildings. "Have you got gas masks?" was his first question which struck me as a little strange.

"A field exercise has just been called at Gütersloh," I said, "so, yes, we have got them."

The army captain now led us into an operations room where he went on to explain that a training exercise in riot control was underway. "Trouble is," he said, "the participants are getting a bit carried away. We make things as realistic as possible here, but if there's a danger of injury we have to call in the Red Caps – military police – who will use live tear gas rounds before separating the two sides. If this happens you might have to don your gas masks. And you may be needed to pick up a squad of Red Caps to fly them here."

"No problem."

"But there's another thing I'd like to try first. If possible, I'd like you to fly above the compound low and slow. Sometimes this acts as a warning sign."

I readily agreed to this plan and soon, with the army captain occupying the Wessex co-pilot's seat, I lifted the machine into a hover before manoeuvring above the Tin City compound as he directed. "The rioters are doing their thing there, there and there," he pointed, "and they seem to be gaining the upper hand. We have radio contact with the leader of the control team but he says that his men are struggling." We gazed down at men armed with sticks, batons and dustbin lids. There was frenzied movement as individuals rushed from one building to another. "At this point," went on the army captain, "the control team should withdraw and re-group, but it doesn't seem to be happening." I flew towards a group of men and came to a high hover directly above them. Faces looked up to stare at the Wessex then, after some moments, the army captain asked me to fly around the compound a couple more times before returning to land near the operations room.

"Thanks for that," said the army captain after we'd landed. "The control team leader has just called up to say that the helicopter's presence seemed to have the desired effect." The army captain went on to request that we remained on standby in case of further trouble, but by mid-afternoon we were released to join our colleagues at 'D' Flight. The distance, soon covered in a helicopter, was not great nevertheless the December light was beginning to fade as we approached the given grid reference, a wooded area beside a farm. An airman came running out to marshal us towards a safe landing spot and after landing and shut-down he helped us to haul camouflage netting across the Wessex.

That evening, as members of 'D' Flight sat huddled around tables in the mess tent, it was a chance for everyone to relax. Some played cards, chess or back-gammon, some read books, some preferred to chat as they drank copious cups of tea and consumed endless supplies of food. Always up for a blarney, Frank liked to talk about his native Ireland and his varied flying exploits there. One time, he said, he'd been sent with his pilot for an unusual task south of the border. Arrangements had been made for them to land at a civilian airfield to refuel, but before the refuelling they had to close down the Wessex to fill in necessary paperwork. They'd just started up again to move to the refuelling spot when a man came running towards the helicopter. "Watch out," Frank had said to his pilot, "looks like trouble."

"I must talk to your pilot," said the man who seemed in a fluster as he entered the Wessex cabin and gesticulated to Frank. Headset clamped to head, the man then spoke with the pilot on the aircraft intercommunications system: "Flight lieutenant," he said, "there's an inspector in the office here, sir."

"An inspector of what?"

"I forgot to ask. He looks quite inspector-ish, though."

"But what does he want to inspect?"

"Why your aircraft documents, sir."

At this, the flight lieutenant leant across, extracted all the documents he could find and handed them to the messenger. "I'm about to fly over to the refuelling spot," he said.

"You know where to go, sir?"

"I think so, it's over there," said the flight lieutenant, pointing.

"That's correct, sir, that's quite correct. You see that pole thing sticking up? Well aim for that then turn left a bit, turn left a bit more and a bit more and you should find what you seek." At this, the messenger left the cockpit and scampered back towards the hangar. The flight lieutenant, meanwhile, spoke to the air traffic controller who cleared him to hover-taxi to the refuelling point. Just as he reached the refuelling point, however, the controller transmitted another instruction: "Shut down immediately and stay with the aircraft!"

Shortly after he'd complied with this latest instruction, the flight lieutenant saw a vehicle race up to the helicopter and screech to a halt. The same messenger as before jumped out of the vehicle and ran up to the Wessex. "Flight lieutenant," he said, "you're to come with me."

"Am I to be arrested this time? Clapped in irons? Sent to..."

"It's that inspector fellow, sir. He wants to see you."

"What's wrong now?"

As they drove up to the company hangar, Frank and his pilot saw the airfield manager come out to meet them. "Don't ask!" said the manager, rolling his eyes skywards. "Just put on your hat, flight lieutenant, look meek, agree with everything that's said, otherwise I suggest that you keep quiet and follow me!" The manager now led the flight lieutenant into an office where, sitting behind a desk, an inspector-ish looking fellow with a fierce facial expression glared at him.

"Flight lieutenant," said the inspector, "I gather you've been flying that Wessex parked over there – over there by the refuelling spot."

"That's correct, sir, that's quite correct," said the flight lieutenant.

"Were you not aware of a serious omission before you got airborne? You've been flying without copies of important aircraft documents on board which makes it an illegal flight."

"Is that so, sir?"

"Indeed it is – why, look! I have the documents right here, right here on my desk."

"Well I'll be blowed," said the flight lieutenant. "Tut, tut. How on earth did that happen, I wonder?"

Amidst widespread hilarity and the camaraderie for which service life was well known, a few more tales from Frank and others kept us entertained until all agreed that it was time to turn in. "It's a dawn start for us tomorrow," said the flight commander. As Frank and I headed for the two-man tent we'd assembled earlier, we relied on our service-issue torches, green-lensed for tactical concealment, as we stumbled around in the dark.

Eventually ensconced in my sleeping bag, many thoughts went through my mind. I thought about today's rude awakening, the subsequent hectic activity, the flight to Tin City, the relentlessness of these field exercises. I thought about the time a few months earlier when I was at home loading the washing machine with the aftermath of another field exercise called 'Pegout'. When the telephone rang I heard my wife's voice as she answered. I thought of our five-year-old daughter as she came running through to me to say something about: 'Mummy sad'. When I went to see what was happening, my wife put her arms around my neck. Her face was pale and drawn, her expression one of disbelief. I thought about the potent image of our two young children staring in bemusement as, between sobs, their mum explained that her own mother had been given just twenty-four hours to live following a stroke, a medical prediction which turned out to be accurate. I thought about the way that the military life, if tough for the serviceman and servicewoman, could be tough for the families too. I thought about my immediate situation, the damp, the cold, the aircrewman in the camp bed next to mine, an aircrewman who had just started to snore...

"Merry Christmas, Frank."

CHAPTER 18
HEROIC RESCUE

Malcolm Soper's emergency callout

RUDELY AWAKENED, Captain Malcolm Soper eyed the telephone sceptically. The tiresome ring, however, was insistent. He glanced at his bedside clock: 0220. After a long and difficult day at work, he'd been at home for around two hours and right now, he mused, he felt less than enthusiastic about being dragged from his bed. The telephone, though, continued to ring and ring. Eventually relenting, he lifted the receiver. "Very sorry to disturb you, Malcolm," said the duty controller at the Aberdeen base of Bristow Helicopters, "but an offshore emergency has arisen. The Transworld 58 oil rig has been dragging its anchors in these gales and heavy seas. They're worried that it might break free and collide with other installations."

"So we need to evacuate personnel?"

"I'm afraid so."

"Okay. I'll be in as soon as I can."

On the drive through Aberdeen's deserted streets on that dark November night in 1981, Malcolm had many things running through his mind. He felt very tired – exhausted – and he was well outside normal crew duty limits. However, the rules changed in emergency situations when decisions were pretty much left to the discretion of the aircraft captain. As a S-61N pilot of many years experience and as one of the few captains immediately available at the Bristow's Aberdeen operation who was qualified to carry out winching on search and rescue missions, he was an obvious choice. From the way that his car was buffeted during the drive he knew that conditions out there were rough. With the Transworld 58 positioned way out in the North Sea nearly two hundred miles from Aberdeen, matters would be a whole lot worse. Clearly this was a life or death situation.

Still deep in thought, Malcolm parked his car at the Aberdeen heliport, hastened with his head bowed against the strong winds to the company buildings, then paced upstairs two steps at a time towards the flight planning room. The room, normally a hive of activity, was eerily empty apart from the duty controller who'd phoned him. "Evening, Jim," said the ever-affable Malcolm as he strode up to the duty controller, "any update?"

"It's not looking good, Malcolm," said Jim. "Very sorry to have to call you after such a long day yesterday, but the Transworld 58 radio operator has just transmitted another urgent request for help."

"Okay. I'll get on with the flight planning."

"Your co-pilot, Bob Bolton-King, is on his way. Also another captain and co-pilot – Andy and John – though they're not qualified for search and rescue winching."

"Two S-61Ns required, then. Will winching be necessary?"

"We're not sure – maybe, maybe not. In case it is, the engineers have allocated you a winch-equipped aircraft and your crewmen for the flight will be Colin and Chris."

Working rapidly at the flight planning details, Malcolm let out the occasional whistle of surprise as his calculations produced unusual figures. The S-61N's normal operating limit was sixty knots, but with that night's reported wind speeds of up to ninety knots and with the wind blowing from a north-westerly direction, the helicopters would reach the Transworld 58 very quickly. The problem, though, was the return. "Our best option will be to divert to Norway," Malcolm briefed his co-pilot who by now had hurried into the flight planning room along with the other crew members.

It was during these planning procedures that Jim called out from the radio room: "Malcolm...Andy...a word, please!" The two captains went across as requested. "I've just received another urgent call from the Transworld 58," said Jim. "Their worst fears have come true: the rig has broken away from its anchorage and is now drifting out of control."

Malcolm, as the senior captain, called together the other crew members to explain the situation: "If anyone wishes to stand down, that is entirely their prerogative," he said. "For my part, I'm prepared to have a shot, but there'll be no criticism of any individual who doesn't volunteer to fly in these conditions." Malcolm then looked at each of the five men in turn. With five nods of assent, Malcolm went on: "Thank you gentlemen. The decision is unanimous. We'll wait for a further update from the Transworld 58 then get going."

So it was that, shortly before 0600, and after difficulty starting the helicopters' rotors because of their tendency to 'sail' in high winds, the two S-61Ns set off on their marathon task with a fifteen-minute interval between take-offs. Violent gusts caused frequent and ominous clattering sounds from the main rotor blades, and sea salt whipped from wave tops began to accumulate on the windshields, a hazard not alleviated by the windshield wipers which caused smearing when operated. Huge waves, illuminated by occasional use of the helicopters' landing lights, looked spectacular as they were swept along by the gales.

After a little over one hour, Malcolm's co-pilot made radio contact with the Transworld 58's radio operator who confirmed that the oil rig was still drifting out of control. "Any more bad news to report?" quipped the co-pilot.

"Yes, skipper," said the radio operator, "no good news, just bad. Very bad. We're well beyond pitch and roll limits for landing, and even if you do land we can't refuel you because our refuelling equipment has been blown overboard!"

Malcolm thought about this for a moment before saying to his co-pilot: "Tell them we'll attempt to land anyway. We'll then fly to another installation to refuel."

For his initial attempt at landing, Malcolm was hampered by poor visibility which forced him to overshoot. For his second attempt, a temporary improvement in the visibility allowed him to hold a high hover to one side of the Transworld 58 while he assessed the situation. He was worried that the S-61N's powerful down-draught would cause debris to fly about. He therefore radioed instructions that the helideck should be cleared of all personnel. He was fearful, too, that the helideck's movement might cause the S-61N to slide about although he noticed periods when the movement was less extreme and it was this, he realised, that would offer the best chance of success.

Manoeuvring judiciously, Malcolm flew the helicopter towards the helideck. Guided by his winch operator he aimed to hold a hover directly above the landing spot marked by a yellow-coloured 'H'. When there he maintained the hover until he judged that the rig's movement was less severe. He then lowered the collective lever firmly to place the S-61N in the exact centre of the 'H'. As his co-pilot later said: "It was a superb bit of piloting and I remember watching the movement of the artificial horizon in total disbelief once we were on the helideck."

The next stage was crucial: would the helicopter hold its position so that personnel could move safely around the helideck? At length, and no doubt amid great sighs of relief, Malcolm decided that it was safe to permit the passengers to board one person at a time.

The first passenger, wearing a bright-orange survival suit zipped-up to the neck, appeared on the helideck. Bending low, this man then crawled on hands and knees as he grabbed the thick rope that covered the helideck. Hand over hand, he dragged himself towards the helicopter where, stationed by the S-61N's air-stair door, the two burly aircrewman hauled him aboard before signalling that the next man should follow. In this way, all the passengers coped successfully with the unconventional boarding procedure, although one man had to be helped when he became entangled in the rope netting. Eventually, and with the cabin seats all occupied, Malcolm was anxious to depart without delay. By now the other S-61N had arrived and the captain was holding a hover to one side of the oil rig. He acknowledged Bob's take-off call after which Malcolm swiftly lifted the S-61N and set heading towards an installation some twenty miles away where he planned to refuel. The second S-61N, after a similarly difficult passenger pick-up at the Transworld 58, then refuelled at a different installation.

At both installations the refuelling process required unusual procedures. The helideck crews were doubled up to move in pairs for mutual support as they crawled around on hands and knees, and three men were needed to drag the refuelling hose to the helicopter's refuelling point. With the process completed Malcolm handed over the flight controls to his co-pilot for the transit to Stavangar in Norway: "Fly at two thousand feet initially, Bob," he said, "but if the wind veers we may have to descend."

With the winds from a north-westerly direction, at first the flight calculations worked as planned. However, as the flight progressed towards Norway the wind changed to a more northerly direction thus reducing the S-61N's ground speed. The wind continued to veer and Malcolm's new calculations revealed that the helicopter's fuel reserves may be insufficient to reach land. To add to their problems, the helicopter's navigation aids failed and radio contact was lost. Reduced to 'dead reckoning' navigation techniques with estimated compass headings and the use of a stop watch to time the distances covered, the prospects looked increasingly bleak. Malcolm, though, was keen not to worry the passengers. "Turn round and smile cheerfully at our passengers, Bob," he said to his co-pilot, "let's at least try to give the impression that everything's okay."

Malcolm decided to take over the flight controls again. He descended to a height of three hundred feet (any lower height caused an excessive build-up of sea salt) and he flew at an airspeed well above the S-61N's stipulated maximum limit; this was their only hope of reaching land before the helicopter ran out of fuel. Glancing down, the sight of giant waves and seaborne flotsam sent a shiver down his spine. With nature in charge, a tenuous destiny awaited if they were forced to ditch in these seas where the helicopter's emergency life rafts would overturn all too readily.

Nonetheless, an intrepid character with a naval background, Malcolm pressed on determinedly. He was not the type to give up and his spirits lifted when one of the S-61's navigation systems suddenly showed signs of life: the needle within a cockpit radio-positioning indicator had ceased its interminable rotation. The needle now pointed on a steady heading towards a selected beacon. At last there was some navigational guidance and the beacon verified that the helicopter was reasonably on track. "There's hope yet!" said Bob as he continued to re-calculate their dead-reckoning navigation for he still had no information about distance to run. Malcolm made a small heading adjustment and he gazed ahead for signs of land. This came without warning for in the very poor visibility it was not until the S-61N had virtually crossed the Norwegian coastline that he realised that safety had been reached. With a sigh of relief, now he knew that if the fuel ran out he'd not be forced into a sea ditching.

It was not long before Bob managed to establish radio contact with air traffic control at Stavanger. The controller confirmed the helicopter's position and he gave priority over other air traffic for by this stage the S-61N's low fuel warning lights had started to flash. This was a rare sight: the helicopters normally operated within strict safety parameters with plentiful reserves. And to add to the crew's anxieties, they knew that the fuel gauges tended to be less reliable at very low levels, a problem exacerbated by the heavy turbulence which caused the needles to flick back and forth erratically. Malcolm decided, therefore, to run one of the engines at a slightly lower fuel level: if this engine stopped he planned to use the other for a controlled landing onto the nearest field. "Keep smiling," Malcolm repeated to his crew: he saw no point in causing unnecessary worry to the passengers.

This, certainly, proved to be a prudent plan for when Stavanger airfield at last came into sight and when Malcolm landed there, both engines were still functioning. He parked the helicopter and as the passengers were cleared to disembark, their nods of thanks, thumbs-up signs and smiles of relieved gratitude revealed genuine appreciation. Malcolm and his colleagues were relieved, too, when told that the other S-61N had just reached Stavanger safely. They heard that all of the Transworld 58 personnel had been rescued apart from a skeleton crew left on board, meanwhile the rig itself had cleared potential collision risks and was riding out the storm. With this news, Malcolm and his colleagues were able to relax at last. Shown to a crew room, they sank into armchairs and gratefully accepted mugs of strong Norwegian coffee.

As he sat quietly sipping his coffee, Malcolm's mind was far from restful. He thought about the coincidence of timing when, twenty-one years earlier to the day, he had ejected from a naval Sea Hawk aircraft into the North Sea. He thought of another coincidence of timing for today was his birthday. He thought about the temperamental Decca and other navigation systems currently fitted to the S-61N, how these seemed to work fine under normal circumstances but failed in bad conditions – the very time when most needed. He thought of the unreliable weather forecasts, how these had misled the crews who, if properly informed, would have arranged a second offshore refuel en route to Norway. He thought of the bravery and commitment of his colleagues, of how, to a man, they had volunteered even though they had every right to refuse the flight…

Suddenly, rushing into the crew room, an agitated member of airport staff asked: "Who is Captain Soper – captain of one of the helicopters parked outside?"

"I am," said Malcolm.

"Sir…you need to come with me urgently."

As Malcolm ran outside he was reminded that the stormy conditions had yet to abate for he had to bend low against the gales. When he looked ahead he was astonished to see that one of the blades of his S-61N had fractured in the strong winds. Despite tie-down ropes, the blade's tip had broken off and fallen to the ground. He could barely believe what he saw: these metal blades were designed to withstand the severest conditions and in theory just would not break in that way. He gazed in wonder for some moments, then he noticed that the rotor blades of the S-61N parked next to his had started to move. Realising that the machine might become unstable and collide with his own, he dashed across, entered the cockpit, sat down in the captain's seat and re-set the rotor brake.

Deciding to remain seated for some moments while he monitored events, Malcolm noticed that some light aircaft about four hundred yards from his position had started to rock vigorously. Despite sturdy ground tethering, the light aircraft were affected by an approaching line squall with associated wind speeds which Malcolm reckoned were in excess of one hundred knots. He made a mental note that if one or more broke free, he'd dash to the back of his helicopter as the best place for self-preservation. Remaining in the cockpit for the present, however, he heard the howl of the wind increase to a shriek as the line squall approached. Suddenly, the S-61N's flight controls, despite hydraulic locking, began to thrash around. Malcolm grabbed the controls and as he did so he saw to his alarm that the rotor blade immediately in front of him was bending upwards, almost to the vertical. The restraining rope snapped; the blade was then flung downwards so that the tip touched the ground. Now the blade sailed upwards again, then down, then up – a cycle of movement repeated several times until, with a loud *craaack,* the blade fractured and its tip crashed to the ground.

It was later, when he spoke with the Stavanger air traffic controller, that Malcolm was told that the wind speeds had increased from a relatively gentle ninety knots to over one hundred and forty knots in the line squall.

By the time new rotor blades were sent along with a team of engineers, the storm had eased. Both S-61Ns were repaired and flown back to Aberdeen. After their return, all six members of aircrew involved in the Transworld 58 rescue flight were invited, along with their wives or partners, to a convention held in Miami, Florida. The aircrew were jointly honoured with the Avco-Lycoming Helicopter Heroism Award in conjunction with the Aviation and Space Writers of America.

Author's note: *with sincere thanks to Mrs Jenny Soper for her co-operation with this chapter on her late husband Captain Malcolm Soper.*

CHAPTER 19
FALKLANDS FEATS

Alan Boulden's South Atlantic experiences

"THEY – THE CRABS I mean – will have to go there…" the Royal Navy captain pointed impatiently. Flight Lieutenant Alan Boulden, who'd overheard this remark, remained silent despite the uneasy feeling that surged within him. The captain glanced back and went on: "I'm sorry," he said as he spotted Alan, "but all of the cabins are currently occupied by naval officers." As the man in charge of military personnel on the MV *Atlantic Conveyor,* the captain had the final word when it came to the contentious issue of allocating accommodation. "You'll be on the aft upper decking," he said to Alan who, as the senior Royal Air Force officer on board, felt less than impressed by this announcement. The unspoken implication, that members of the Royal Navy enjoyed priority over the Royal Air Force ('crabs' in naval parlance), was hardly likely, he reckoned, to encourage respectful relationships with an atmosphere of hearty co-operation. Furthermore, when Alan's accommodation turned out to be a Portakabin welded to the deck, and when it proved to be crowded with an eclectic mix of personnel including three Chinese laundry men (who, parenthetically, made a small fortune from the ship's company), his spirits were hardly lifted.

However, on that late April day in 1982, if Alan felt instant antipathy towards the Royal Navy captain, the opposite turned out to be the case for the *Atlantic Conveyor's* master, Captain Ian North. Affectionately known as 'Captain Birdseye' (his resemblance to the man in a certain fish fingers' advertisement was uncanny), fifty-seven-year-old Captain North was a mariner of great experience. Alan learned that Captain North first went to sea in 1939 and that he was held in high regard as one of the best masters in the Cunard fleet. Evidently when the *Atlantic Conveyor* was requisitioned for the Falklands campaign, all of his crew volunteered.

It was shortly before the *Atlantic Conveyor* set sail on 25 April 1982 that Alan was ordered to fly a shuttle of two Boeing Chinook helicopters onto the ship to join other aircraft which had already been delivered. After this, he was instructed to remain on board as a member of the hundred-ship task force destined for the South Atlantic. When the Chinooks had landed (a tricky exercise in the confined conditions), the helicopter's mighty main rotor blades had to be removed because, unlike naval machines, there was no blade-fold facility. Each of the six blades was heavy and the procedure, complex under normal circumstances, was fraught with difficulty on the *Atlantic Conveyor's* restricted deck. Halfway through the de-blading of the second Chinook, Alan and his colleagues felt the ship lurch as it was cast off. The hazards now multiplied so Alan rushed up to the bridge to speak with the Royal Naval captain. "My engineers are really struggling, sir," he said, "and we risk damaging the Chinooks." "The task force has been ordered to set sail," said the captain sternly, "your men will just have to get on with it."

The air force men, therefore, did 'get on with it', fortunately without injury or damage, but the incident hardly helped to improve Alan's opinion of the naval 'four ringer'. If he found himself fuming, perhaps he sought solace in conversations with Captain North for as the passage from Devonport, Plymouth, to Ascension Island got underway, a voyage of just under two weeks, Alan seemed to spend many of his days on the bridge chatting with the master. One time, Captain North explained some of the unusual aspects when merchant vessels were requisitioned. "For instance," he said, "my civilian crew, just as with the Royal Navy personnel on board, come under the naval discipline act." Then there was the issue of 'split captaincy'. While the ship's master had greater expertise at sailing his ship, the Royal Navy captain knew more about naval warfare. "A good working relationship between the two of us," said Captain North, "is therefore rather important."

The task force made progress in generally good weather apart from one day when a storm blew up. The sea's surface that day was streaked with foam which Alan observed with a sense of awe. When waves reached up so that their white froth, caught by the wind, was whipped against the side of the ship, perhaps he reminded himself that the *Atlantic Conveyor*, a twelve-year-old merchant container and vehicle transporter, was a structure of near fifteen thousand tons, intrinsically stable, as tough as old boots, an engineering feat designed to stay afloat under the most adverse conditions. If he ventured outside to walk along the deck, he had to grip handrails. Nature, he realised, could put on a thrilling show. The elements provided an earthquake of the senses which even the most dramatic Hollywood film could not replicate. He'd watch the ship climb each giant swell then hang at the crest before a sudden drop made the whole hull judder. From within the ship, deep structural groans created an eerie symphony. When the largest swells crashed through the ship's railings, the sea water would bounce off the superstructure to send up spectacular fountains of spray. Crew members caught in the maelstrom had to tense their bodies to take the blows as water cascaded from the deck to tumble in a rush of grumbles and gurgles towards scuppers.

At one point during the storm a violent lurch caused a bladder tank on the forward decking to rupture. The tank's contents, thousands of gallons of aviation fuel, began to spill across the deck, alarmingly close to aircraft, until the mixture of fuel and sea began to drain slowly overboard. As there was little that could be done, Alan headed back to the bridge where Captain Birdseye appeared unperturbed. The waters persisted to rage, froth, and surge against his ship like a riotous crowd, but he took the situation in his stride. Captain Birdseye had seen it all before.

The following day, as was typical of the mercurial conditions experienced by mariners, the sea had calmed, the storm had passed and the *Atlantic Conveyor*, as if with a shrug of the shoulders at all the fuss, proceeded serenely onwards. The feeling of comparative safety, the glory of the light, the stillness in the air provided a contrast that could seem surreal. Now, though, with the need to refuel, the ship headed for Freetown, the port city and capital of Sierra Leone. The ship's crew, banned from visits to Freetown with its tempting bars and discos at the likes of Lumley Beach, were prudently kept on board and the ship soon resumed its passage to Ascension.

It was early May when Alan and his colleagues first spotted the distant outline of Green Mountain, the near-three thousand feet high point of Ascension Island. By this stage Alan had been briefed on the procedure for so-called cross-decking, the process whereby equipment was transferred from one ship to another in order to reorganise the disarray created by the task force's hasty departure from the United Kingdom. Planners now wanted to ensure optimum 'tactical unloading' when the war zone was reached and, as part of this, Alan was ordered off the *Atlantic Conveyor* to fly a Chinook for the cross-decking process. When completed, and in a move that would have profound implications, he was ordered to remain at Ascension to help with the second wave of ships destined for the South Atlantic.

When the task force set sail again, Alan's first assignment was to fly a Chinook to the peak of Green Mountain as part of plans to install an air defence radar unit. Access to the mountain peak, which was covered by the only tropical vegetation in the island's barren, volcanic landscape, was limited. The radar system, though, was seen as necessary because in theory it was possible for Argentine forces to launch an attack. When a site had been selected and prepared, Alan flew his Chinook with the radar equipment underslung then, after judicious manoeuvring, released his load following which the unit was soon installed and operational.

As Ascension's role in the Falklands War became increasingly significant, the stage was reached when the air base (Wideawake) became one of the world's busiest airfields with up to four hundred movements of all types each day. Alan flew regularly to ships, most of which were anchored a mile or two off the Ascension coast. A notable exception, however, was the *Queen Elizabeth 2 (QE2)* which arrived at Ascension with three thousand troops of the Fifth Infantry Brigade as well as six hundred and fifty volunteer crew members. The ship's master had been ordered to remain beyond the visible horizon as the British government did not wish to advertise the *QE2's* involvement in the war. Alan was briefed that, as part of the ship's preparation for war service, a refit at Southampton had included installation of two helicopter landing pads. He learnt, too, that fuel pipes had been installed through the ship directly to the engine room to facilitate refuelling at sea. Other modifications had included the transformation of public lounges into dormitories, the laying of some two thousand sheets of hardboard to cover the ship's carpets, a section of hull reinforced with steel plating, and anti-mine precautions. "All sorties to the *QE2* must be flown in radio silence," said the briefing officer.

"Does this apply to any other ships?"

"No, just the *QE2.* Be aware, too, that the ship has been blacked out and its radar has been switched off." Surprised by this, Alan realised the reason on his first sortie: not too far away he noticed a vessel with Soviet markings and festooned with aerials.

On 25 May Alan and his colleagues received the news that, in the vicinity of the Falklands San Carlos Water, HMS *Coventry* had been sunk by A-4 Skyhawks of the Argentine air force. Shocked by this, Alan then heard the further news that the *Atlantic Conveyor* – 'his' ship – had been struck.

Later, he learned that it was early evening when the air raid warning was sounded and Captain Birdseye had ordered an immediate turn through forty degrees to present the *Atlantic Conveyor's* strong stern doors towards the direction of threat. The 'emergency stations' signal was piped and the ship's siren was sounded. An air of growing suspense must have been palpable as Captain Birdseye on the bridge frantically focused binoculars in the direction of the threat. A minute ticked by. All watched, all waited. Naval ships in the vicinity fired off chaff decoys, but the *Atlantic Conveyor's* crew had none to fire off. A Sea Harrier combat air patrol was launched from HMS *Invincible.* Another minute ticked by but two pilots, Captain Curilovic and Lieutenant Barraza of the Argentine navy, now had the *Atlantic Conveyor* in their sights.

The time was 7.42 p.m. when the *Atlantic Conveyor* was struck by two AM39 air-launched Exocet missiles fired by two Super Étendard fighter aircraft. The missiles penetrated the ship's main cargo deck causing a fireball to sweep through the structure. The ship, though, lacked the damage-control systems fitted to warships and the fire proved impossible to suppress. Thirty minutes after the missiles struck, she was abandoned. Most of the crew members were rescued from the water, including the Royal Naval 'four ringer'. However, a dozen of the ship's company died that night, men whose circumstances might have been dictated by the flip of a coin or by drawing straws, men who included Captain

Birdseye and the three Chinese laundry men. The latter's profitable takings ultimately proved tragically pointless. Although Captain Birdseye had evacuated the ship successfully, by the time rescue reached him he'd succumbed to the waves. If there are places on earth where people away from the bustle of city existence learn the truth of man's fragility, one of these must surely be within the pitiless clutches of a seething Southern Atlantic Ocean.

In moments of solitude, Alan would try to recall his conversations with Captain Birdseye, the intriguing accounts, some humorous, some not, all of them enthralling as the sum of long experience at sea. Posthumously awarded the Distinguished Service Cross, the ship's master had finally found a new place and now Alan realised just how deeply he'd been moved by the loss of his friend.

Two months later
Some two weeks after the Argentine surrender on 14 June 1982, Alan reached San Carlos Water. He arrived as a passenger on board the MV *Astronomer,* a container ship and former 'lift-on, lift-off' ferry converted to an aircraft transport vessel. As all but one of the Chinooks he'd helped to load onto the *Atlantic Conveyor* had been destroyed, the *Astronomer* was packed with replacements. The one surviving Chinook from that traumatic night, aircraft 'BN', by chance had been airborne for an air test. Since then, this aircraft had flown many hours and now needed expeditious support.

When Alan started up his Chinook on the *Astronomer,* a technical fault became evident. He knew, though, that rectification there and then would create problems. After discussion with his co-pilot the two agreed that they could operate the helicopter safely, if with difficulty. Alan announced all of this on the aircraft radio, perhaps with a slight air of hubris, after which he was soon airborne to fly the machine to the Chinook detachment site at San Carlos. After landing, however, he felt abashed when he realised that most of the helicopters there were operating in a far worse state than his Chinook. All of the machines had been in more or less perpetual use with just emergency servicing. 'BN' was no exception and continued to be flown without a pilot's door.

Later, Alan learnt details of the war mission which had led to the loss of the door. The crew were tasked to fly 105-mm howitzers to a Special Air Service unit pinned down by enemy fire. Assured that the landing site was flat and secure, the pilots were briefed for a night operation using specialised night-vision goggles. Three of the howitzers would be transported inside the helicopter while ammunition pallets were carried underslung. The Chinook pilots took off as planned and encountered no problems en route but the landing site, when reached, proved to be covered in boulders and far from flat. In the words of the co-pilot: "Then the fog of war intervened." With nowhere suitable to land, the pilots spent time manoeuvring to an appropriate spot to drop the underslung ammunition pallets. As the artillery guns already on site were hard to move on the rough terrain, the pallets had to be dropped in exactly the right place. "I distinctly remember troops firing their weapons as they ran around under the rotors," the co-pilot reported later, "which was not part of the plan." The pilots nonetheless managed to drop their load before flying back to San Carlos to pick up more guns and ammunition. However, during the approach to Teal Inlet, the Chinook hit the sea. A bow wave came over the cockpit window and the engines partially flamed out but, remarkably, wound up again. The pilots were able to climb away successfully but had to jettison a damaged door. Eventually the door was replaced, but by unconventional means (a door 'borrowed' from an Argentine Chinook abandoned at Stanley).

Alan and his colleagues were soon established at the San Carlos base after which they began a routine of intense flying for the next few months with the Chinooks programmed from dawn to dusk. Crews regularly achieved seven flying hours a day after which, exhausted, they retired to sleep in the accommodation provided at San Carlos – pens of sheep sheds with two or three aircrew per pen. This was no Shangri-La and the area was hardly flush with plush places awarded five stars – other than those above which, incidentally, shone with particular brilliance in the clear, pollution-free skies of the southern hemisphere. Perhaps surprised by their own capacity for inventiveness, the crews' earthly comfort levels were ingeniously improved by occasional items acquired from cargo carried in the Chinooks. Next to each man's bed, ex-Argentine ammunition boxes made convenient lockers to store individual treasure. Alan recalled how one young pilot developed, bizarrely, a torch fetish and liked to fill his Argentine ammunition box with countless numbers of torches. The circumstances of that anomalous environment evidently affected different people in different ways.

One afternoon in mid July (the depths of winter in the Falklands), Alan's tasking for the day was nearly over when he received an urgent 'all stations' message. Available helicopters were required to converge on Stanley to assist with an evacuation. Evidently soldiers from the Seventh Gurkha rifles were unable to reach their accommodation (a ship moored in Stanley Harbour) because the harbour master had decreed that stormy conditions were too dangerous for the small boats normally used to ferry the men. Faced with the prospect of hundreds of men spending the winter night on land in the open air, the powers that be decided to summon help from the Chinooks. All were anxious to complete the task before nightfall, so the timing was tight. The large loads which the powerful Chinook could carry meant that the soldiers were squeezed aboard like sardines in a can. One time, when given the call by his crewman: "Clear above and behind...you're clear to lift," Alan routinely asked for the number on board. He expected between twenty to thirty men so was surprised when the crewman replied: "I've absolutely no idea."

"What none at all?"

"Afraid not. I lost count after ninety!"

Eventually, so-called accommodation coastels were chartered. Prepared in the United Kingdom, the coastels were towed to the Falklands together with a pre-fabricated walkway to allow troops to walk aboard directly. One time, Alan was intrigued to hear a conversation on the aircraft radio between the coastel's ground staff and some recently arrived instructors from the Chinook operational conversion unit. The instructors had been asked to manoeuvre their Chinook to help reposition the coastel's walkway. "Sorry, but it's too heavy," said the instructors eventually. What nonsense, thought Alan, that walkway's not heavy – maybe a couple of tons – easy for a Chinook. With dark, if unkind, thoughts along the lines: 'those that can do, those that can't teach' he was later about to remonstrate with the instructors when he heard a small but significant detail. The walkway had been welded to the coastel for the sea transit. Even a Chinook would struggle to lift the entire coastel.

Over the next few years Alan returned to the Falklands several times, initially on Chinooks, then later as a search and rescue pilot on Westland Sea Kings. The Sea King and Chinook units in the Falkland Islands were combined and re-designated 78 Squadron when Royal Air Force Mount Pleasant was opened. Although the brand new accommodation at Mount Pleasant offered the benefits of a cinema, gymnasium, swimming pool and comfortable rooms, Alan reflected that his best memories were from the days of Port San Carlos and the sheep sheds with their rough, tough ammunition boxes and that torch collection. The new set-up undoubtedly deserved a star or two, nevertheless the spirit of cama-raderie he'd experienced at Port San Carlos was something, he knew, that was worth more than any number of stars.

CHAPTER 20
BALKAN BURDENS

David Lanigan in Croatia

"A CRUCIAL BUT uneasy truce," said the briefing officer, "is the best way to describe this current ceasefire in Yugoslavia." Seated in the briefing room and listening intently were members of the Dutch company KLM/ERA which had been awarded a United Nations contract to operate two S-61N helicopters in Yugoslavia. The helicopters were needed to carry UN personnel and equipment involved with monitoring the ceasefire, and as part of background inductions the briefing officer was explaining the significance of the company's role. One of those listening was Captain David Lanigan, a former search and rescue pilot recently employed by KLM/ERA as a first officer for the period of the contract. It was now spring 1994 but some months earlier David had spotted a newspaper advertisement announcing the need for pilots for the contract. At the age of fifty-two he was seven years older than the maximum stipulated in the advertisement but this was waived in view of his past experience. Later, he learnt that KLM/ERA managers had struggled to find enough pilots; evidently the company's own union-dominated pilots had not considered a military-orientated operation in Yugoslavia to be to their liking preferring instead to stick to their secure way of life based at Schiphol in the Netherlands from where they flew out to North Sea gas installations.

"Both of your helicopters will be based in Croatia," went on the briefing officer, "at Zagreb in the north, and Split in the south. As you may know, the independence of Croatia was recognised officially a couple of years ago, in January 1992, and current boundaries across the former Yugoslavia will have implications for your flying routines." David thought about this, about the region's complex layers of division, the resultant intense passions displayed by local folk. Regrettably, he mused, truth appeared to be distorted by rumour, facts veiled in allegory. He'd read about the political upheavals and conflicts which, over the last few years, had led to the disintegration of Yugoslavia's federation of six republics – Bosnia and Herzegovina, Croatia, Macedonia, Montenegro, Serbia and Slovenia. He was aware that with the death of President Josip Tito in 1980 Yugoslavia had lost a key unifying figure and that unsolved issues now persisted to cause bitter inter-ethnic fighting with explosive consequences – a cycle of revolution, xenophobia and violence which seemed to be repeated in an endless sequence as if trapped within some apocalyptic odyssey.

"With the federation of Yugoslavia now in the process of dissolution," said the briefing officer, "borders between newly formed independent states will have to be recognised as international borders. This, naturally, will complicate the peacekeeping task of the United Nations although plans have been made to ease, hopefully, the progression of your flights across the region's nascent air traffic control regimes." The briefing officer went on to explain that the UN force, known by the acronym UNPROFOR (United Nations Protection Force), was formed two years earlier in February 1992 with nearly thirty-nine thousand personnel from some forty different nations including, for example, Argentina, Canada, Kenya, Nepal, Russia, the Netherlands, the United States and the United Kingdom. "De-militarised safe havens, ceasefire lines and so-called pink zones, have been set up to try to establish suitable conditions for ongoing peace talks, and you will be flying across and into these areas."

The briefing continued and others followed but eventually, when concluded, it was not long before the KLM/ERA flying operations commenced. So it was that David, with the elaborate background information no doubt uppermost in his mind, was tasked one day to fly due south from the company base at Zagreb to a position near the town of Knin, a distance of some one hundred and fifty nautical miles. While his aircraft captain checked and signed the technical log, David carried out external checks on the white-painted S-61N. As he did so, streams of sunlight cast strong shadows although he noted that the airfield's fine weather contrasted with cloud build-ups over distant mountains.

Soon, with the helicopter's engines and rotors running smoothly, and with clearance from the duty air traffic controller, the captain manoeuvred the S-61N away from the dispersal area towards the runway take-off point. Various aircraft types were passed in the process, including a line-up of the ubiquitous Bell 212 operated by the United States military, and a giant Russian Mil Mi-26 (NATO code-name 'Halo') reputed to be one of the largest and most powerful helicopters to have gone into series production. As the S-61N approached the runway, the controller's clearance allowed the captain to take off with minimum delay after which a further transmission instructed: "Turn left onto north and maintain one thousand feet." This involved a turn away from the desired direction but perhaps, speculated David, the turn was designed to avoid interference with a fighter aircraft about to be scrambled. Eventually cleared to proceed on the planned route, he concentrated on re-aligning the helicopter's twin GPS systems with a map supplied by the US military.

The S-61N now headed towards a crossing point on the ceasefire line (CFL) at which juncture David and his captain knew that their flight's progress could become a little tricky. David used the aircraft radio to check in with the controller on board an airborne warning and control system (AWACS) aircraft which, he'd been briefed, was circling over the Adriatic Sea at a height of thirty thousand feet. "You're identified", growled the controller in an accent which David reckoned was South African. At the crossing point itself he changed radio frequencies and called the air traffic controller at an airfield ahead. However, there was no reply. He called again but with the same result. He knew that the airfield was Serb-controlled and he knew, too, that the controllers always listened but replied only if the mood took them which wasn't very often. There were rumours that these controllers were not paid which maybe explained their lackadaisical attitude.

Despite the lack of communication, the S-61N's captain maintained his authorised course and the flight above the airfield proceeded without incident. At that stage a crewman called Hans, a new recruit from KLM/ERA's base at Schiphol, presented each of the pilots with a mug of coffee. The crewman, who was also a qualified engineer, had to bend down onto his knees as, clutching the mugs, he leant through the narrow cockpit entrance.

David glanced back at the passengers. Some tried to sleep although most of them read newspapers. None appeared to look out of the windows to enjoy magnificent views of vineyards, colourful fields, and hilltop villages – a benign and idyllic scene when observed from a distance. Less idyllic, though, was the reality for those on the ground who faced fearsome destruction of homes, hotels, factories and vehicles. David noted the lack of road traffic, the absence of tractors and normal farm activity. Instead, all appeared eerily quiet, a sad spectacle which emphasised the recent destructiveness. It seemed doubly cruel, thought David, that in the couple of decades before Tito's death Yugoslavia was known as a regional industrial power, an economic success. He'd read about the country's healthy economic growth during that period, a time when medical care was free, literacy was over ninety per cent and life expectancy was over seventy years. With a unique position straddling the East and the West, Yugoslavia had acted as a buffer between the Soviet Union and the West, and the country had earned international respect in this role.

"Ask the AWACS for clearance to climb," interjected David's captain. Ahead, the mountain passes they'd hoped to use were obscured by cloud piling up over the mountain tops. When authorised by the AWACS controller, the captain climbed to an altitude of eight thousand feet at which height the conditions were clear. "How far to run to Knin?" he asked David.

"One hundred nautical miles."

"We should be able to talk to the Canadians soon." With this remark the captain referred to the S-61N's planned destination, the Canadian battalion based near Knin. When David established radio contact with a Canadian controller he was told that the weather was good there with a light and variable surface wind. Before long, as the miles ticked by, permission was given for the helicopter to initiate a descent.

"Thirty nautical miles to run," said David eventually, "and we just can make out the old town of Knin ahead." In the northern Dalmatian region of Croatia, Knin was known as an important rail and road junction for routes between Zagreb and Split. The town was known, too, for dark deeds during the recent Croatian War of Independence when most of the non-Serb population had been ethnically cleansed. As the helicopter continued to fly towards the town David spotted occasional road traffic but the railway lines looked rusty with no signs of trains.

"I'll fly down this valley to the landing site," said the captain who manoeuvred judiciously towards a makeshift helipad – a large concrete slab placed above a water reservoir which supplied the Canadian contingent and other military units. The base was part-Serbian and part-United Nations controlled and as the S-61N touched down, David was aware of armed guards observing closely. Not until the machine's engines and rotors had been shut down completely were the passengers allowed to disembark into waiting coaches. Hans now assisted ground crew with the helicopter's refuelling procedures after which he and the two pilots secured the S-61N. When satisfied, they set off towards the base's Canadian orderly room, ensuring as they walked that they kept to the concrete paths to avoid the danger of mines concealed in adjacent grass. During the walk, they nodded 'good morning' to Canadian soldiers who were cleaning their heavily armed vehicles. The Canadians stared back suspiciously but the three aircrew were allowed to continue unchallenged thanks to UN passes.

At the orderly room, the three were told by the duty officer: "You'll not be required again until four o'clock this afternoon, but don't wander off too far, please. There might be a sudden casualty evacuation task."

At this, the three aircrew decided to head for a local café run by a Serb and his Croatian wife. The couple's ethnic mix, so David had heard, evidently had caused them problems in the past. He'd been told that two years earlier the couple had run a holiday hotel on the coast but when the Croatian War of Independence broke out they were given twenty-four hours to leave or their hotel would be torched. With other families they'd boarded a bus which drove them to a position near to the front line of fighting. The resourceful couple, though, had managed to make their way to Knin where they established a café on the UN base and began to put their lives back together again. Now, David and his colleagues enjoyed good coffee as they sat under the thatched roof of an open-sided wooden building. The air was warm and full of the scents of spring while the men discussed the latest events in Croatia as well as recent news from KLM/ERA, a company formed some thirty years ago but which was now rumoured to be up for sale.

An hour or so later, when the three left the café, they made for the United Nations canteen where, so they'd been told, one United States dollar would buy a hot lunch for UN-badged personnel. This, indeed, proved the case and the three joined a queue from where they watched an intriguing melange of languages, uniforms, customs and people from across the globe. The queue moved slowly but eventually the three, clutching loaded food trays and searching for a place to sit in the crowded canteen, found space by a group of Canadians and joined them.

"Are you guys the helicopter crew?" One of the group said.

"Yup, we've flown down from Zagreb."

"Best way to travel," said the Canadian who continued boldly: "Real awkward moving any other way. The enemy's everywhere! Jus' last night there was trouble."

"What was going on?" asked David. The Canadian hesitated then gave a short cough as if to signal that he'd decided his listeners were reliable. "A situation with one of our ground patrols," he said. With a nod of his head he went on to describe how armed groups of young men were known to roam the local area threateningly at night. Consequently the Canadian commander, renowned for a tough approach in his sector, had ordered an ambush to be set up. An illegal armed group had been duly intercepted and when challenged, the group's response had been to open fire with automatic weapons. The Canadian troops returned fire and after a brief but intense fire-fight six gunmen lay dead. "Unfortunately these encounters are not so unusual," said the Canadian. "The bodies were checked for ID but none was found."

David thought about the gunmen, their young lives cut off in their prime – and for what? "What happened next?" he asked. "The weapons were gathered up and the bodies were buried without markers near the site where they fell."

Some moments of silence followed the Canadian's description and it was not until later that the three aircrew discussed his account. They needed no reminder that their operating environment was hazardous, but the Canadian's matter-of-fact portrayal had been, to say the least, thought provoking. The descriptions had stimulated, too, a discussion about the somewhat meagre equipment supplied for the aircrews' own protection. They wore no body armour when flying although a layer of Kevlar, a synthetic fibre of high strength first used on racing tyres, had been placed on the floor of the S-61N's cockpit and cabin. Fortunately, to date only one of the two machines had collected a bullet – a .22 shot in the tail.

By mid-afternoon the three decided to make their way back to the Canadian orderly room where the duty officer announced: "You've been tasked to fly back via Split." David knew that the airfield at Split, located west of Kaštela Bay on the Adriatic Sea, was divided between military and civil operators. He'd heard that the latter's use of the airport had dropped dramatically from over a million passengers in 1987 to near-zero when the civil war broke out. "After you've landed at Split," continued the operations officer, "you'll be required to shut down for an hour or so before the onward flight to Zagreb."

At length, when the passengers were driven up in coaches and escorted to the waiting S-61N, the crew swiftly went through start-up routines. Shortly after take-off the watchful presence of the AWACS aircraft was evident when the South African voice, even before the helicopter's undercarriage had been raised, abruptly interjected: "I see you lifting from Knin for Split."

"Affirmative."

"Call when level."

After ten or so minutes of flight over what looked like semi-desert country-side, Split Airfield came into sight. In stark contrast to the semi-desert area, David could see that the airfield itself was set in a superb spot with azure-blue seas before a backdrop of mountains. Indeed, the halcyon scene prompted him to make a mental note that one day, when all the troubles were over, he should return here on holiday. The current reality, however, was a chain of white United Nations observation posts which marked the ceasefire line. As the S-61N flew above the line, David double-checked the helicopter's identification setting and radio frequency then called the Split approach controller. A long pause ensued but this time the controller at least had the courtesy to respond as he gave clearance for a visual approach to Split's easterly runway. At the airfield boundary David noted a number of Royal Naval and Royal Air Force helicopters lined up for daily operations into Bosnia. The S-61N touched down from a 'running landing' after which the captain taxied to a crowded dispersal where he shut down the machine.

An hour later the S-61N was airborne again. Cleared to fly due north before a turn inland for Zagreb, the designated route followed the picture-postcard topography of the Croatian coastline. With the Adriatic Sea to the helicopter's left, the machine flew above an area crowded with a seemingly endless series of islands and islets. To the right, the Dinaric Alps with a high point of just over six thousand feet stretched north and south as far as the eye could see. Over past weeks David had flown regularly above these rugged mountains where he'd observed with a sense of fascination the desolate gorges, cataracts, deep ravines, shale and scree interrupted by occasional goat paths that twisted and turned through a wilderness of thorny shrubs bursting into spring bud. At times he'd felt as if flying at the edge of an abyss, a curious analogy to the country's troubled politics.

Still following the coastal zone, at one point the S-61N flew above a modern shipyard with a half-completed, rusting vessel stuck on the slipway. There was nobody about and the shipyard's cranes stood forlorn and stationary as if frozen in time. A nearby marina appeared to be deserted, the Mediterranean's million-aire yachts nowhere to be seen. Eventually turning inland towards Zagreb, the captain, as before, was obliged to climb above cloud build-ups. With reports of hazy conditions at the airfield he requested an instrument landing system (ILS) but was offered instead a step-down radar-guided approach, a satisfactory, if old-fashioned, system.

After landing at Zagreb, the S-61N taxied past a varied mix of aircraft types, including a Russian-built passenger jet which, David speculated, had probably flown into the Bosnian capital of Sarajevo that day. This city remained under siege and in scenes of tragedy still ongoing, thousands of Sarajevans had lost their lives under constant bombardment and sniper shooting by Serb forces. The Russian-built passenger jets sometimes returned to Zagreb from Sarajevo riddled with bullet holes. David had heard that the Ukranian flight crews were equipped with flack vests and were so well paid that after two years some elected to retire.

When the S-61N reached the dispersal area, the captain closed down the engines and rotors then leaned forward to recover a talisman – a small toy bear – which he'd concealed behind the cockpit coaming. "Always brings me luck," he said as he looked up at the skies then glanced at David.

Following post-flight formalities, David decided to walk the mile or so distance to his company house near the town of Velika Gorica, a name which, roughly translated, meant 'large vineyard'. He knew that Velika Gorica, which was positioned near two airports, had played a significant role in the civil war and just this year would be upgraded to city status.

Tramping stoically across country, David used the walk as an opportunity to gain perspective and to think through his diverse experiences in the Balkans. The S-61Ns normally covered two main routes, today's southerly one and a route to Osijek near the town of Vukova. The latter, he knew, had been the focus of a ferocious battle in the civil war and the current force representing the United Nations was supplied by a Russian paratroop battalion, men who were very fit, good at unarmed combat and fearless. If a football ended up in a minefield along-side the airfield, they would cheerfully set off to recover it. Perhaps inevitably, therefore, these men were among the casualties which the S-61Ns flew from time to time to a mobile army surgical hospital (MASH) unit near the helicopter dispersal at Zagreb. This unit, just as in the TV series *M*A*S*H,* was a tented facility where many lives were saved. Manned by volunteers from a United States Navy base at San Diego, Southern California, the young Americans enjoyed life and seemed happy to serve in Croatia for a six-month tour. If they went off base, it was in groups of six or more in view of potential local antipathy towards UN personnel and their white-painted equipment.

David himself, however, had begun to feel confident on his own for he'd made local friends including at a popular pizza café. Now approaching the café, he made a spontaneous decision to call in but first, as a precaution, he hid his UN pass. Pushing open the café door, he was met by a buzz of conversation. Suddenly surrounded by a group of burly men, he was shuffled towards a table. As he sat down, a glass of beer was thrust in his direction. He glanced at surrounding faces and grinned when he recognised some of the Dutch engineers from KLM/ERA. They talked about the company and what it was up to but apparently no-one wanted to buy it yet. They talked, too, of the hazards faced in Croatia but at length David bade goodnight to his colleagues and left the café to resume his walk to the company house.

As he walked along, he pondered the problems so earnestly discussed although he was keen to place a positive spin on the situation. He felt the need for optimism and to think in a confident, sanguine way. Even the climate, he mused, though tempestuous early in the year and insufferably hot in the summer, felt heartening just then in the balmy spring with wild flowers blooming in impossible places – and tomorrow's prospects, he reckoned, were surely good.

About one year later, by the spring of 1995, such optimism had regretfully proved overambitious. At the beginning of the year the Croatian president, Franjo Tudjman, told the United Nations that, from 31 March, he was terminating the agreement which permitted UNPROFOR to be stationed in Croatia. Violence erupted again and in early May Croatian offensives caused Serb forces to attack Zagreb with rockets. This triggered the withdrawal of the KLM/ERA operation. The company's Zagreb-based S-61N was in Split at the time and the crews were ordered to fly across the Adriatic Sea directly to the Italian seaport at Ancona, a distance of just over two hundred and fifty miles.

The next day, the crews continued their flight to Graz Airport in Austria where all personnel involved with the operation were directed to reassemble before returning to the Netherlands. It was an opportunity for the Dutch army to return personal effects which their troops had managed to rescue including, in David's case, a large travel bag where he'd hidden several months' worth of allowances. The Dutch troops also packed and transported to Graz over a million pounds-worth of helicopter spares from the company stores at Zagreb Airport.

David and his colleagues then flew the two S-61Ns across Austria, into Germany and eventually to Dan Helder in Holland. The operation was over before the planned time, nonetheless they felt that they'd 'done their bit' for the United Nations. Caught in the crossfire of uncertain alliances, complex algorithms with shifting ethnic and national identities, their position and that of other United Nations' personnel had been more than a little challenging. As a conduit for future peace, though, they felt that their presence as part of the UN had helped the Croatian government to attain their objective: the eventual withdrawal of Serb forces. With independence and the preservation of borders, Croatia had achieved its goal although the process had meant the loss of thousands of lives, an economy in ruins, enormous damage to infrastructure and thousands of refugees.

However, over the next decades Croatia would demonstrate resilience and determination to the point that the country became a safe, independent and tourist-friendly nation with a strengthening economy and a stable government. In July 2013 Croatia was elected as the twenty-eighth member of the European Union. Traditional folklore festivals were revived to take the place of guns and weapons of war. Zagreb was no longer a focus for rocket attacks by Serb forces but instead became renowned for an international folklore festival with dancing, music and songs dedicated to the Croatian folk tradition.

When David and his wife visited the new Croatia on holiday, he'd observe the improvements, the tourists in the streets, the marinas packed full of yachts. Perhaps with mixed feelings he'd think back to the days he'd spent there in the slipstream of war, for he'd witnessed bad events, miscellaneous memento mori of an anguished period. But that was in the past. Things were different now. Life had moved on. With a sigh and with a curious sense of reassurance he'd listen to the still of the night as he glanced up at the stars that shimmered in an early evening sky.

CHAPTER 21
KOSOVO

Richard Pike on a Balkan mercy mission

WE STARED AT the vehicle sent to collect us. "It's a great big Macedonian rust-bucket!" said someone.

"Not the best," I agreed, "but it should get us there." There were six of us altogether and as we clambered into the ancient taxi, I glanced up at the early morning sky. The rising sun had started to spread a riot of colours across the horizon, and I sensed a timeless quality which seemed to be carried across the still air. A great chorus of birdsong was mixed with other sounds of dawn and in many ways the atmosphere was idyllic.

This, though, was deceptive, as if a ploy of nature. For just a few miles from our comfortable accommodation, a hotel in the centre of Skopje, Macedonia's capital city, were less than comfortable scenes, dark, ominous ones.

As the taxi set off to drive at speed through the streets of Skopje, I thought about the potent, almost tangible tang in the Macedonian air that morning... intense and unsettling. Gazing through one of the taxi's windows I could see in the distance, about ten miles away, the outline of the Sharr mountains which indicated the border with Kosovo. A hundred miles or so beyond that lay Kosovo's contentious and perilous border with Serbia. I took a deep breath and sighed. The general mood within Skopje was heady and exotic, yet on that July morning in 1999 I held disturbing images in my head – mental pictures of the recent chilling campaign of ethnic cleansing by Serbian troops against the Albanian population of Kosovo. The Serbian actions had led to hundreds of thousands of people, mainly ethnic Albanians, seeking safety in huge refugee camps set up in Macedonia and elsewhere. The scenes inside these camps were pitiful, furthermore the situation had created unrest within Macedonia itself.

It was about five months earlier, in March 1999, that NATO aircraft had initiated air attacks against Yugoslavia and just ten or so weeks after that when the president of Yugoslavia, Slobodan Milosevic, had conceded defeat. Now, as a consequence, displaced Kosovans had started to drift back to their own country. Their country, though, bore grim scars from scandalous and brutal acts by the Serbians – acts that amounted to a systematic campaign of terror which included murder, rape, arson and severe maltreatment.

An international effort to assist Kosovo had begun. This effort involved, under a United Nations World Food Programme contract, a team of pilots and engineers from Bristow Helicopters. As a helicopter pilot with that company, I was part of the team and it was our task to distribute, by Sikorsky S-61N helicopters, food in the form of bread-making flour to remote communities in war-torn Kosovo. Normally we were employed to fly to North Sea oil installations, so to operate in far-flung, often mountainous, corners of Kosovo was, one could say, an interesting contrast.

That morning, as the drive continued towards base camp where our two S-61Ns were parked, the six of us talked about this and that, including a character employed by the United Nations World Food programme to facilitate the helicopter operations. An unlikely individual with a rather bloated look, nobody really understood the nature of his task, least of all him. He blundered about like a big lost sheepdog and earned the nickname 'Pink Elephant' (as an Icelander, his complexion, poor fellow, did not cope well with the potent Balkan sunshine). His English, we all agreed, was often hard to understand. "Too many of that stuff make you plumpy..." he'd said yesterday as we hastily consumed sandwiches while the helicopter was loaded up for the next task. With a chip-toothed grin he'd patted his ample midriff and added: "...like me! But better much than skinny."

"You're talking tosh as usual," one of the co-pilots said.

"Too thin, too hunger, drop down dead! Ha! Ha!" His pink cheeks had appeared to glow; there'd been a buzz of reaction to the comment and an awkward shuffling amongst bystanders. The co-pilot had shrugged his shoulders which began to shake with amusement. Someone else had stifled a guffaw...

When the taxi driver suddenly braked hard, we fell silent for a few moments. Conversation, though, soon resumed for there seemed much to discuss. "The numbers of kids that appear from nowhere when we've landed near their village – it's amazing!" said one of my fellow captains.

"Seems a bit dodgy when some of them try to climb into the helicopter," said his co-pilot.

"If they're supervised, I don't see the harm," I said, "bad things have happened in Kosovo – terrible things – so small acts of kindness should..."

"Surely our job is to deliver flour not to entertain kids."

The conversation quietened again as we watched the taxi driver pull out to overtake a long convoy of lorries, a mix of military trucks with white-painted 'K4' signs, Red Cross vehicles and various civilian lorries. The convoy was heading for the Macedonian/Kosovan border and from there into Kosovo itself to reinforce the NATO-led peacekeeping Kosovo Force (KFOR) which had entered Kosovo on 12 June 1999.

We'd read in the newspapers that KFOR troops had been preparing for combat operations but that in the end the mission had become purely a peacekeeping one.

We'd learned that during the first days of entering Kosovo the NATO soldiers were greeted by ethnic Albanians cheering and throwing flowers as KFOR vehicles rolled through their villages, and we'd seen pictures of marines followed by crowds of local children. There were press reports, too, that the KFOR troops, as they moved from village to village uncovering atrocities across the country, were gripped by a grim sense of outrage. English was a common language, and some spoke German, so from school teachers and others the troops listened to stories of people, crazed with fear, being dragged out of their homes. "No!" a young ethnic Albanian woman in one village had pleaded, "have pity!" But pity was scarce. A Serbian soldier, excited by his power, had cried: "Vermin! Come to me!" If he felt any sense of triumph, it must have been shockingly tainted. Other villagers, powerless to intervene, were compelled to stand aside in rage and distress.

But it was not just present atrocities that fuelled the hatred, for with long histories of feuds, of old scores to be settled, past quarrels bubbled up and petty issues escalated into life-or-death altercations. The KFOR troops came across corpses spread-eagled and twisted, as though they had never contained a life, and they uncovered mass graves. To their dismay, the troops learned of the darkness that can lurk at the base of the human soul.

After the war, the Independent International Commission on Kosovo reported:

'Yugoslav forces were engaged in a well-planned campaign of terror and expulsion of the Kosovan Albanians. This campaign is most frequently described as one of "ethnic cleansing" intended to drive many, if not all, Kosovan Albanians from Kosovo, destroy the foundations of their society and prevent them from returning.'

"Nearly there now", as the taxi tackled a roundabout, one of the co-pilots pointed towards the complex expanse of tents and mobile huts that formed a base camp for the diverse agencies supporting the international post-war effort. The hut was already full of sound and movement when we arrived, for the engineers, as they prepared the S-61Ns for flight, had arrived ahead of the pilots. Inside the hut were telephones, a fax machine and lists of current flight information, radio frequencies, weather forecasts, details on areas known to be land-mined. Space was at a premium; flight planning and engineering management had to share the basic facilities. This, though, did not compromise the high professional standards we were accustomed to applying to North Sea operations, and I sensed a familiar businesslike atmosphere as we got down to work.

Once the scrupulous flight planning had been completed, I walked to our allocated S-61N registration G-BFRI with my co-pilot and a third pilot who would act as crewman. It was unusual to employ a pilot in this way but in view of the special and unpredictable hazards, the reason was not hard to figure out. We had been scheduled to take off first; the second helicopter would follow in about ten minutes.

The S-61Ns had been painted from stem to stern in a fetching shade of white with 'UN' at the helicopter's front and, at the rear by the tail-rotor, 'WFP' next to the World Food Programme's insignia of olive leaves around a hand clutching grains. Soon, with the engines started and the rotors turning, my crewman, secured by a special 'long' strap as he stood by the open cargo door, called: "Clear above and behind...you're clear to lift." He then closed the door immediately for we were parked in a confined area and committed to a so-called 'towering take-off'. Pale and choking dust filled the air as, with my left hand, I raised the collective lever to lift the S-61N into a vertical take-off manoeuvre to clear the area as rapidly as possible. At our landing site in Kosovo the helicopter would be loaded with around two tons of flour and HDR (humanitarian daily rations – cardboard boxes laden with high calorific foods), but just now the powerful, load-free helicopter swiftly towered upwards and I turned onto a northerly heading for Kosovo.

At this point a refugee camp came into view. A vast, sprawling network run by the United Nations High Commissioner for Refugees (UNHCR), we'd heard that when Kosovans registered in the refugee camps they were asked where they would like to be relocated. Most, apparently, chose Germany, an interesting selection in view of the history of Nazi activities in the region during World War Two. People smugglers were evidently active in the refugee camps, cashing-in on the tide of human torment with promises to take people to the European country of their choice for a fee of five thousand US dollars.

As we continued to fly northwards, the border with Kosovo quickly became evident, readily identified by long traffic tailbacks. The S-61N provided an ideal queue-jumper and we soon passed the border point which, like the helicopter, was covered in white, though for rather different reasons: a nearby cement factory had been a casualty of NATO bombing and the surrounding area was powdered in white layers of cement as if tiny white mites had decided to infest trees, factory buildings, fields, crops, houses, vehicles. As we flew on towards Priština, Kosovo's capital city, country villages in superb surroundings would reveal less than superb sights: individual houses selected as targets for revenge burning. The war may have ended, but retaliation had not. In merciless scenes where former neighbours had become enemies, occasional black clouds of filthy smoke rising upwards marked where another property had just been torched. Sometimes we'd see villagers clustered helplessly together, dazed, seized by dread, no doubt, as they observed the war's aftermath produce prolonged horror.

For some miles we followed a good navigational feature, a railway line but one, sadly, abandoned apart from occasional 'K4' military trains. Before long, high-rise blocks in the distance indicated that we were approaching Priština. Flying close to the city we could see where strategic targets including the post office, police headquarters and military barracks had been hit during the NATO air campaign, and it was clear where certain districts had been selectively shelled by Serbian paramilitaries and Yugoslav ground forces. We'd seen the newspaper accounts describing how these forces, together with Serbian police, had carried out widespread looting and destruction of Kosovan Albanian properties as well as large-scale expulsion of ethnic Albanians. There were reports that trains had been brought to Priština's main railway station for the specific purpose of transporting ethnic Albanians to the Macedonian border for enforced exile.

I flew towards an area just south of Priština where a large field had been set up by staff from the United Nations as a base for helicopter operations. Fuel bowsers, forklift trucks, vehicles loaded with flour bags and HDR were organised by individuals who scurried about looking extra efficient in their United Nations light blue caps and jackets. When I spotted a marshaller begin to wave his arms energetically, I followed his directions to land in the required place. As soon as I'd landed then closed down the S-61N's engines and rotors, a forklift truck drove up and numbers of personnel converged on the helicopter to commence loading flour and HDR. Meanwhile, I climbed out of the cockpit to meet up for a discussion with the Pink Elephant and with Leo, the United Nations interpreter.

Leo, an ethnic Albanian in his mid-thirties, was an interesting character. There was a sterling quality in his approach, in his vigorous, healthy attitude which revealed a determination to overcome the traumas suffered by his kinfolk. He had owned a successful printing business before it was destroyed by Serbian paramilitaries but now, instead of bitterness, he expressed his sense of privilege as an employee of the United Nations.

"For our first task today," said Leo as we studied a local map, "we'll fly due west from here. We'll land by some villages which we've heard are in urgent need." He pointed at a defined zone on the map that had been roughly highlighted in pencil. "Right," I said, "that should be okay. Is there a current update on minefields in that area?" Leo pulled a face. "We've got an approximate idea," he said, "but we'll have to be careful. As you know, not all of the war's minefields have been identified."

It was not too long before we received word that the helicopter had been loaded. Anxious to proceed with our mission of mercy, I hastened back to the cockpit while my co-pilot conducted external checks on G-BFRI. With these and other checks swiftly completed, we were soon airborne again and as I headed due west we used the aircraft intercommunications system to chat with Leo who sat on a jump seat between and behind the two pilots. He remarked on the way that the bright day appeared to brighten further while we flew westwards. I maintained a height of around two thousand feet which gave a good overview of the landscape before us. Marked by mid-summer colours of yellows and greens, the trees, fields, hedgerows of central Kosovo continued to present wonderfully attractive scenes. As we'd seen already, though, these were marred by the occasional sight of smoke spiralling upwards, perhaps an innocent bonfire but maybe the sign of another revenge house burning. We'd grimace with knowing looks but, generally keen to avoid negative conversation, usually we did not comment.

After some twenty minutes of flying due west, we started to make out the city of Peć (or Peja) with the Rugova mountains beyond. Before then, however, several country villages were the focus of our attention that day. I began to reduce airspeed and to circle the chosen area as Leo stared apprehensively ahead. "Possibly that village..." he pointed, "or that one over there." It felt like a scene from the film *Sophie's Choice:* who should we save? When, eventually, we'd made our choice, we searched for a suitable landing site, perhaps a football pitch or a flat-looking field used for other sporting activities which, with luck, indicated a mine-free environment. I flew the S-61N towards the site chosen for a 'spot' landing (hover manoeuvres were precluded by the combination of a heavily laden helicopter and high ambient temperatures) anticipating, shortly after touchdown, the often remarkable and rapid local reaction. That day, indeed, was no exception: as if hidden eyes had watched our every move from secret hiding places, suddenly all hell was let loose as we landed and as adults and children converged on the helicopter. Sometimes we closed down the engines and rotors but that day, with the helicopter's engines and rotors still turning, at once I handed control of the S-61N to the co-pilot and hurried back to the air-stair door with Leo. The 'crewman' pilot, meantime, opened the air-stair door and the three of us stepped outside to assess the situation and to form a plan of action.

Leo spotted a man who, he guessed, was a village leader of some kind. The two swiftly entered into deep discussion which, later, Leo would translate and summarise for us during the flight back to Priština. I watched a fair amount of hand-waving and I noted fierce facial expressions as Leo listened to a harrowing account. In these often tearful situations people had to be allowed time to talk, nevertheless time was limited and as tactfully as possible, therefore, Leo needed to get down to practicalities. How much flour was needed by this village? Was one delivery sufficient or should we return with a second load? Using the formula of one kilogram per person as a rough guide, we agreed details with the village leader. Leo explained that the flour mixture just needed water and salt to be added before baking and he said that boxes of HDR would be left for immediate relief.

At this stage, strong-looking lads were beckoned into the helicopter to help unload the HDR and flour bags, each bag clearly marked with 'Gift from Japan', for example, or 'Gift from the USA': 'not for resale'. The unloading did not take long and when it was completed children could be given an opportunity to look inside the helicopter briefly before we took off for reloading. I was struck by the way the children, against all odds, looked cheerful and interested. Despite dark times and great loss it seemed that the wider world still offered appeal and the adults, too, appeared in generally good spirits although occasionally the staring eyes and worried looks of some revealed latent truths.

By now, though, it was necessary to get on: the next task awaited. Ever conscious of the need not to lose precious time, Leo spoke to the village leader again who encouraged onlookers to move to a safe distance while the four members of the helicopter crew prepared for take-off. Within a short time the air-stair and cargo doors were slammed shut and the S-61N, now two tons lighter, was ready to be lifted into a hover and towered away from the villagers who persisted to wave their hands vigorously in grateful farewell.

Meanwhile, back at the Priština base, the next batch of HDR and flour had been prepared so that reloading could begin as soon as we'd landed and shut down the engines and rotors. A fuel truck drove up to G-BFRI and, while refuelling took place, the helicopter crew took the opportunity to confer with the Pink Elephant while Leo made for a nearby office.

Leo now re-joined us and said: "There's been a telephone call and they want the next load to be delivered to a particular village not far from the one we've just visited." He paused and gazed at me with serious, searching eyes.

"Okay," I said, "should be no problem."

"No…"

"What is it, Leo?"

"Something not very nice, I'm afraid. After the flour delivery we've been asked to fly towards the hills beyond Peć and look for something."

"Look for what?"

Leo hesitated before he went on in a low voice: "It's been reported recently that there's an area beyond Peć where it's believed that a mass grave, so far undiscovered by the authorities, has been dug secretly. We've been asked to look for signs." I nodded grimly for I'd been told about Peć, about the very tense atmosphere that had developed there from the start of the internal armed conflict in the spring of last year. Atrocities had been carried out on both sides and it was said that some eighty per cent of houses in the city had been heavily damaged or destroyed. Many ethnic Albanian folk had been forcibly expelled and some had fled to the nearby Rugova mountains to seek shelter and as a way to make contact with the Kosovo Liberation Army (KLA) who could help in various ways including voluntary evacuation into Macedonia, Montenegro or Albania.

"Sure thing, Leo," I said eventually. "We can have a look but our time will be limited by the helicopter's restricted fuel state."

At this, we all walked back towards G-BFRI which by now had been reloaded and refuelled. We swiftly restarted the helicopter and, when ready to take off, spoke to the mobile air traffic control set-up manned by members of the Royal Air Force. Soon cleared to proceed, the take-off technique had to be flown with particular care for the day's ambient temperature had begun to soar towards the high thirty degrees centigrade and beyond which affected the helicopter's performance. Before long, we headed west to fly, as before, at a height of two thousand feet while we made for the specific village.

While flying along we struck up conversation with Leo again for it was evident that he was beginning to enjoy the freedom and flexibility offered by helicopter flying. He seemed intrigued by the necessary flying skills and clearly he admired the power for good provided by our operations, as if the antithesis of the power of evil that had swept through his country. "Why don't you become a helicopter pilot, Leo?" said the co-pilot at one stage.

"That would be fine," said Leo shrugging his shoulders, "but I'm probably too old to start that now."

"Will you aim to re-build your printing business, then?"

"Oh...I don't know. Things will be difficult for quite a while yet."

Ahead, the brilliant colours of the countryside, the natural beauty of the surroundings, seemed to eclipse the worries of the moment so that for a while we sat in silence listening to the familiar sounds of the helicopter as we observed the local scenery. At length Leo piped up again: "We should see this village soon." I began to reduce airspeed as Leo pointed and cried: "That's it over there!" at which I started to fly around the village to assess a good landing spot. In one field a small crowd had already formed so we chose this as the best mine-free option. I flew a further circuit then set up for a landing, conscious of the 'critical point' beyond which the heavily-laden S-61N had insufficient power for a safe overshoot. However, the 'spot' landing worked out well and within moments the helicopter doors were opened, Leo walked outside to confer with villagers and the unloading of HDR and flour was quickly underway. I saw one man throw off his jacket and roll up his sleeves as he hastened to help with the unloading, perhaps symptomatic, I reckoned, of a village in considerable need. I noted the faces around me which, as before, seemed mostly cheerful and stalwart with only the occasional sign of underlying trouble. I noted a man with a livid scar across his face, and I saw one young woman standing away from the helicopter, her fists clenched as she stared with fixed, demented eyes at what was happening around her.

The unloading proceeded efficiently and soon it was time to take off for the second part of our task. The flight to the pre-briefed area did not take long and as we approached the hills beyond Peć, Leo guided us towards the specific place we'd been asked to check. At this stage crew conversation petered out apart from Leo's occasional directions. As we flew low and slow around the area, the lack of conversation and the strange situation appeared to evoke a mysterious atmosphere. The clear, warm sunshine, interrupted only by shadows of clouds moving over the woods below us – extensive woods marked by scattered leaves and dried moss – produced a paradoxical sense of serenity. We came across a property which had been boarded up; part of the building was covered in dense creeper the dark green of which helped to counter-balance the bleakness of the house's isolated position. Not far from the property I flew across a forest clearing and tried to assess whether it would be feasible to land. After some discussion, however, we agreed that it would be best not to land there but to continue to fly around the area and observe from the security of the S-61N in a low hover.

If the atmosphere was sinister, maybe this was exacerbated by the lack of people for there were few signs of life, just long stretches of empty forest, territory that felt forlorn, lost, insentient. Suddenly, with an outstretched hand, Leo pointed energetically at something. It was hard at first to see what had caught his attention for the perspective was distorted and detailed features, darkened by shadows, were hard to make out. As I manoeuvred the helicopter, however, we soon realised what Leo had seen. To one side of the forest clearing, quite close to the tree-line, it was evident that the surface earth had been disturbed. A series of extended trenches, recently dug then roughly camouflaged in apparent haste, stretched for some distance and one glance at Leo's face, his compressed look, his frowning forehead, the line of his mouth revealed as explicitly as any words what the trenches contained. Leo remained tight-lipped and he did not look at me; he just stared ahead. I experienced a curious chill despite the high summer temperature, as if the place was haunted by the ghosts of exterior existence with the air full of phantoms. The whole scene appeared devoid of reality.

I glanced again at Leo and this time he gazed silently back at me. It was clear that he did not wish to make any comment, but his facial expression was equally clear: "We've found what they asked. There's nothing more we can do now. Let's return to Priština." I nodded, applied power to climb the S-61N and turned due east. The glimpse of that place may have been fleeting, but the impression persisted. There was another impression too, or perhaps it was an illusion, in either case I couldn't avoid the sensation that an unknown, unsought companion was beside me. I experienced a moment – I won't say of vacillation, but of poignant pause – when time seemed to distort as implications sank in. Some weeks later, by which point I had left Kosovo, it was by chance that I heard the haunting melodies of *In Paradisum* from *Fauré's Requiem,* and the memories of that remarkable situation, the thoughts of the unknown faces and figures associated with it, came rushing back so that I was transported in an instant to a lonely ghost's walk lying deep in the shade of that dark forest.

A single imperative at the time, however, was a desire to get away from the place as speedily as possible. There was no crew conversation as we flew along, just four individuals with their own thoughts interrupted by radio calls with the Royal Air Force air traffic controller. Perhaps this was a good thing for it brought back a semblance of normality, as did the routines when we landed at the Priština base.

It was late afternoon, after deliveries to several villages and with the time approaching six p.m. that Leo announced: "Okay, everybody. Thanks for all your hard work – brilliant! I've just made a telephone call and we can call it a day for today." There was no time to lose for we needed to fly back to Macedonia where the helicopters had to be checked, serviced and cleaned ready for the following day. So after a brief adieu, we hastened back to the two helicopters and soon, in apparently no time at all, we'd started up and taken off to head south for Macedonia.

With over seven hours of flying time logged that day and after operating in such conditions with unusually high temperatures, all six pilots were more than a little fatigued after landing at the Macedonian base. Nonetheless, in the spirit of 'all hands on deck' we helped with a number of laborious tasks which included the need to vacuum the flour-dusted cabins, wash the helicopters' outside and assist, where practical, with the engineering turn-round and other technical procedures. The time was approaching eight p.m., therefore, when taxis drove us back to the hotel where, after a much needed supper, some of us liked to enjoy the evening air as we strolled along the streets of Skopje. Dusk was falling by then with colourful streaks across the sky as the sun slipped down below the horizon. As we walked along, nature's potent images somehow encapsulated those experienced earlier in the day, raw images that, for me and I suspect for others, would never go away.

I did not spend much longer in the Balkans and when I returned to my home in a safe and civilised Scotland, it was with heady memories and a strong sense of job satisfaction. All the more sobering, therefore, was the news announced briskly, brusquely, brutally that some fifty company pilots were to be 'let go' because of a downturn in the oil industry. Senior captains, they said, were the most costly and the ones, therefore, to be affected. "How about the 'last in-first out' principle?" we asked. "Principle?" retorted the boss, "what are principles!" "We don't want to be let go," we protested. It was no good, though; the fickle fingers of the fates seldom gave us what we wished in the way that we would wish. Years later, if I peered at the path before me, at its shortening reach as the end crept closer, and if I glanced back at the twentieth century's twilight months, I'd picture the mighty waves crashing down, a notion understood only too well by the good citizens of Kosovo.

INDEX